God Bless Mrs McGinty!

God Bless Mrs McGinty!

My Life *and*
<u>The</u> Sunday Post

Bill Anderson ("The HON Man")
and Editor of *The Sunday Post* 1968–1990

God Bless Mrs McGinty!

First published 2016, by Waverley Books, an imprint of
The Gresham Publishing Company, Academy Park,
Building 4000, Gower Street, Glasgow G51 1PR
www.waverley-books.co.uk
info@waverley-books.co.uk
Find us on facebook/pages/waverleybooks

Published simultaneously in Braille by The Scottish Braille Press www.
royalblind.org/accessible-media/

A catalogue entry for this book is available from the British Library.

ISBN 978 1 849343 90 9

Printed and bound in the EU.

Contents

Dedication

To all the staff of *The Sunday Post*, past and present.

Introduction

My darling Bill died on February 2, 2012.

In the summer of 2014, I was clearing out my desk – not before time, as Bill would have said – when I found a manuscript hand-written in his distinctive scrawl. It was headed "Who The Hell Is Bill Anderson?" and as I started to read, I felt so confused. This was Bill's life story. Why was it in my desk? How had it got there? Why did I not know he had written it? I put it down to dry my tears, and then saw another folder. This one contained the typewritten copy and this time I did not put it down until I'd got to the last page.

When Bill retired, in 2003, he was asked several times to write his autobiography. He always laughed off the suggestion that anyone would be interested. But now, here it was, and it was a fascinating account of childhood in working-class Scotland in the 1930s and 40s, of the wee boy who would grow up to edit the best-read newspaper in the world. I can only assume Bill had put it in my desk, wanting me to find it eventually, but knowing that might take a long time, as I very seldom did a "clear-out".

He wrote it in 1982, several years before I met him, when he was recovering from a near-fatal car accident. So here it is, in his own words, and I know he wouldn't mind me sharing it with you.

Maggie Anderson

Preamble

The Sunday Post – Reporters' Guidelines

What The Sunday Post Is All About:

It is about people.
What can happen to them.
Has happened.
Might happen.
Will happen.
Happened when they hoped it wouldn't.
Didn't happen when they hoped it would.
It is about what people do – or have done to them. Or didn't do.
It is about birth, death, marriage, baptism, food, health, money, leisure, holidays, problems, weather – all the things we all talk about, and telling us something about it to make us all talk about it.
It is about the extraordinary that happens to the ordinary. Your wife. My wife. The woman down the street. The man in the pub. The auld buddy in the multistorey. The young wife in the supermarket. The butcher, the baker, the candlestick maker.
It is taking something we all know about and telling us something we don't know about it.
But it must be a story, with a beginning, a middle and an end.
It must have climax or anticlimax.
Nobody listens to blethers. Everyone listens to gossip.

That's because blethers have no bite.

So a Sunday Post story must have conflict.

It must produce some reaction in the reader.

It must make the reader laugh or cry, or be angry, agree or disagree.

It must be written simply with sincerity and sympathy.

It must be unique in some way.

Ask yourself – would "Mrs McGinty" be interested in what you have written? Mrs McGinty is our typical reader. We mustn't upset her, offend her, shock her or mislead her. We must intrigue, entertain, comfort and support her. Never forget Mrs McGinty – she is our best friend.

Knowing what it's about and how to go about it. There is only this to say. It is not a 9–5 job. A Sunday Post reporter always has his or her eyes and ears open for the unusual.

That is what sets us apart.

W. Anderson, Editor, The Sunday Post.

CHAPTER 1

Don't Worry, You're Only Dying

It was more than a scream; a bellow, deep, low and animal. Someone was in pain, deep-down dying pain. It couldn't be me, could it?

Yet it had seemed like any other Thursday night in the office. Late in November, true. But why should that make any difference? I always worked late on Thursday nights. I was a busy man, a successful man, at the height of his career as editor of a Sunday newspaper. The "best-read newspaper in the world", according to *The Guinness Book of Records*. I had a good wife, three fine sons, a grand home (with a dream kitchen my wife had designed herself) and all the trappings of success in a three-car family. My goodness, I had two Alan Hayman originals on my wall, a young Scottish bird artist of growing reputation.

When I drove home in my Princess 2.2 Litre GHX for dinner I could have smoked salmon caught myself from an exclusive beat on the Tay, or trout for the fish course from a private angling club of which I was a member, followed by venison – shot personally, of course. I had held the Queen's Commission. I was the sleeping partner in a licensed restaurant I'd bought for my family to ensure a future for my sons and to keep me in my old age in the style to which I was becoming accustomed. I was wondering how big a yacht I could afford; on a marine mortgage, I might just squeeze a Sadler 25-footer to cruise the Greek islands next summer. I'd just spent a thousand quid on my eldest son's 21st birthday. We entertained 260 people that weekend. Even my ball-point pen was a gold Parker. Oh, yes, I was successful. Everybody knew that. Everybody in my own circle, that is. They knew how important I was, always meeting important people. An invitation to the Royal Garden Party every year, naturally.

I was an intimate of the MP who was to be the next Secretary of State for Scotland as the Conservatives were certain to win the next general election. We had a tacit agreement that when he took high office, I would go "into public service", offering my talents to the nation in a not-too-demanding-but-very-well-paid sinecure at the head of one of the many state bodies (I rather fancied the Scottish Tourist Board) which would lead in time to my much-deserved knighthood. Not bad for a steelworker's son. Oh, yes, I was successful and important and powerful. I only had to pick up the phone ...

I picked up the phone. What was holding up the presses? "You can't have that heading in 72-point, it won't fit," said the case-room overseer. In the newspaper world, he's a powerful man, too. "It'll have to wait. I can't give the up-makers any more overtime. You know how management feels about overtime." Indeed I did. The successful, important, powerful editor humbly pleaded. I got my heading. Another page of *The Post* was put to bed, ready for the five million who couldn't wait for Sunday to devour the story of the Auchtermuchty train-shunter who had run away with the stationmaster's wife, which was as far as a family newspaper could even hint at the salacious.

I had one page to finish editing before I went home. A feature called "The Honest Truth" in which we quizzed the rich, the poor, the famous, the infamous, the happy, the unhappy, the downright eccentric and persuaded them to bare their souls to satisfy the curiosity of the rich and the poor, the famous and infamous ... It was a popular column that had been graced by not only every Prime Minister since the last war, but just about everyone who came into the public eye. Now I was preparing one for the Christmas issue. It was November, remember, and we worked well ahead on the "early" pages inside the paper that wouldn't become dated before publication day, when they only needed news and sport wrapped round them to go to the presses. The heading I wrote out was "The Honest Truth About The Luckiest Housewife Of The Year". Memory dims when you've subbed as many Luckiest Man/Woman/Boy/ Girl/Dog/MP/Pop Star/Footballer/Golfer/Minister stories as

I have, but it was probably about the Newcastle widow who fell from the ledge of the three-storey window she was cleaning – and had her fall miraculously broken by the Littlewoods man bringing her news of a £72,000 pools win. That was the kind of story my readers loved and I gave them what they wanted. God bless Mrs McGinty! I put the last par mark on it, wrote the sub-headings and scribbled the type-setting instructions across the top. "Questions 8-point metro-black. Answers 8-point imperial, reverse indent", as I had done a thousand times before. That was it. Another Thursday night. Given a disaster or two for the front page – and I had great faith in human nature – with another £1 million transfer for the back page – and I had great faith in the spendthrift men who run football – another edition of *The Sunday Post* was "measuring up" as I chose to call it.

But my mind was still buzzing with it all as I left the office. A good editor has to have a butterfly mind, capable of flitting instantly, but with total concentration, from a threatened libel suit by that mail-order merchant you know is a crook but can't quite prove, to the reason why British Leyland shares suddenly dropped three points in a bull market; from the Auchtermuchty train-shunter to the Newcastle widow; from the sale-of-work that raised £27.50 at Darkhead Red Cross annual fete to the evil machinations of the Chancellor's latest Budget. It is a knack you develop with time. But it meant a constant clutter of clambering facts and figures careering around in your grey cells like a runaway computer.

It also had a tendency to make you pass your wife in the street without recognising her. Other family and friends had no chance. Even your colleagues of many years were turned into casual acquaintances whose names you couldn't remember because the computer had fused on those Budget figures. It made you a strangely withdrawn kind of man, with a strained, worried look, (yet all those facts and figures flashing in a pair of bright staring eyes,) as you mistakenly said "Good morning, dear" to the doorman. Many is the Thursday night I searched all five storeys of the car park where I usually left my car, only to remember it was at the back door of the office, or my wife was using it because hers was in for a service; or it was in for a service! Such is the strange world inside an editor's brain – quick as a flash, but eccentric.

But I was quite sure my car was in the multi that Thursday night. As I left the office I stopped to light the 57th cigarette of the day. The match flickered and died. Brrh! I shivered. There was a cold sharp wind blowing that cut to the bone. I hadn't even noticed it until it blew out the match.

I shrugged my shoulders against the wind and stepped back into the shelter of the doorway to light the cigarette. Was that what did it? Was it those few seconds that brought me so close to death and changed completely what was left of my life? Or was it that damned heading that didn't fit? The burned toast at breakfast? The restaurant cashier who didn't have change for a fiver at lunch? Maybe the car park lights always being switched off at six o'clock which meant I had to fumble in the dark for my car keys and the lock? I'll never know. I'd like to blame somebody or something for putting me in the wrong place at the wrong time. Probably myself for not realising the significance of that icy wind on a night in late November …

I had moved to a house in the country, halfway between the city that housed the head office of *The Sunday Post* and the town that held the high hopes of the family's licensed restaurant. The city and town were joined by a fast dual carriageway, notorious for its accident black spots. It was bad for the blood pressure but the move to the country was still one of my better decisions. What a joy it was to drive through the changing seasons of the countryside, a world of nature away from my own artificial life. The surge of joy at the first green buds of the renewal of spring. A curlew calling in a corn field. A flash of a weasel's tail disappearing into a hawthorn hedge. The bewitching scent of pine and spruce after summer rain. To think the city folk have to buy it in a bottle of disinfectant. A bonny orraman's wife, standing at the crossroads with her three neat children, all waving a cheery good morning as she waited to see them safely onto the school bus. The cheery postwoman, looming eerily out of an autumn morning mist, a ghost pedalling her old bike back into the more leisurely past before postal codes.

But it was November. Dark, dreary, unfriendly November, so I was hurrying home to the warmth of the fire and glass of Talisker. I left the roundabout at the end of the city's ring road and pulled onto the dual carriageway. Everyone else was hurrying home too, impatient with that kind of madness that afflicts us all when we get behind the wheel of the car and try to drive away from all our worries. And I do drive fast. Motoring seems such a waste of time when there's so much to do.

Hello, what was this? A big lorry and bus slowing down the inside lane and so close together they were making it just that bit harder to overtake in all that traffic. Ahead I could see a chap in a yellow "1100" of some sort. He wasn't hanging back. He pulled out to overtake, alongside the lorry with the bus still in front. Good. I'd follow him and get past the other cars between us who weren't making any move. Out I went and accelerated to catch up with the yellow car and got past the big two just behind him. Oops! I was getting too close to Mr Yellow. Touch the brakes. Just enough to slow down, enough to leave a safe distance behind him. That's my recollection of it. But I should have been content to wait a few seconds more for my glass of whisky.

As soon as I touched the brakes, the car went into a vicious slide to one side, skidding out of control. Ice – a solid sheet of it. Black ice, the kind where there's no warning hoar of white frost on the grass verge or sheen on the road surface. The first of that winter, so sudden, unseen and deadly it had caught everyone on the hop, not only the drivers, but the police and ambulance services and the local authority roads department that should have been out sanding and gritting the roads, especially at accident black spots.

There were fourteen accidents on those roads from the city that night, because of the icy conditions. Enough to have questions asked in Parliament. Most were bad bumps with troops of walking wounded, mostly minor bumps, cuts and bruises, jamming up the casualty department of the city hospital. Two were serious. Mine was one of the two and furthest from the city, which could have been crucial. It had happened where a shallow left-hand bend in the carriageway led into a slight dip where the ice had set fast and cruelly into the tarmac in the shadows of some trees. A week later, in early morning, another driver hit ice at the same spot. His car flew off the road, hit a tree and he was killed instantly.

All this I didn't know then. All I knew was that my car was sliding out of control towards the lorry on the inside lane. I tried to correct the skid away from it. I wasn't too worried. After all, I was an Advanced Motorist with a badge on the radiator grille to prove it.

I did all the right things, I kept calm, no desperate jerking of the steering wheel or any of those panic measures. Turn smoothly into the skid, wait until the spinning tyres pick up some grip, then pull out of the skid and away. Only the tyres didn't pick up grip as the book said. OK, pump the brake quickly a couple of times to break the wheel lock, but that didn't work either. So much for the good book. I was inches away from the lorry. Panic! Forget the brakes. Wrench the wheel over. Get away from that bloody lorry. Thank God. That worked. Sheer panic worked. The car turned away from the lorry, only to go into an even more wicked skid in the opposite direction, towards the central reservation. This time turning into the skid did work. But by then, it was too late. The car was fishtailing; the rear end flicking from left to right and back again like a whale out of water. I missed the lorry but the offside wheels caught the low kerb of the central reservation, jerked to the right and ploughed two long snaking shallow furrows across the strip of grass that separated the two carriageways. But the grass was brick hard with ice, too. The car didn't stop, but flew out onto the other carriageway, still turning, side on to the oncoming traffic speeding along into that black ice …

Now I knew I was in a heap of big trouble. If only I hadn't been in a hurry. If only my mind hadn't been filled with the muddle of working late. If only I'd realised just what that freezing cold wind might mean. If only I'd switched on the car radio for a road weather forecast from the local station. If only I hadn't been there and then. If only …

It was all over in seconds. But as anyone will tell you who's been in that situation, it seems to happen in slow motion. No, there wasn't time to see your whole life flashing in front of your eyes. But too much time to see the headlights, big and small, oval, square or round, dipped and undipped – all in differing degrees of brightness, but all getting bigger and bigger, powered towards you by God only knows what behind them. And me in a dark blue car, side on, sliding towards them, almost invisible in the gloom. "What a silly bloody way to go," I remember thinking. "Not with a whimper, but great big bang." My editor's mind still working to turn the telling phrase.

For I knew one of these pairs of headlights was heading straight for me, and whatever was behind them had no chance of stopping on that ice. The closest pair were big, beaming, screaming "Here I come, ready or not" in the excited way we started the childhood game of Hide and Seek. Only there was nowhere to hide. "Pray it's an invalid car," was my last rational thought. I wasn't wearing a seat belt. In a last despairing gesture of self-preservation I tried to throw myself away from IT across the front passenger seat. IT hit me just behind the pillar of my driver's door. I could say with an almighty bang. But bang, however almighty, is the poorest of poor descriptions for the noise that filled my ears as though the gates of hell itself had closed behind me. Just as there are no words to describe the force of the collision; you can only experience it, like childbirth in a woman, I dare say. The effects of it were enough for any dramatic description. That side of the car bananaed inwards, pulling the front, engine and all in towards me and curling the steering wheel somewhere down into my right hip. The roof bulged up. The pillar of the driver's door caved inwards, clawing and digging at my side and back – which would have been rooted to that pillar if I had been wearing my safety belt! The windscreen, with the window on the driver's side, shattered into a million flying fragments.

It had never been a Friday car, full of the niggling faults from that rush of the production line to finish for the weekend. It had been safe and reliable from new. Now, one side mortally wounded, it was tossed brutally aside by the rushing bull, and thrown back onto the central reservation which it had so rashly crossed into the forbidden territory.

It was cold, oh, so cold. A man's voice, almost angry. "He's had it." A girl's voice, fearful but concerned. "Are you all right?"

Is who all right? Why is it so cold? Who's that screaming? No, it's not a scream; more a bellow like a wounded animal. Who are all those white faces in the dark? What's that small red light? Of course, you know. It's the oil warning light. Why is it important? Wait. A hand on my shoulder. The girl again. "Tell me where it hurts." Hurt? It doesn't hurt. I'm just cold. Very, very cold. Wait. It does hurt. My back hurts. My hip hurts. My knee hurts. So does my head. My neck. That groan again. Someone's in agony. The oil light. Why is it on? THE ACCIDENT! I've had an accident. In the car. That groaning. Someone's dying. Oh, my God. The other car. I've killed someone. He's somewhere in this mess with me. That girl again. "You'll have to tell me where it hurts. Can you breathe all right?" Of course I can breathe all right. No, I can't. My lungs are crushed. My back hurts like hell. I've never known pain like that. There's no-one in this wreck with me. It's me that's making those animal noises. "My back," I croaked from my gasping lungs as I came round to the full awful realisation. "It's my back. Don't move me. For God's sake, don't move me."

The other car had been a big powerful Volvo, the one with built-in roll bars and an impact absorbing engine compartment. A brute unless you were the one inside it. It wasn't his fault. There was no way he could avoid me. A sheer accident. He'd been jogging along in the outside lane of his carriageway, bound north, when he was confronted with my car. When he'd catapulted me aside, he'd skidded on to a halt. I don't even know his name to this day, for it was many months before I could even bring myself to wonder about it. Someone told me in hospital that his car was towed to a garage for repair. He was treated for shock and bumps and bruises. I can imagine the fright he must have got. But, he was fit enough to take the train home to Aberdeen that night. I must meet him some time, the stranger who was chosen by fate to change my life. I don't know the girl's name, either, but she was the heroine. The man, I suppose the one with the slightly angry voice, organised the traffic round the accident until the police came. The girl, and I have a notion she said she was a medical student, did all the right things.

I was lying across the front two seats with my head and shoulders against the edge of the passenger seat. My right leg was trapped somewhere down there in the tangle of steering wheel and front door. After the door pillar had caved in and caught me in the side and back, I had been thrown away from it again, so I was still sitting, trapped, in the driver's seat, with my back to it. Someone switched off the engine. The faces came and went. The girl stayed. It was all a blur, not only because my head was still spinning with the force of the impact, but my spectacles, those expensive photometric spectacles, had been blasted to the four winds, never to be seen again, despite a search of the wreckage of the car and all around next day. I am unusually short-sighted. I can read the finest of print, but, without my specs, anything more than six feet from me is a blur. Also, there was blood pouring down my face, into my eyes, which didn't help much. She checked my breathing first. I was having difficulty, but I was breathing.

She must have known her first aid, for she lifted my head from where it hung on my chest and laid it back on the seat. That helped. But what was wrong with my mouth? Something was rattling about. She opened my mouth gently and put her fingers in, realising something might be choking me. It was my false teeth, shattered in pieces. She forked her forefinger and hooked out all the bits. It was the first moment I really became aware that it wasn't all some dreadful dream, for I felt self-conscious at the sudden thought of a young girl seeing me without my teeth. What a sight I must be. But to feel that, I had to be alive, if only just.

The pain had been numbed by the first stunning impact. Now it was cruelly confirming I was alive in wave after wave. Shock and the freezing cold were soon to numb it to the bearable again. But that was one of the worst moments, especially the pain in my back.

It was time to do a mental check. I might as well know the worst. Was my back broken? Was I paralysed? No, it couldn't be broken. I could feel pain in my legs, especially the right one. I could even feel something running down that leg. Something hot at the top and cold at the bottom – blood? I groaned a message to the girl. She checked my leg. "No, it's not blood," she said. "I can't really see, but I don't think you're bleeding badly anywhere." "What about my head?" She wiped at my face and head with a handkerchief. A couple of cuts from flying glass, nothing desperate. It was as she did this, I suddenly realised about my leg. If it wasn't blood, it couldn't be oil or petrol. It had to be – my own urine. I blessed her discretion, my unknown angel, and worried about my bladder and other more privy parts. But no bones sticking out anywhere that I was aware of, so I came to a conclusion. I was badly hurt. Very badly hurt. I knew that. And it was mostly to do with my back and my breathing. If I could just hang on until the ambulance came and not let anyone do anything silly about moving me, I might make it.

Come to think of it, that's what my father had said when he had his accident in the steelworks. Trapped by a leg, too. If he could just hang on and stay conscious. OK, Dad, let's do some hanging on. But I would have to put out of my mind what his accident had done to him.

Now I was slipping into deep shock. It was getting so hard to breathe properly. I wouldn't go. There was something I had to do. My wife, Meg, someone would have to tell her. That man had come back. Somehow I managed to tell them and give them my phone number. Whether they were just humouring me to keep me calm or there was some misunderstanding I don't know. But Meg never got the message.

The police, at last. They'd do something. It wasn't a lot, but it was the best they could do. They were overwhelmed by the trail of accidents that night, all inside an hour or two after dark and the descent of that first black ice of winter. They came, checked I was alive, and being looked after. I wasn't drunk. Or the other driver. Made the accident scene as safe as possible and went on to the next accident up the road, which might be far worse. "We've sent for the ambulance, sir, it'll be here soon," one of them told me. "Don't worry, sir. You're not dead, yet." An overworked, underpaid Scottish bobby, trying to be kind in his own gruff way in the middle of a nightmare for all the authorities that night, and the victims, human or mechanical, strewn along the roadsides. Nor was I to know the ambulance was stretched beyond the limit, leaving on a call for one accident, only to come across another before they reached it. All on those ice-trapped roads that made it as dangerous for police cars and ambulances as anyone else. The more hurry, the more havoc!

Yes, the traffic policeman meant to be kind, but only made me angry. How dare that comforting flashing blue light leave the scene of my accident. Look at all these idiots driving past my wreckage, on either side of where it lay on the central reservation; still driving far too fast for the conditions and taking their eyes off the road to gawp at me as they passed. Me. Not dead yet, but dying. It may not have been quite that way, for I wasn't really there to see it. But that's how it seemed to me. Looking back, that anger probably saved me. It drove me back up to consciousness. Damn the pain in my back. And I could breathe well enough to whisper demands. "When's that ambulance coming?" Soon, they kept telling me, soon. "When are the police coming back?" Soon, they kept telling me, soon. Reassurance wouldn't save me.

Don't they know who I am? I'm Bill Anderson. I'm a successful man. I'm an important man. I know important people. Why, I know the Chief Constable personally. I lunched with him only the other day. How dare they leave me here dying?

But I might as well have taken a heart attack naked in a Turkish bath. There would be no label on me then to say "Very Important Person. Handle him with care."

I'm told it was 40 minutes before the police, who had far from forgotten me, did get an ambulance through to me. It seemed like 40 years, or 47 if you call it a lifetime – my lifetime. They had a lot still to do. It was quick, efficient and excruciating. It didn't take them long to decide I had to be got to hospital fast. The tangled metal was wrenched away to free my leg on the driver's side. The undamaged passenger door was opened and a blanket laid over the seat. I was eased over onto the blanket and lifted out to the waiting stretcher. The pain in my back as they lifted me out of the car was the worst yet. That chap was bellowing again. It was too much for me. I slipped into merciful oblivion. I hadn't even been able to say thank you to a girl I didn't know, and still don't. Thank you, from the bottom of my heart, whoever you are, sweet maiden of the gentle voice. You will make a wonderful doctor.

The bumps and jerks of the ambulance brought me round again. The agony of every movement another knife in my back. But lying flat I was breathing better. Just get me to hospital. For God's sake, we'd stopped. Yet another bloody accident. They had to stop. No-one hurt badly enough to need an ambulance. Thank God. No more delay. Grit your teeth. It can't be far now …

CHAPTER 2

It's No Joke Being Joe O'Soap

There are three classic symptoms of middle age in any man.

When his false teeth click as he chews because his gums are rapidly receding inside them.

When he has unrealisable sexual ambitions brought on by the sight of a girl's bottom in skintight jeans.

When he takes a close look at himself in the shaving mirror and doesn't like what he sees.

You can quote me as an authority too, for not only was that poor chap we left in an ambulance suffering all the symptoms, but I invented the midlife crisis for men when bras were being burned all over the world and we needed some sympathy. It is something that happens to most men, however successful, somewhere between 45 and 55.

That awful man next door to you is having a midlife crisis. That's why he growls when you say "Good morning." He knows it is not a good morning. He has just opened the rates demand and his wife is still yapping behind him about needing new curtains for the lounge. He knows the car won't start and, because of it, bangs the door closed before he even tries the ignition key. Whatever you do, don't smile. Kindness will only make him have his nervous breakdown there and then.

Nor is MLC any respecter of rank. Prince Philip had it badly. Remember when he snarled and swore at photographers; moaned about his salary; told us all to get our fingers out; then swanned off round the world alone to get away from the wife? That was MLC, my friends, and a right Royal case of it. I had to invent the midlife crisis for another reason. *The Sunday Post* was a family newspaper.

Certain words or phrases were banned for fear of giving offence to the narrow-minded and, much more plaudable, to protect parents from the embarrassment of awkward questions from children whose eyes might stray from the comic section. "What's menopause, Mummy?" So it was never menopause, but "the change of life" on the women's page. Even ministers' wives could mention that at the Woman's Guild. And if it provoked a question from a precocious offspring, it could be fobbed off with "Oh, it's just something to do with Mummy's headaches."

So, too, it was never "menstruation", not even "period", but "monthly occurrence" or "periodic pains". Any form of affliction below the waistline became "tummy trouble" or "lower tummy trouble", with enough discreet words to indicate the true part of the anatomy under discussion. Homosexuals, who might have to be mentioned in the news, became "men who misbehaved" and breasts might be on full frontal view in other publications, but were never uncovered in *The Post* and, if they had to be referred to, became dull, unsexed "chests". The prissy obsession not to offend reached its height in my predecessor's tenure when the penis and testicles were painted out to remove them from the side view of a prize Aberdeen Angus bull before publication, which puzzled the farming community mightily and led to an angry letter from the owner demanding damages if he failed to sell his pride and joy to Argentina because we had castrated it. Sorry, sir, but what if some innocent child had asked what they were?

Mind you, even *The Post* recognised that the language of a maiden aunt in 1921 was far removed from that of similar staid spinster in 1981. So as the times became more permissive, the euphemisms grew fewer and there was even a historic day when "womb" was used for the first time. You could at least tell a 1981 child it was "something to do with Mummy's tummy".

I thoroughly approved of this. I was proud of the fact that *The Sunday Post* could be left around the house for any of the family to pick up, read and enjoy. Not tucked under the cushion of Dad's chair with those latter-day rags of Fleet Street known in the trade as the "bum-and-tit" brigade.

I always found perfectly acceptable ways of mentioning the unmentionable. So, when it seemed men were discovering they had a menopause, it became the "midlife crisis for men" in *The Post*. So what about all these dirty words in this book? Don't send it to your maiden aunt for Christmas unless she's a very modern maiden aunt. The restraints on an editor do not apply to an author licensed to spill all. "Tut! Tut!" as much as you like. Hide it from the children, burn it or read it in the loo. But plain speaking it is from here on in.

Conscience clear, I can proceed to the many other symptoms of the male menopause. For a start, there is a far more morbid interest in health than counting the hairs on your comb, mate. If your father was a baldie, forget it. There are far worse ails in store. Only this week, I had two coronaries, cancer of the bowel and a hiatus hernia. True, they all turned out to be various manifestations of flatulence, but they sure put the wind up me. So you go ahead and worry about your high blood pressure. It keeps your mind off your ingrown toenails.

Another symptom is that any woman seems more attractive than your wife, who is still very demanding, even if it is only every second Sunday. This sad sag in your sex life becomes all too revealing if you ever look at the naked ape in the full-length wardrobe mirror after a bath.

You may smell as fresh and youthful as Brut can make you, but whatever happened to the man who made love five times on his honeymoon night? Those varicose veins look like a relief map of great rivers of the world.

As your burgeoning belly reveals, you haven't even kept in trim like Gregory Peck and you can't afford to go to Switzerland for the monkey gland treatment. So you are not going to feature in gossip columnist Nigel Dempster's dirty dozen escorts of Bianca Jagger. You are, face it, just another dirty old man who has to cut the hairs out of his nose. You may have given your best baritone ever of "My Way" in the bath, but you're never going to have as many women, as much money, or more friends in the Mafia than Sinatra, the Old Groaner. The groans coming from you when you bend to tie a shoelace are because you're old.

There is not a snowball's chance in hell of you ever becoming Prime Minister, bringing the House to its feet in cheers and rousing the nation to wring some chicken's neck. You are never going to stride down the 18th fairway at Augusta, only a four-inch putt away from beating the likes of Jack Nicklaus in the PGA Championship.

Not for you a decision whether to sell all your oil wells in Venezuela and the Greek shipping line to get in on the Arab deal to buy Manhattan Island and lease New York to the Chinese for overspill.

In short, you have knocked your pan out for 30 years and have little to show for it but a nasty letter from the bank manager and that faded photo of Rosie which you keep in the back pocket of your wallet so your wife will never find out what a good time you had at the only Transport and General Layabout Annual Convention in Blackpool to which you were ever appointed a delegate.

Doctors, who should keep their opinions to themselves, do say that statistics (of which there are lies, damned lies and doctor's opinions) show the average male reaches his peak at 22 and thereafter it is downhill all the way. You don't need any bleeding doctor to tell you that. You know. You know why you are so intolerant of youth; so darned tired you can't be bothered taking the dog for a walk; so heavy-handed with your children; so cussed you never talk to your wife because what the hell is there to talk about with her?

I tell you this because I suspect that you may be suffering from that last, but most soul-destroying symptom of all, the dreaded Joe O'Soap syndrome, named after the initial letters of the disease – Jealous Of Every Other Son Of A Prick (or Pro).

So this is written that you will not have any twinge of envy at the emergency treatment room of a hospital casualty department. He is just another middle-aged, pot-bellied slob like yourself, with a smoker's cough and hardening arteries, fighting for his life. Death neither knows nor cares who he is …

The nurses stripped me gently, but quickly, like a careful boy peeling a banana. They were cleaning me up as the doctors came and went. "What happened?" I tried to tell them, but I was confused by pain and shock. "My back, it's my back," I kept saying, as if it explained all the hurt in all my body. I was x-rayed, examined, poked and probed. That hurt, too. The doctors became more demanding. "You'll have to tell us exactly what happened, exactly where it hurts. Here? Here? Here?" They had to know, for I was rapidly becoming a puzzle (which I've been to my family, friends and colleagues all my life, so why should the medical profession feel out of it).

Their problem was I didn't seem to have been in as serious an accident as they'd been told it was. I had none of the horrendous lacerations I should have had. My cuts were minor – one high on my forehead; one in my eyebrow; several on the backs of my hands and a mysterious small deep hole in my left side.

I had no limbs hanging askew. No bones sticking out of me. (They were all sticking into me.) I didn't need bandaged or plastered. The only outward sign of any serious injury was massive angry red bruising down my back, later to turn into a giant Picasso of purples, yellows, reds, blacks and blues. And that breathing. Like a very old man dying of very old age. Short and shallow. So it had to be crushing damage. Internal injuries. But how serious? A ruptured spleen is always a probability in such cases. Or a punctured lung. As my condition deteriorated, there was talk of an exploratory op. But to explore where for what? The sensible decision was made. Wait and watch. "Stabilise and support." The injections started. The drip for shock and any internal bleeding.

It was three hours after the accident before my wife found out the hard way. The police phoned her. She hadn't been too worried. She hadn't lived with me through three thousand ruined meals for nothing. She'd left my dinner in the oven. (She found it still there four days later!) You can imagine the shock of that telephone call out of the blue. It was worse when she phoned the hospital. No, don't come, she was told. You won't be able to see him. Serious? Well, some broken ribs, but his condition seems to be stabilising. No, he's not critical. Phone in an hour. In fact, they didn't want her to come for good reason. I was now beyond the ken of casualty. They'd done their duty. They'd kept me alive. Now I was a job for the experts, but that meant transferring me to the teaching hospital four miles away.

I was never actually told the full extent of my injuries, either. I had to pick them up in bits and pieces later, just as the doctors had to do at the time. Three ribs in my back had been fractured in two places and the other ribs where that door pillar had hit me had been flayed, cracked, bruised or otherwise knocked about. I had a "stable" fracture of the pelvis on that side, too. If you imagine your pelvis as a soup plate with a big crack through it, you can still hold it together in one piece with your hands. My muscles were holding the crack together, so it was stable. In the countless x-rays that were taken later a doctor told me, "We've found another fracture in your femur, Mr Anderson. At the top, where it goes into the hip joint." What did one more matter? I was far more worried by another consultation, at which I was a drugged overhearer, in which it was announced, "Some damage to the pubis." Drugged or not, I immediately put my hand down to my most privy part to make sure it was still there, and worried about it for days until I discovered it was the bone behind it. As long as it was OK, the bone would just have to heal with the rest of me, dammit. Needless to say, all the soft organs inside me had been bashed about, too. Try putting some apples, plums and oranges all in a big plastic bag inside the spin dryer and see how they feel about it.

Also, the modern theory is that strapping or plastering (or even the old dodge of wiring) broken ribs can do more harm than good. So my injuries would have to wait until my survival was certain. The problem? I'm no expert, but as I understand it, casualty hospitals are becoming more aware of a phenomenon called "shock lung" in layman's language. When a lung gets an almighty dent as it did in my accident, it protests with countless mini haemorrhages in the lining of all those tubes. Tiny spots of bleeding. But put together, they can add up to a lot of blood which chokes the smallest branches of the air passages. It is a problem to which heavy smokers are most prone and for whom it is most dangerous. All that tar and other goo sticking to the tubes starts to break away, too. And me a sixty-a-day man. So I had shock lung. On top of that, while none of those damaged ribs had punctured the lung, they had pinched and nipped it on the outside, causing bleeding and swelling. What's more, I had another little complication called "flare breathing". Your whole rib cage, muscle and bone, plays a vital part in breathing, helping your lungs to expand and contract. My rib cage was in such a state that it was going in when it should have been going out and vice versa, and even my good lung wasn't doing what it should, tar and all. Sooner or later it would stop telling the rest of me to stay alive. To put it bluntly, either I was going to be mighty lucky and survive direct personal assault by another car at a combined speed of somewhere around 100 mph with neither disfigurement nor disablement or I was going to be mighty unlucky and stop breathing before I could prove how lucky I was.

Not so many years ago, in my state, the minister would have come to the hospital to say a few words over me and the doctor would have written a few words like accident trauma, pneumonia and shock on the death certificate and that would have been that. But this was 1981, and I was a fully paid-up member of the NHS. Help was at hand.

Professor Alfred Cuschieri and his sidekick came from the teaching hospital for a consultation. It is surely the greatest merit of our National Health Service that, poor or rich, we can get the best treatment (free, at a moment's notice and without hesitation) when we really need it. I wouldn't be ill in America for all the oil in the North Sea. They did do a check on internal bleeding. I have a fuzzy recollection of whether it was better to go in through my navel or not. But they decided to make a fresh incision just above it to put some magic-eye instrument into my abdomen and have a shuftie at what was happening there. The specialist decided on a transfer to the better facilities and knowledge of Ninewells General Hospital.

My wife, by that female instinct which defies explanation, phoned as the decision was made. As I was transferred, she was driving to the teaching hospital with my eldest son, Ewan. It must have been a nightmare for her, driving along those still icy roads, past the trail of accidents and the very spot where my accident had happened. Fortunately, what was left of my car had been towed away.

They were told nothing, but put in a side room to wait with a cup of tea and the reassurance that they would be able to see me soon, "but only for two minutes!" When they did see me, it was, they tell me, a shock they'll never forget. The husband of 24 years and father of 21, the powerful and important, devastated with the face of an old, old man, fighting to breathe. They tell me my first gasped words were "Well, they think they've got me where they want me now." I have always been a perverse man. There was time to hold hands, then they were hushed out and went home on the promise that there was nothing they could do by waiting and whatever my condition, I wasn't going to pop off without warning. They'd be phoned if there was any change.

I lay there all night, in deep shock, barely aware of the comings and goings around me. Only the pain and the gurgling wheeze of my own breath. Hold on to that, Bill. Breathe in, breathe out, breathe in … out … in … out. My middle son Graeme came at 8 am, saw, broke down and left and I knew him not.

When Meg phoned at 9 am she was told of my "breathing problems". Somewhere around the same time, they were all round me again. "Well, Mr Anderson, we're going to have to do something about you." I recognised the Professor's voice, that voice. Wise and wonderful man. You are so right, sir. I've done my stubborn best. But this time Bill Anderson is not going to be able to make it on his own. It was all very smooth and efficient once the decision was made.

By 11 am Meg and my youngest son Alan were allowed in to see me; I was in the intensive care unit, all tubed up and wired in.

I was not a pretty sight. I was on the ventilator. A stainless steel tube had been inserted deep down my throat into my lungs. From the complicated mechanics of the attachment that covered my mouth, a concertina tube led to the machine behind my bed, where a pump hissed and puffed, up and down, as it did my breathing for me, pushing oxygen into my lungs and drawing the carbon dioxide out.

Another tube was led down my nose. An intravenous drip led from a strung-up bottle onto my left arm. Another finer tube, of unknown purpose, was sticking out of my right wrist. There was something that looked like a transparent garden hose pipe inserted into my side under my armpit and a smaller one lower down, out of the side of my abdomen. Since I couldn't eat, I had to be fed through a tube. A catheter snaked discreetly from the small linen sheet that covered my embarrassment. Otherwise, I was naked.

When I first became aware of all the tubing, my initial instinct was to phone my stockbroker to buy Dunlop shares. But it was no joke to my nearest and dearest. I now looked as I'd felt, desperately ill.

A nurse took them gently aside. Don't worry. It's not as bad as it looks. Nothing could be done about the broken ribs. No operation or any other surgical interference. Nor was I in any condition to do anything about the other injuries. Nor did they really need any emergency treatment. But I did need help with my breathing. That's why I was on the ventilator. To help me to help myself.

I will only add this. I have never been afraid of death, only of the dying. Some time in that dark night, I had known I was dying, slowly but surely, and found it wasn't all that hard to take; to let yourself slip away from the pain and perplexities. The only regret that you wouldn't be around to read your own obituary to see what a fine fellow the impossible man everybody knew was a bit of a bastard had become in death. I had refused the temptation not out of any great desire for life, but sheer bloody-mindedness. Now I was on the ventilator, pulsing behind me as regularly as my heartbeat, I knew I was going to live. So look out world, there's life in the old dog yet. Which, with the drugs, shock and everything else, might account for my rather curious conduct on that first visit of my family to the ICU.

First, I kept lifting my hand to sign in dumb language – the kind you use to indicate someone talking too much – to insist that they talk to me, and keep talking. Don't stand there looking at me in brave silence. Smile, damn you. And talk to me. Keep me from slipping back into that tempting, too deep sleep. My next sign was for paper and pencil on which, in halting scrawled block letters I put down my first clarion call to warn the world of my second coming: TEETH. SPECS.

I couldn't have used the teeth anyway with all that gizmo between my gums. But with my spare specs, I could see a little of what was going on around me. Not that there was much to see. Intensive care is an eerie, inner world without windows, of constant, regulated heat and drug-induced immobility in which every bodily function is performed for you. The population of patients – never more than five in that big, low room – came and went silently and mysteriously like thieves in the night, either to leave by the door marked "Way Out" or, like the little girl, leaving by the door to nowhere. The little girl in the other bed I never saw and never knew and never heard about until I had won my battle and she had lost hers. Why do I find myself crying now as I think of her when I so selfishly survived?

There was no time either. Nor was I allowed the watch I wrote another note for. Unhygienic, worrying and where would they put it on wrists plastered with tubes and whatnot? Drugs every hour, blood every two hours, x-ray every four hours and the physiotherapist, the bloody physiotherapist. She came every two hours. In every shape and size, from a blonde Teuton who should have stood trial at Nuremberg to a mousy brunette who almost cried herself because she knew how much she was hurting me. I always knew when she was coming, whatever shape she took, because a painkiller and pacifier were hypoed straight into my intravenous drip tube shortly before she arrived, always walking smartly, smiling, but never really daring to show any sympathy or she just wouldn't get anywhere with me. She was the most evil necessity in my kind of case.

She had to force the blood and other yeugh out of me through all the tubes that led from my body into all those bottles below my bed. She would flog my chest with her fingers, pressing and poking, then turn me partly onto my side to do the same to my back.

Can you imagine the exquisite agony of that, with all my broken bones, battered lungs and bruised organs? And she did not stop until the tubes were "emptying nicely" of the gobs of blackish purple, yellow, green and red and miscellaneous other fluids that the wounded beast exudes. Indeed, she did not stop until my lungs coughed up their quota, up into the neck of that life-giving tube in my throat and started to block it, and stopped the ventilator breathing for me until the hovering nurse uncapped a duct, slipped in yet another tube to suck it up and away and let me breathe again. It was a purgatory that petrified me, even though I knew she was doing me good. Until, one visit, high on morphine and low in patient patience, I demanded my notepad and wrote a billet-doux to, as it so happened, the blonde stormtrooper. It was short, sharp and to the point: "I HATE YOU."

I took the coward's way out and arranged for my wife to flood them with apologies, wine, flowers and chocolate afterwards. But at the time, all I was aware of was a slower, far more respectful approach to the bed of the body that dared to speak back.

At home there was a flood of goodwill, too. The cards and flowers overpowered the local postie as well as my wife, and the phone never stopped. Good lord, I wasn't as unpopular as I thought. Vanity, vanity, all is vanity!

So the days passed, with only the odd hiccup. My wife never got quite used to my suddenly going red in the face and flapping my arms in a distress signal to the nurse when I coughed up another blockage and had to be sucked out. One of the squad of doctors who worked in shifts in the ICU had a fair old time getting one of the countless blood samples. It had to be arterial which, for safety, was taken with the finest of needles, from the finest of arteries in the wrist. I watched in drugged detachment as he had seven attempts to hit the one slim straw in the haystack with his needle until the tiny spurt of capillary red flushed his face with success. Which was the first time I knew the Chinese could blush, since that he was. Maybe he's practising his acupuncture, I remember thinking as he left. I was improving when I could joke about it!

My wife tells me she watched the bottles under the bed and when the discharges started to clear she knew I was on the mend, too. The one thing she could never get used to was my habit of pulling my knees up to make myself more comfortable, thereby making a flapping tent of the small sheet that covered my nakedness and flashing my all. As those who could see had seen my all before, prudery had no place in the ICU as far as my comfort was concerned.

My sons started making cracks. "When are you going to stop imitating a North Sea oil rig, Dad?" "Isn't it time they changed your nappy?" One, knowing my hatred of inactivity, even brought in one of those children's Join-the-Dot books. "This must be about just your strength, Pop. You can do it one-handed." Which found its way to the children's ward. (But not before I'd filled in the first page to prove to myself it was an elephant and I hadn't suffered any brain damage.)

There was one more crisis, when the chart of my blood chemistry suddenly went haywire. To let you understand, the ventilator feeds a cocktail of gases to your lungs – air enriched with oxygen and with nitrous oxide as a sedative and painkiller. This "cocktail" changes as the patient's needs change. He is also being fed through his veins and there are all kinds of drugs being pushed into him; let alone the "poison" passing into his blood from all the damaged organs. All this only really shows up in the arterial bloodstream which is why it is so regularly monitored.

My blood chemistry suddenly revealed problems. The conferences and consultations started again until it was tracked down to a vital valve in the ventilator. It wasn't giving me the gas "cocktail" the doctors had ordered and was not exhausting the carbon dioxide it should. The life-saver was asphyxiating me. It was replaced and I didn't grudge the £200 someone told me it cost for the valve alone.

One of the more curious side-effects is what all this does to your skin, which becomes babyish in texture and feels curiously hot most of the time. Pressure points become unbearable and one day the family were treated to the laughable sight of yours truly with a new and unusual feature added to his nudity. Sheepskin bed socks and a sheepskin pad under my backside. They were heaven and I became as attached to them as a child does to a "sooky" comforter.

On the fourth day (or was it the fifth, or sixth?) my lungs were put to the test. I "came off". The ventilator was switched off. Then the nurse used the bladder bag – the one you see in all those hospital movies – to keep me breathing by squeezing it. Then I started breathing and she kept pace with me until she was sure I could breathe on my own. Then she stopped. I was now all on my ownio, with an oxygen mask to help. And I was OK, my lungs were healing. I was breathing for myself. And I was able to take my first unfettered drink from a feeding cup. Nothing ever has, nor ever will, taste as sweet as that cold, so beautifully cold, water with a touch of orange and glucose. My God, I'd give up the Talisker for that any time. No solid food. That was too risky. Imagine a fish bone stuck in my throat.

But the spells off the machine got longer and longer. They were all very proud of me. The doctor said "You are one of those patients who understand what's happening. You have helped us to help you. You have been very good, really. You have made remarkable progress." The "really" I suspect was to do with the cursing and swearing of those physio sessions. But for me that "really" was the one in "really on the mend". I still had a long way to go, but I was over the hump. I would have liked to say thank you properly but it wasn't possible. There had, it seems, been several tubes up and down my throat even before I'd been put on the brute that goes with the ventilator. My vocal chords were damaged. I could only speak in a croaky whisper and that was banned to avoid further damage. I couldn't shout for joy yet.

CHAPTER 3

It's A Helluva Way To Stop Smoking

Even a doctor inured to the most curious workings of the human body raised an eyebrow when I mentioned that, every time I passed wind, my right knee hurt. I mentioned it only because, after being maintained by fluid through tubes for a week, there was no other movement possible in that direction. I have no doubt that Billy Connolly could have made an hour on stage out of the ensuing conversation, hospital humour being almost as coarse as the wild one's lavatorial funny bone. But there was an anatomical explanation. Some big nerve, ending in "…ceptor", I think, passes through the pelvis and down the leg. The damage there. So when I pressed to relieve the pressure of pent-up gases, ouch, in my right knee. The doctor's explanation satisfied my irrational, but I hope understandable, fear that, somehow, in ICU a spare tube had got stuck inside me, leading from my bowel to my kneecap. Unfortunately, someone passed on this titbit. So whenever life was getting dull for the bedpan boys, some po-faced wit only had to ask, "How's your knee today, Bill?" for all to fall about laughing – dangerous for men only held together by a plethora of metal, plaster and bandages. You can't really laugh in an oxygen mask!

As you have guessed, I had been moved upstairs from ICU to the first six-bed cubicle in the male surgical ward, so I'd be handy in case I still needed some surgery. The first thing I did was to look out of the window. I think that I shall never see a poem lovely as a tree. The world!

I have certain unfailing tests for marking your progress. Hearken well, for the doctors won't tell you. The nurses don't know. And beware of the cleaners who polish the floors of a morning with yon bumping machines, who will tell you your whole case history at any hint of asking, but with embellishments from neighbours, friends, family and the woman at the bus stop who lost her man in just the same way that will only bring on an immediate relapse.

But first, Anderson's basic rules for survival in hospital, once-you-know-you're-not-going-to-die:

Rule 1 Do not be misled by the fact that "pressure points" when you're very ill suddenly become bed sores. That's to be expected and only an excuse for turning you over and smacking your bottom with putrid potions.

Rule 2 Do not be misled by anything the Professor says to students round your bed. He is only trying to impress them, not frighten you to death.

Rule 3 Do not be misled by anything visitors tell you that the doctor/sister/nurse/cleaner told them confidentially about your condition. (See Rule 1.)

So, who do you trust? And how do you know whether who you trust is telling the truth? If you are in male surgical, put not your faith in people, but in baths.

When you are very, very ill, the youngest, sexiest nurse available is assigned to give you the full bed-bath treatment, gently washing you all over, albeit with a very large sponge, even in the most intimate regions. This is because there is absolutely no chance of any response whatsoever from the inanimate flesh, which gives her much-needed training in giving bed baths without blushing.

When you are a little better, a bed bath is given as above, only the sponge wielder is the ugliest old bat you ever saw who wouldn't blush in a Singapore brothel.

You know you are much better when a nurse somewhere between the two gives you a bed bath in which the sponge is handed to you to wash the bits you can reach, thus avoiding any possibility of proving how much better you are.

Finally, though still confined to bed, a basin, water and sponge are thrown at you from a safe distance by any nurse and you are told to get on with it, whether you can reach all the parts or not. You are now almost convalescent.

This system is infallible. If by any chance there is a reversal of this, you can be absolutely certain you have had a serious relapse and had better send for your lawyer, crook though you know him to be.

Of course, if you're fit enough to get out of bed, you are fit enough to go to the bathroom and do-it-yourself. The only danger then is that you are not allowed to lock the door and, barred from any excitement in her life, a sex-starved frustrated spinster in her mid-thirties who just happens to be a nurse, may burst in without warning "just-to-make-sure-you're-all-right-and-can-she-do-anything-for-you?"

If you say no, she will promptly tell all who have anything to do with your care that you are much better, and you will get home a lot earlier than you bargained for, which she knows (hell hath no fury).

If you say yes, you will have to go through the whole bath regime again, which is a bit of a bore, since you end up trying to block the door closed with a wedge of wet toilet tissue, and may have a heart attack in the bath, which is why the door isn't locked in the first place.

There are no exceptions. In the course of all this, any interference with your person by a nurse's hand bearing surgical spirits or talcum powder is purely incidental and for good medical reasons. Besides which, if you dare to move, they know the surgical spirits will run into the wrong place and you will miraculously rise from your bed, about three feet straight up. Thus only advancing you faster to the next stage in the bath regime, which suits them fine.

I was a problem. Why should I change the habits of a lifetime just for some silly old rules about baths? I stuck firmly at stage 2 of the bath regime.

Every day in every way I was getting better and better. But

remember all those unplastered, unbandaged ribs and various other stable and unstable fractures left to their own devices and healing in their own good time? With the best will in the world I could not reach any of those parts which still posed problems but were slowly returning to life. And even the biggest teaching hospital in Europe is limited in the number of ugly nurses. So when they ran out, they resorted to low cunning.

When they were fairly sure I wouldn't actually fall apart, I was lifted out of bed into a wheelchair and taken to a special bathroom reserved for any who dared to defy the bath regime. From the wheelchair I was supported, stripped to my birthday suit and lifted into a contraption not unlike a bosun's chair with a back and sides, but attached by chains to a hoist on what looked like a portable lifeboat derrick which the nurses then manoeuvred above the bath to lower me (by turning a winch handle) until I was in the water, bosun's chair and all. You'll get the picture quicker than most if you ever saw that Frankenstein film where the monster is lowered into the bath of fluid for a quick flash of lightning.

Oh, it was lowdown and sneaky. For a start, not a shred of human dignity is left to him who is transported naked like a rhinoceros bound for a new home in the Serengeti. Moreover, the plank of wood on which you sat always dug painfully into that zone referred to as erotic, so even the youngest, sexiest nurse was safe winching the handle (and usually much amused). She could even wash your back safe in the knowledge that you were placed in such a position you couldn't reach her but could reach the rest of you and so could be handed the sponge to do so in the offhand manner pertaining to stage three of aforesaid bath regime. It was some palaver just to make sure you obeyed the rules, but hospitals are like that.

But it was worth it. Even though the reverse process was just as undignified. Those baths were heavenly, unbelievably soothing to a bruised and battered body. Even the Picasso on my back began to fade as I went through this performance every day. I lived for those baths. I couldn't wait to get in. I begged not to be taken out. "Just a minute more, nurse. Please." If I sat very still, with my eyes closed, and tried to imagine I was floating in soothing, supporting warmth it was the one place in the world I was free from pain. Whatever the devil was wanting for souls, I would have doubled for my daily bath and trebled to keep *her* away. For the dreaded physiotherapist was still coming in her different disguises. Twice a day. "Oxygen mask on, please, Mr Anderson." Adjust the moisturiser to fill my lungs with steamy air. Open the front of my jammie top. Slap! Slap! Slap! "Now lean forward, Mr Anderson." Lift my jammie top up at the back. Slap! Slap! Slap! "Now cough it up, please, Mr Anderson." And the torture was then repeated until she was satisfied my lungs were clear again.

It was the sheer relief when it was only once a day that made me suddenly realise. I had not smoked a cigarette since the crash. I couldn't when I was in ICU. I hadn't when I went up to the ward. Perhaps those drugged days on the ventilator had flushed the nicotine from my system, too. Maybe I'd had the withdrawal symptoms without knowing, or been too busy surviving. But I hadn't even noticed that I had stopped and I didn't even want a cigarette. No craving of any kind (except for another bath). From 60 a day, it was a miracle.

What's more, she was the one helping to make my lungs, if anything, healthier than they'd been before. A blessing in disguise if ever there was one. So God bless and thank every one of her.

Thereafter, when all and sundry asked if the rumour could be true; that the editor who set his wastepaper basket on fire 60 times a day with carelessly discarded matches had really stopped smoking; my wife with wry and, for her, rare humour, would say "Yes, it's true. He took a crash cure, you know." Crash cure, to be sure, dear. But it's a helluva way to stop smoking.

Enough of that. I have to mount one of my pet hobby horses for a moment, which proves I was getting better. You cannot read this next important statement and watch *Coronation Street* at the same time. *Coronation Street* would overtax your concentration.

There are plenty of people to tell you what you can't do. There are plenty of people with a thousand-and-one reasons why you shouldn't do it, even if you can. Give me the friend who knows you can't do it – but tells you that you can. Or if you can do it, tells you to do it. And whether you can or can't, do or don't, stays your friend. He is your best friend, believe me. Sadly, it is the reason why bureaucrats have such few friends. They are specially trained from birth to tell you you can't do it whether you can or can't, even if you ask them in triplicate.

They are only ever happy if you don't do whatever it is you even started to wonder if you could do. (Before I'm finished with this brilliant thought, I can see it being set as a particularly difficult passage for interpretation in Higher English.) I have to be quite honest about this and say teachers, traffic wardens and most wives fall into the same category. So do hospital ward sisters since the reorganisation of the National Health Service which had as a top priority the creation of more bureaucrats. It is not their fault. It is the system which now stretches from sanitary disposal officers, formerly known as dustbin men, right to the very top, where hereditary bureaucrats can even tell Prime Ministers and Chancellors, not to mention their own wives, what they can't do (such as free beer for the workers, or free champagne for the bosses).

Now hospital ward sisters may struggle against this. Sometimes they may even forget themselves and wipe a fevered brow. But only to remember in time and dash back to the desk that has transformed Florence Nightingale into Deputy Senior Nursing Officer, Provisional Grade III, Sub-section Va (Male Surgical), where she has so many forms to fill, her pen needs held together by surgical tape, which is the nearest she's been to dressing a wound for a long time.

So never cross a bureaucrat by asking for a bedpan. Indeed, insist she reads your form most carefully before she comes anywhere near you. Otherwise, you may find yourself being told that all post-operation patients must get out of bed as soon as possible, no matter how many unsupported broken pelvises you may have, until she finds the right form and discovers you are not the post-op prostate who should be on his feet to avoid a clot. I did not say which clot he should avoid. I shame her wrongfully, of course, and I exaggerate.

We are all human, even bureaucrats, and she was an absolute angel of mercy who triumphed over all the forms in the end, including those lying in beds and especially the one who refused to do as he was told. But it made for a bad start in our relationship which made us eye one another with suspicion from then on. I would also respectfully remind her that there is no point in suing me as I would swear I wrote this at the time under the influence of drugs. Though I'd still like to know where she hid that half bottle of whisky smuggled in to me buried in a basket of fruit.

I also suspect a touch of form-filling about my sheepskin bed-socks and bottom-comforter. I had become so attached to them I was allowed to take them with me from ICU to male surgical; and needed a minor operation to remove them for prompt despatch in a sealed plastic bag to the laundry. The socks came back and I wore them to the bitter end, but the other end was never to know such comfort again. Had sister taken foul revenge? Never. It was obvious some bureaucrat spotted my bottom-comforter on the laundry list and since it was not on the inventory for male surgical, had it restored to ICU. How his eagle eye missed the bedsocks I shall never know, but my heels were happy he had a blind spot and could go on glowing in the dark knowing they were not actually going to burst into flames.

How are the mighty fallen. Once I had worried about how to explain the perilous state of the economy to the massed armies of unemployed. Now my only concern was sheepskin bedsocks. Hospital does that to you. It is basic stuff, boyo.

In any case, sister had me moved out of her sight to the middle six-bedder of the ward. I wasn't quite sure what to make of that. I knew where I was with the bath. But did this mean I was well enough not to need her constant scrutiny? Or that she was sick of the sight of me? If I wasn't careful, I could be cured here but end up a total neurotic obsessed by bedsocks and bureaucracy.

Not to mention bedpans. I was now a seven-day wonder. Not because of my spectacular retreat from death's door. But because it was seven days since I had come upstairs and started eating solids and I still "hadn't been". This also gets the bureaucracy upset. There is a space on the form to tick it after all – the have-been and the have-not-been. The form can't wait forever. What do you mean, you "haven't been"? You can't do that. You're so right, nurse. It's beginning to feel as if I'll never do that again. Anyway, if it took God all of seven days to make the world, why worry about my laggard innards.

It was a trying time. "I think maybe … now, nurse." Ring the alarm. Mr Anderson wants the commode. Sparks would fly from the wheels as it was rushed to my bedside and the curtains closed on me, which was hardly fair if they wanted me to perform. Open the curtains and let them see Will Shakespeare at work. To-have-been or not-to-have-been. That is the question. After all, you can hardly stand, sorry, sit, there stage middle and cry "I haven't had a (insert-suitable-euphemism-to-suit-yourself) for a fortnight."

I was on and off that perfidious commode like a yo-yo. The round of applause that rang round the ward when the lid was banged shut was silenced only by the glum faces as the curtains opened once again on failure. Impatience was creeping in. Veiled threats being muttered. It was all very well for the Professor to say it would take time. Just look at all those empty boxes on Mr Anderson's form. As for my part, I wanted no other claim to fame in *The Guinness Book of Records*. I was desperate. Have you ever sat on a commode with a cracked pelvis? Indeed, I got so desperate I seriously thought of sending for her again. She had moved mountains.

Stop laughing. It isn't the least bit funny. It hurt like hell to be lifted out of bed onto the commode. It hurt like hell hanging on to it, hoping and praying. It hurt like hell having to admit defeat. "Sorry, nurse, it's no go," as though confessing to some awful crime, and adding "You have not won tonight's star prize. Can you come back next week?" Show your sense of humour wasn't costive. It hurt like hell being humped back into bed. It hurt like hell being pushed around until my pillows were apple pie, even if I wasn't. It hurt like hell having to face the accusing eyes when the curtains were open. Who was I to let the side down?

Come the tenth day and I could fend off the form-fillers no longer. This was a serious breach of hospital discipline. And after that bath business, too. The doctor was consulted. Orders given. To put an end to this painful episode, and draw the final curtain. I can only add that when it did happen – it hurt like hell!

From then on, every day showed improvement. When casual visitors asked how it happened, I could say "Oh, just a bit of a bump with my car," in that modest understatement we use to prove how-brave-we-were, but-we-don't-care-to-talk-about-it.

It was Santa Claus who made me realise how quickly time was passing. I woke one morning to find him at the end of the ward. Well, a big dummy of him wearing an oxygen mask and tubes leading from unseen orifices. So they were decorating the ward. Oh, lord, I had to get out. Imagine having to suffer one of those awful hospital pantos where the chief surgeon always hauls sausages out of a redundant tailor's dummy.

I was shunted into a side room that same day and wheelchaired from my bed to the common dining room for meals. Before I could escape, I had to get on my feet.

I eased myself into a sitting position on the edge of the bed, grabbed the locker and heaved myself up. I was standing, but couldn't budge. The pain came flooding back. Forget it. But I didn't. I persevered with the locker until I felt confident enough to fall across onto the chair, using my left leg as a support, for my right still hung useless. From the chair to the long handle on the loo door. Open it and fall onto the loo. And reverse the procedure.

When I could do that, I got round the rest of the room, resting on whatever came to hand when the pain was too much. I did it and did it until I was soaked in sweat. Then from falling about, to hopping about on my good leg. With the croak that still passed for a voice, I looked and sounded like a bull frog. But it was still the wheelchair if I wanted to leave the room.

"Why can't I have one of those metal contraptions the old folk use to start walking again after a hip transplant?" I asked the next round of doctors. Whispers. Shaking heads. All the x-rays out again.

"We're not sure you're ready to be on your feet, Mr Anderson."
Oh, no. Watch this. I did my bunny hop round the room. I got my
Zimmer frame next day. *She* brought it and showed me how to use
it. Grasp the support bar firmly. Push the frame out in front of you.
Take the weight on your hands as you pull your legs forward into
the frame again and so on. I made them take the wheelchair away.
From then on, I Zimmered round and round the ward corridors
with all the cubicle eyes doing a Wimbledon watching me passing
to and fro. I even made one daring dash for freedom, pushing
through the ward into the outside corridor. But they caught me
and tortured me cruelly by saying they'd take my Zimmer away.

There wasn't much time left. Even staff nurse was rehearsing her
lines for the panto in the sluice room. A new strategy was needed.
On every round, I would time my run so the doctors were at the
far end of the corridor when I left my room. Head high, shoulders
back, I'd Zimmer straight at them, as quickly as possible with a
cunning flick of my waist to throw my right leg forward as though
it was walking, too. One of them was sure to say "Slow down, Mr
Anderson." "Got to get my exercise," I'd say. "Won't be long now"
and I'd whip round the corner to collapse unseen over Mr Zimmer
with the effort it had cost me.

The ENT gave my vocal chords the OK two days before Christmas.
They would heal in time. Another set of x-rays showed my lungs
were clear. My bone fractures had knitted, but would still take
time to heal.

I begged and bullied. I pleaded and made a pest of myself. I
promised I'd be careful. I'd go straight to bed and watch the telly.
I showed them yet again what a wonderful partnership I'd formed
with Mr Zimmer. At the evening round, all three of my parole board
came to my room. Was that really my file? It looked like the manuscript for *War and Peace*. Heads together. One shook. Two nodded.

They had said a couple of months anyway. I was out of hospital
in less than five weeks. I came home on Christmas Eve, packed
like an egg in a corrugated box of pillows and blankets to protect
my frail shell.

We had to pass the spot. I could see the furrows of the car's skid across the central grass reservation. I had held it all back. Tried to make fun of it. Laughed, even when it hurt. Now it all came back, welling up from deep inside me in a flood that wouldn't be stemmed. First the sobs that shook me as I tried to stifle them. Then the tears of recollection, relief and release, coursing uncontrollably down my cheeks. Oh, sweet Jesus, I was alive and going home. And I feel those tears again as I recall it.

Reborn, and out of the womb into the harsh cold light of winter. To a bed couch downstairs in the sitting room where all I could see out of the window was snow – and those early clematis should have been pruned by now. And inside, the realisation crowding in fast. Bills. Medical forms. Insurance claims. Police (to say I was innocent, I hasten to add). Letters to write. Nobody meant to hassle me. Quite the opposite. They were kindness itself. But the important, powerful successful man was home from hospital and, only if you feel up to it, of course, could you just … decisions, decisions, decisions.

I paid the penalty for leaving hospital early. The strain on my muscles and bones of using the Zimmer like a mad man in those last two days had set their healing back. There was a hot spot in my back that was starting to give me gyp. My wife looked at it. "There's a bump, Bill." First, a small bump then it swelled up to a big bump. It was so painful I couldn't even bear the weight of my pyjama jacket on it.

The hospital said I still had to sleep almost sitting up. So every night, my wife had to spend an hour adjusting my eight pillows, leave a hole for that bump, until I found a position that was bearable enough for me to drop off. Even with the prescribed handful of sleeping pills and painkillers, I was only getting an hour at a time. If I did doze off again, it would be fitfully until, sure as guns a pillow would slip – down on to the hot spot. I cannot tell you how often I sat there, out of my mind with drugs in a waking sleep, crying with pain and frustration. And if I did sleep, the nightmares.

Eventually my doctor phoned the hospital. More consultations. It wasn't an abscess. I had somehow displaced the broken ends of a rib which were bulging out into my skin. There was nothing really could be done about it unless I went back into hospital and had a spinal anaesthetic above the bump which would take away the pain and let me sleep. But keep me flat on my back. And work my way through the bath regime again? Was there no alternative? OK, double the sleeping pills and painkillers and we'll see. But Mr Anderson will have to accept that he has been very badly knocked about. It will all take time. He shouldn't really be home. He was very seriously ill, you know. Thank you, doctor, I will grit my teeth and grin. I virtually had to start again. It was weeks, but the pain did ease in time. It still comes and goes a year later. I have it now, nagging at me, when I can still just feel the bump.

As I healed and the weather cleared Mr Zimmer came into his own again. It was a milestone when we manoeuvred together down a doorstep and out to feel the fresh wintry air on my face, with that faint scent that marks the country from the city! Dung being dumped on the fields. Winter is passing. So too other milestones. All the way down the garden path. To my neighbour's for a coffee. To the end of the road. Then Mr Zimmer went off to make friends with someone else and I got two sticks with spiked rubber feet to make sure they wouldn't slip on any surface. I set myself targets. First the loose brick on the first corner. Then the lamp post opposite the butcher's window. Then the post office where I could read what was happening in the village. I always lingered there. Then the house with the green fence. Then right round the village. It was the end of February. Three months. And I could go to the pub for a pint. It may not sound much to you, but I celebrated with a small cigar, which was a terrible mistake. There is no fool like a healing fool. I casually asked mine host for a packet of Hamlet, the small panatellas. There were five. I lit one and sat there, proud as punch. Oh, I didn't inhale the filth down into those lungs that had nearly cost me my life and were now healthier than they had been. But I was still so guilty I hid the other four from my wife when I got home, and didn't dare go near them again well, for another month anyway – and I felt somehow uneasy.

I also had a certain disquiet about the fact I could scarcely bear to look at *The Sunday Post*. My life. I had put my whole being into it for 25 years and what did I have to show for it? A catastrophic car crash on an icy Thursday night because my mind was too full of it! And not even a line in it about the Editor's accident or parlous state of health. Part of that passion for secrecy that shrouds the Thomson family for whom I worked and their many publications. Bill Anderson I might be, down and so nearly out. But the Editor of *The Sunday Post* it would appear is not Bill Anderson but some nameless immortal. The King is dead. Long live the King. I felt curiously anonymous.

Yes, I was feeling sorry for myself. And, in my humble opinion, rightly so. Let us return for a moment to where this odyssey began – to take a closer look at that important, powerful man, with all the trappings of success. Under that flashy façade hid just another harassed, high pressured company man, a heart attack looking for somewhere to happen, with hacking cough from too many cigarettes; bloodshot eyes from too many Taliskers in the middle of the midlife crisis; snapping at his wife and children; sneering at his friends; waxing sarcastically at his staff; the house on mortgage, the holidays on overdraft, the business near bankruptcy. Even that blasted car I crashed was the company's. The only way I could live was by shuffling credit cards. This was success? When first we practise to deceive, the tangled web we weave is usually round ourselves. And, oh brother, had I been fooling myself. Even all that talk about the knighthood. The aforesaid influential MP lost his seat at the election, so that was out the window too. Face it man. All you are is a convalescent has-been.

So I argued with myself in that post-fatal depression. Oh, I know what you're saying. Stop feeling sorry for yourself. You've had a good life. Travelled the world. Mixed with the high and mighty. Seen more and done more than most. And Fleet Street has a healthy respect for your journalism even if nobody else knows who you are. Did you learn nothing from your accident? That the most important and valuable thing in life is life itself. Your life isn't over yet, not by a long chalk, and you've had it no worse than many since the day you were born, and a lot better than most. Hmm! You may have a point. Since the day I was born. I have to think about that …

Have you ever walked into a cinema in the middle of the main feature? You've just worked out what you think is happening when it's "The End", and then you've to sit through from the beginning to get your money's worth, knowing the ending. I wouldn't like to spoil this book for you, so maybe it's not a bad idea to go back to the beginning!

FOOTNOTE:
If this life-or-death drama now has to go back to the day I was born, in fairness I must warn you that this book will take a turn for the boring. If you actually paid hard cash for it (no credit cards, please) or borrowed it from a friend who can prove he paid for it, feel free to skip the boring bits. There are more funny bits, and even dirty bits, if you look hard enough. If the book is borrowed from a public or other lending library, the author insists you must read every sweaty, bloodstained, tear-dropped boring line – if only to get your rates worth and if you don't think it is worth it, be comforted by the fact the author has not earned a ha'penny royalty from you.

CHAPTER 4

So What If Your Mother Is A Bastard

Before Alex Haley bared his African soul, I didn't bother about roots. I knew they held up trees – any fool knew that – or were squared at school; or worried your sister because she wasn't as fair-tressed as she made out and was always doing something to hers with evil potions from sinister dark green or brown bottles that smelled vaguely of the bleach Mother used to whiten the wood round the sink.

It never occurred to me that I must have roots. After all, I was busy making my way in the world, wherever the way led. A born itinerant. Wherever I happened to lay my head was my home and I was content to be able to trace my ancestry back to my parents. But Mr Haley made me wonder. Who was my Kunta Kinte? And my convalescence gave me time to find out.

Actually, once you decide you want roots, it's not too difficult to dig them up, providing your library ticket is valid and you don't have too many overdue fines. (I must remember to return *No Orchids for Miss Blandish*.) Simply browse through a few reference books on the origins of names and the like and, whether you actually find any skeletons, you are certain to uncover a few bones.

I must confess as a boy I liked to think I had Viking blood in me. It stemmed from my voracious reading, when by torchlight under the bedclothes I lapped up the lurid tales of marauding Vikings who rowed across the North Sea in their big oary boats. Then rampaged ashore, looking like very wild long-horned Highland coos, to plunder Scotland with two-handed battle axes. I warmed to heroes who enjoyed a spot of raping and pillaging. I had only the vaguest notion of what raping involved, but it sounded fun from the illustrations of women with bulging breasts. As for pillaging, it had to be bloodthirsty since it was something to do with pillows (or was that raping?) and I had often fought my brothers to tears with a feather bolster. And what laddie didn't fancy a Viking funeral?

That's what my picture book said they gave Leif Erikson after he discovered America. That tickled me because I wasn't too keen on that chap Columbus. He was a funny foreigner who went round begging from kings and queens just to feather his own nest.

My favourite Viking story was about Ragnar, the legendary Norse king. He preferred the life of a Viking to staying at home and running his country. Who wouldn't, apart from a certain grocer's daughter.

What I liked most about Ragnar was that when he wanted something, he took it. He never had to see if there were enough cakes on the plate to stretch to seconds for me.

Now Ragnar fancied the fair maid called Thora. Except her dad had surrounded the house with frozen lakes and heather hoaching with adders so Ragnar could get at neither booty nor boobs.

Cunning lad, he stuffed his jerkin and shirt with hair – horse or whatever I know not – and wrapped more hair round his woolly leggings up to his thighs and down round his baffies, so that the ice couldn't freeze him or the adders bite him. So he won the fair lady and all that went with her.

A modest enough adventure, you might say, and I would have to agree, bar for the punch line. Thereafter, he was known as Ragnar Lodbrok. And Lodbrok, dear reader, is Norse for "Hairy Breeks". Say it to yourself. It rolls off the tongue with a rare Scottish burr, doesn't it? And so evocative, especially for a laddie who had to wear short, scratchy, Co-operative flannel breeks himself. Yes, Hairy Breeks was my hero. He had my sympathy as well as my admiration.

Moreover, as I revelled in the tales, not only of HB but of Thorfinn the Mighty, Sigurd the Stout and Magnus Barefoot, I noticed not a few of the Northmen had names ending in "son". Was it too much to ask that I was "Son of Anders", great-great-great-grandson of Anders the Mighty, descendant of a Viking chief, maybe even old Hairy Breeks himself? I even drew up a family tree to prove it, and vowed to grow a beard. By the time I was old enough for that, it became a Clark Gable moustache because I was in love with Doris Day by then.

To my utter surprise, when I made my foray to the public library all those years later, I found a great deal of evidence to support my boyish fancy. The sentence jumped out of the book at me. "Anders was a not uncommon name in early Denmark." As everyone knows, the Vikings came from Denmark, Norway and Sweden. The reference went on to reveal that, thereafter, Andersson had become a not uncommon name in Scandinavia and even had much the same spelling in Norway, except there was a snag to that. The scribe rather tended to the theory that the Norwegian Andersson was a corruption of Andrewson, meaning Son of Andrew and definitely of Scottish origin, which seems to infer that the Viking raids weren't always one-way, with some Andrewsons up to a spot of you-know-what in their airt. Or maybe they were captured prisoners shown a few favours by the wives back home while the Vikings were off on another raid. Never mind, it was just possible that Hairy Breeks had been my Kunta Kinte.

Alas, rather than any confirmation, I came on evidence that only confused the issue. A tome on the clans of Scotland was emphatic that Anderson was derived from the Gaelic Mac Andrea, meaning Son of Andrew, that patronly saint of Scotland; or Gilleandris, meaning St Andrew's cup-bearer. A Gael. This left me with more in common with the Welsh and Irish than the Norsemen. Not that I've any objections to the Welsh or the Irish, except at football!

The tome further revealed that the more ambitious of the MacAndrews and Gilleanders, realising there was more to life than peat, porridge and usquebaugh, migrated across Scotland to become Andersons and take over Aberdeenshire as powerful lairds, tenant farmers and other useful citizens. That was better. If I had to be a Gael, I'd prefer to be an Anderson of that ilk.

Unfortunately, I didn't leave it there but turned to another verbose volume on Scottish surnames wherein it averred the Andersons not only owned large swaithes of Aberdeen-Angus territory, but were big in the Borders, too. Ah, cattle thieves. The skeletons at last. But no. This branch seemed to have sprung from a French bloke called David le fiz Andreu, who came over with all those nasty Normans to grab a slice of the cake in Sir Walter Scott country and started a line through Andreu to Androsoun, Androsone and so to the latter-day Andersons.

On trying to track down this Franco-Norman, I found myself back with the Vikings who had seized most of Normandy in AD 911. Full circle. Now I knew why *Roots* was such a long TV series. But, if you think about it, this link did bring Hairy Breeks back into the picture. Could one of his progeny have sired Monsieur Andreu in a session of R and P (not to be confused with the R and R of the American forces in Vietnam, though it has been alleged there were many similarities)?

If you're with me so far, realisation must be dawning that any Anderson has to face a rather nasty truth. Chances are he or she is a mongrel mixture of Viking, Franco-Norman and Gael.

I then investigated my other paternal bloodline. My other great-grandfather on my father's side was a Colvin. None of the experts disagreed about this name. A vernacular pronunciation of Colville, of Norman origin. Back to Normandy but also to the Vikings! For this name originated in the form of Colleville in Normandy taken from a farm owned by a Scandinavian called Koll.

The first of this bunch of Normans to turn up wearing tartan trews was a Philip de Coleville, who somehow acquired a brace of Baronies in Roxburghshire around 1159. His other claim to fame was that he offered himself as a hostage for William the Lion under the Treaty of Falaise. I leave that to the historians, but the Colvilles were grander folk altogether: barons, lords, lairds, gentlemen and assorted religious dignitaries, although one managed to get hung for treason. This was more like it. All in all, the Colvilles definitely added a touch of pedigree to the breed.

Anyhow, wherever the Andersons originally sprang from, they were prolific. By the middle of the 19th century, they had become one of the eleven most common names in Scotland, along with the McDonalds, Mackenzies, Stewarts, Campbells, Robertsons, Scotts, Thomsons, Millers and, would you believe, Smiths and Browns (so that explains the frequency of their appearance on hostelry registers).

Now I had the general picture up to about 1850, I had to be more particular to the present day. It can be a mistake to find out too much about your antecedents! But you can do it for yourself by getting hold of the oldest birth certificate in your family and working back from there through Parish registers and other public records. Wills, of which you can get copies if you have a date of death, are not only splendid sources of family background, but also explain for the first time why your mother never writes to her brother's widow in Baltimore and wouldn't even speak to her if she did come home for the first time in 47 years, flashing her dollars.

I was lucky. I only had to go as far as the attic. As one of the dubious legacies of being my aunt's executor I had fallen heir to a Fry's Chocolate box, packed with faded bromide snaps, funeral bills, yellow newspaper cuttings and other whatnots of memorabilia. Aunt Nan was a magpie. She even cut the bone buttons off Uncle Wull's old semmits before using them as dusters. Just as well. The chocolate box I'd stuck in the trunk with scarcely a glance was bulging with clues to my past.

But an hour's analysis of Auntie Nan's hoard made one thing crystal clear. From all those romantic beginnings, my Andersons had thrown my titles and fortunes to the wind. I was solid working class, son – and what's wrong with that as long as you can keep proudly quiet about it and get rid of your glottal stop?

Somewhere around the middle of the 19th century, a couple of stout Scottish artisans were birthing the current Anderson dynasty, though they were not to foresee the end product or they might not have enjoyed it at the time. John Anderson was an east coast fisherman hauling haddock and cod from the North Sea grounds which was a rather more honest endeavour at sea than that of the progenitor, Hairy Breeks. James Colvin, impoverished descendant of those rather grand Colvilles, was heaving coal from the mines of Lanarkshire.

John, the God-fearing fisherman, spawned a lad called Alexander Anderson, while the pneumonocious miner coughed up a lass called Janet Colvin. In that month alleged to be merry, in the Year of Our Lord 1865, after what passed for romance in those days, Janet (spinster, dressmaker), aged 20, married Alexander (bachelor, hammerman), aged 24. What did pass for romance in those days appears to have been a brief touching of hands on the couch in the front parlour, on a Sunday night, after church, under the eagle eye of a priggish Presbyterian mother and a frowning father who had somehow been transformed into a self-righteous Bible-thumper from the leering, lurching drunk of the night before.

Nevertheless, Janet and Alexander had managed sufficient cursory good-night kisses on the cheek at the front door to finally pledge their troth. But what was a hammerman? Did you notice that, too? It's a pity they ever stopped the TV series *What's My Line?* I'd have loved to have seen Gilbert Harding cross swords with a hammerman. For all I know, I'm passing hammermen in the street every day. Or if Alexander had been a hammerman in Glasgow at the time of the Gorbals gangs, I could have guessed what he did for a living. Where was that chocolate box? Were there any clues to this curious occupation?

Indeed there were. A much folded and unfolded letter with a business heading whose contents are shown opposite. What a wealth of information. But I could take time to savour it. For what struck me immediately was a fine print line at the foot of the letter: "All quotations subject to the usual strike and stoppage clause."No doubt you cottoned on to that "usual" too. Man may have been on the moon. Women may have burned their bras. The Russians and the Americans may have threatened to blow us all to kingdom come. But nothing has changed really, and I find that faintly reassuring.

But there were riddles in the letter, too. If my grandfather had

Dalzell Steel & Iron Works,
Motherwell,
3rd October 1900

Alexander Anderson has been employed at this Works for about ten years, chiefly about the melting furnaces. He has been working as a second hand, taking turns occasionally as a first hand and has shown himself to be a good workman.

D.M.M.

For David Colville & Sons Ltd

STEEL MANUFACTURED BY SIEMEN'S PROCESS ONLY
ALL QUOTATIONS SUBJECT TO THE USUAL STRIKE AND STOPPAGE CLAUSE.

been a hammerman when he married in 1865, but had worked for ten years in the melting shop in Motherwell up until 1900, that meant hammering men or anything else was something he did in the 25 years between 1865 and 1890. A gap I would have to fill.

I thought I knew part of the story. Part of the family lore was that, for a time, he had been a self-employed "wrecker", a demolition ganger, knocking down not houses and other buildings, but any erections with steel in them, such as bridges. Was that what he had done in the missing period? Then settled for a steady job in the steelworks? Now he was starting to take on flesh I had to know, for he was dead before I was born. But who was there to ask, as both my parents are dead now? And that still left hammerman.

Meanwhile, one name on that reference I did know. Colville's. The largest steelworks in Europe, indeed, barring Germany, in the world. A sprawling, ugly, pounding, steaming, hissing conglomeration of mills and engineering shops that carved the heart out of Lanarkshire, spouting red, yellow and oily black smoke from countless chimneys during the day, and firework and furnace glow at night that reddened the sky wherever you looked. Yes, I knew Colville's well, for I had lived in its noisome, grimy grey shadow for 17 of my formative years. The alchemist's inferno that turned the iron, brought in on the ships of the River Clyde, into the steel that built the even greater ships that went steaming round the world, ringing out the paean of "Clyde-Built with Colville's steel", with names like the *Queen Mary*, *Queen Elizabeth*, *Queen Elizabeth II*; building railways that built the British Empire and the locomotives that carried the troops to defend them, the bridges that joined nations together and the shells that knocked them down again.

Yes, I knew Colville's well, for that name had cost my own father a leg. But if I was ever to find myself, there were years to fill before I could dwell again on that ghastly night.

So next to the final irony of that letter. The name again. You may have spotted it as quickly as I did. That curious twist of fate that gives life an almost scary pattern. For in those years, wasn't there a certain James Colvin, a poor scion of the grand Colvilles, howking the coal out of the ground at Wishaw, in the shadow of the steelworks, to feed the mills that made a fortune for the grander branch of his own forebears? I wonder if he knew. I wonder if that feeling of under-privilege – of having to tip the bunnet to the bowler-hatted foreman and bow the head to the Derby-hatted boss in case you lost your job – was what led to Red Clydeside and all that followed. Equally, I wonder what James Colvin, miner, and Alexander Anderson, hammerman and second hand, would make of the trade union leaders of today, with their limousines and shiny modern offices and bloc votes that they wield in the one-man power that smacks of the opposite of the democracy it is alleged to defend. Don't start me, for I have no time for the extremes of any political persuasion, or anyone who tries to sell me any political philosophy ending in -ism. Nor can I put any more flesh for you on James Colvin. Perhaps another time.

However, if only half the stories passed down in the family are true, Alexander Anderson is about to grow larger than life before your very eyes. He was a big man, by all accounts, with a shock of white hair to the end of his day. He had hands and a thirst to match his size. In all modesty, he could claim the biggest hands and thirst in Scotland. In those days, most working men spent any spare moments from a three-shift 60-hour week in the pub, to get away from the drudgery of work and nagging wives. So what's new? (Carpets instead of sawdust. *Space Invaders* instead of skittles. Malibu in cocktail glasses instead of cheap gin in jugs. And wives in the pub!) When they had to make their own amusement, they devised games, one of which, called Span, was very popular in the industrial central belt.

It was simple enough. The adversaries each bought a pint. The pints were placed a little apart on the wooden counter that served as the bar. First to play put his hands palm down between the glasses, thumbs touching in the middle, each pinkie touching a pint. Then he splayed his hands, pressing them down and out, to push the pints as far apart as possible. If the second player, on his turn to do the same, couldn't touch the glasses with his pinkies, he lost. Or if he pushed the pints even further apart, he won. The winner drank both pints and collected any side bets he had laid, which could be as much as a bob (shilling), a considerable sum when cigarettes were around 3d for a twenty packet.

For all the other champions brought to his local from pubs far and wide, my grandfather never lost, which also accounts for his alleged prodigious capacity for beer and his proverbial generosity from his jingling pockets to anyone but the wife who waited for him to reel home, champion of Span and, as far as I can gather, any other challenge to his fists.

Janet must have been a tolerant woman for, despite my grandfather's failings, she bore him seven children of whom the second youngest was my father, John. He was a smaller man physically than his father, but big in every other way. And while he didn't have his father's hand span, he did not too badly in the other hereditary department. And so, son followed son unto all the generations and at the tender age of 14 my father was dispatched to the selfsame Colville's steelworks where he laboured for 43 years to the high rank of roller in No 4 Bar Mill – until that night in 1950. If my father and grandfather left me no other legacy, and they did, it was my ambition when asked about my background, to brag at a cocktail party at 10 Downing Street that one was a hammerman and a second hand at that, and the other a roller in the steelworks, you know, and then watch the faces.

So much for my father's side of the Andersons. My mother's side was more mysterious. I could leave you on that intriguing note, but if I have to tell the truth, the whole truth and nothing but the truth, the reasons for the mystery were far from romantic. My mother was illegitimate.

Here I must digress. Yes, I know that's exactly what you are told not to do in Lesson Four of "How To Be A Writer In 24 Hours" (Money Back Guarantee If Your Novel Is Not Published Within Seven Days). But in the first place, I have always tried to lighten the blows of life with a little digression. And it is no easy matter for me to confess I am an SOB, which may end in bitch in America, but is indisputably another word for me. What's more, my mother would never have told anyone, never, for in her day bastardy was the next worst malady to leprosy. There were no short-form birth certificates then to hide the shame of the mother, the poor bastard, or anyone else who ever had reason to see it, which is why I must take you down a byway to explain how I came to know my mother's dark secret.

I was five when the world last went mad for the umpteenth time in 1939. It would take another book to tell you about it. Suffice to say, "the land of hope and glory" was cut off from all hope and not much glory for a few years and there was a scarcity of all manner of things including food. A device called "rationing" was introduced to dole out the few supplies that managed to get through the U-boats. This meant I never knew what a banana was until 1945 because I was too young to remember when the war started and never saw one again until it ended. Worst of all, sugar was strictly rationed to about 2 oz (metrify that yourself, for I can't be bothered) per person per week, and sweets the same. You even had to hand over funny wee ration coupons at the sweetie shop for as much as a gobstopper. It was hell on weans with a sweet tooth, like me. At times I was reduced to a laxative chewing gum called Bonomint which was sold "off-the-ration" in chemists because it was medicine. I suffered many dire consequences for the sake of my craving!

The only other substitutes were small Ovaltine® tablets in a tin, whose real purpose was for making the famous before-bed beverage, and liquorice stick. Not the modern confection, but an actual twig from the tree which we chewed and sucked for hours until it was a stringy pulp, but with poor reward in flavour or sweetness. Babies were mighty lucky to get their dummy teats dipped in sugar then, I can tell you. The craving was only made worse by the fact that the wartime diet was a weird, bland, tasteless gathering of make-dos from powdered egg to snoek which, if I recall correctly, was a brown nameless piece of fish meat in a tin.

The sweetie coupons cut out of the ration book were supposed to last me a month. Sometimes I managed to get to the second day even when one month, in desperation, I told my mother I'd lost my sweetie coupons when I hadn't. She hauled me off to a neighbour who was a Justice of the Peace where I swore blind to my loss, and my mother signed affidavits in triplicate to confirm it. So I got a double ration that month. It was my first essay into real crime. I think it was a hanging offence in wartime (like "Careless Talk Costs Lives") but that quarter pound of cinnamon balls that I sucked for ages was worth the guilt. Though it was a long time before I could convince myself I hadn't let Adolf Hitler win the war.

Imagine my shock after the war when my mother, of irreproachable virtue all her years, confessed that she, too, had got extra sweeties through an "arrangement" with Peggy in the Co-operative whereby those "in the know" put their shopping bags up on the counter in such a way Peggy could slip into them a highly illegal packet of pan drops, or maybe even a bar of Bournville dark chocolate. To such depths of depravity do mothers and children descend when men make fools of themselves playing soldiers.

That, you will be glad to hear, brings me to the old picnic case under the bed in my parents' room. Forbidden territory to a child, for it truly contained the ancient mysteries of life itself. They actually sleep together in the same bed in there, I remember thinking, but what for? But I was a child of insatiable curiosity and whatever was forbidden had to be investigated. I dared to go in. I wonder if they need a potty under the bed, too. If I just take a peep … and there it was, not a chamber pot but an old blue case, wrapped round with a broad buckled belt.

I recognised it. In the early years of the war, it had been carried out to the family bomb shelter buried in the back garden. It was named the Anderson shelter after Sir John, its designer (and no known relation unless he, too, went back to Hairy Breeks). Six sheets of corrugated galvanised metal, curved at the top, were joined up, three a side, with straight front and back, and erected in a big hole dug in the garden (or anywhere convenient) then covered with earth, turf or any other material to make them if not proof from a direct bomb hit at least from a near miss or any blast. It was fitted out with bunks, a heater, usually a solid fuel stove with a chimney poking out above earth, and other conveniences to make life tolerable during an air raid. When the warning siren went I was carried from my bed to the shelter in blankets and often slept through it all, oblivious to the fact those nasty Nazis were trying to end my young life while they strove to wring the chicken's neck. There the family stayed until the all-clear sounded. Being near the steelworks meant we had our share of alarms, though the unmistakable rise and fall of the Vroom-Vroom-Vroom meant the Junkers never found them.

The old picnic case always went, too. And I often wondered what secrets it held. The family jewels? We had none. Emergency food supplies in case we were buried alive? They were left in the shelter. My father's life savings? He was always skint by pay day, which was why my mother kept a packet of Co-operative Gold Flake hidden for when he ran out of cigarettes, as he always did. So what could be so precious that it had to be protected from Herr Hitler?

Now I didn't need x-ray eyes, like the chap in *Film Fun*. I could find out for myself. I could open it, if I dared. But what punishment would it rate if I was found out? I knew I would be found out. It was one of my mother's favourite axioms. "Be sure your sins will find you out." And she always did. There were three known punishments. If I used a "bad" word, told a lie, was cheeky or otherwise misused my mouth for any verbal misdemeanour, my tongue was rubbed with soap. Literally and none of your Palmolive®, but rough red Co-op carbolic, fittingly used for all the other dirty places in the house. I was then sent "to wash out my mouth".

The next punishment was a tablespoon of castor oil and bed. This was definitely a far more serious sentence. Stealing homemade ginger biscuits from the Coronation tin, for example. Remember, it was wartime and biscuits were precious. Or for a serious lie, such as saying you had paid half of your Saturday sixpence into the savings bank at school when you'd spent it on Bonomint. The castor oil served a double purpose. It not only purged you of your evil ways, but everything else as well. Castor oil or sulphur and treacle were a weekly relic of the old Scots myth that they "cleaned the blood", like carrots being good for your eyes. So this punishment was often quite unfairly applied for what seemed to me were carbolic offences at most. It also got you off to bed early, which was no bad thing if visitors were coming. I hate even a whiff of castor oil to this day.

The last resort was the belt. Not any old belt, but *the* belt. I can still feel it. It even had sub-divisions of application. The first degree was across the backs of your bare legs as you ran for it. The second degree was when your trousers came down and your bare backside got it in that painful burst of temper which every Scottish parent seemed to need to persuade themselves that it was necessary. The miscreant prayed that the temper wasn't such that it was the buckle end that was used!

The third degree was when you were sent to bed without your tea or supper to wait for it. That only happened when my father was on the "back-shift", from 2pm to 10pm. For when he went to work, the belt went with him. Not round his waist, but just below it, on his hips, like a weightlifter's support. And it served the same purpose. To support the stomach and muscles in the lower back in the bending and lifting of his labours. So it was wide, supple with use and blackened with sweat and acrid fumes from molten steel. It also had a strong bronze buckle. When I read all the uproar about some latter-day thug still being threatened with the birch on the Isle of Man, I remember that belt. I lived in screaming terror of it. But, by God, you did go out of your way to avoid it.

When my father didn't work, it hung on a nail behind the glory-hole cupboard next to the larder in the kitchen. So handy, if only to be waved at you as a threat. That's why any belting offence which occurred on the "two to ten" meant going to bed and waiting, every hour a century, for his step on the street, which you heard from a 100 miles, and not because they were heavy studded work boots. Then the voices below. The sneck of the cupboard door and my mother coming up the stairs and into the room, as white-faced as me. It was always my mother. "Be glad it's me, for if it was your father …" a sentence that was never finished. No temper. It was all so cold and deliberate that I'd be bent over the bed before asked, resigned to my fate. But I'd squeal like a stuck pig at the first blow, because I knew that what could be done in a temper was a different story now. "It's got to be done, William, or you'll never learn." One more. Squeal harder. "It's for your own good." A third. Howl like hell. "It's hurting me as much as it's hurting you." A fourth. Squeal, scream, howl and throw in a few sobbing "I'll-never-do-it-again, Mum." Contrition usually worked, if you timed it right. And so to bed.

All this I considered as I crouched down on my knees, looking under the bed at temptation. What could be worse than the belt? I felt the same cold shiver that I'd had when I'd read about a German spy being hanged. But I had to know. I hauled out the picnic case and opened it before I could stop myself.

What a let-down. Just a load of old rubbish. Or so it seemed to me. Letters; penny-a-week Prudential insurance policies; photographs; school certificates; National Savings Certificates from the school bank; a small red book on Freemasonry; bank books; Co-operative share book; medals. As you've guessed long ago, it was all that my mother reckoned should be guarded from destruction. But for me, there was nothing that was worth more than a castor oil job. Until I lifted a photograph of my father, posing proudly as Captain of Colville Park Golf Club, to take a closer look at it. I saw the handbag first, a square flat bag, like a big square purse, made of scrolled leather. Honestly, the flap almost fell open.

There were brown manila envelopes inside, each with a name – William, Ian, Barclay, Betty, Mother, and Father. I had to look in mine. It was my birth certificate. I'd seen it before. I don't know what made me pick my mother's next. It was so old and yellow I unfolded it gently for fear it might tear or fall apart. And there was the unexploded bomb that my mother carried into the Anderson shelter for fear it might blow up in the outside world and send her secret soaring up into the sky in scarlet letters over the town. Better buried with her if the worst happened! For there, under the perfect black copper-plate of "Father Unknown" were the neat red, printed letters of "ILLEGITIMATE". My mother was a b … I couldn't even say the word to myself. I knew what it meant. A fate worse than death and also it was the worst swear word there was. All the carbolic soap in the world couldn't clean it off my tongue. Nor all the castor oil in the world purge it from my mind.

As soon as the first shock passed, I just knew I had to forget I'd ever seen it. I was trying to, even as I thrust everything back into the case. It was my hurry that was my undoing. For as I shoved the case under the bed again, it knocked against an old shoebox. The lid fell off to reveal – Mars® bars. So that's where they were. The store from which we all got half a bar a week as a mouth-watering extra to the sweet ration, half-filling the box – so many surely one would never be missed!

But it was. My mother had them counted. My mother had everything counted. She knew it was me, the youngest, with the sweetest tooth. It was back-shift belting, too. For being selfish and greedy, she said. For telling a lie about taking it. But I wonder now if it wasn't also a warning about what would happen if there was more to it than a Mars® bar.

She never said. She never would, to anyone. As she never spoke of her mother, I have never said, until this moment. So she took her secret to the grave. I can only hope she'll forgive me. Perhaps it would help her to know that, with the maturity of years, it was a key that was slowly to unlock the mystery of much of her behaviour towards me.

At the time, the Clydebank blitz fell on us a few nights later and the picnic case went to the shelter. But I was far more interested in the piece of shrapnel which went right through Mrs Hislop's dustbin lid. They lived next door. Imagine a German bomb that close. "It's a bit of one of our own anti-aircraft shells," pronounced my father, wearing all the authority of his ARP tin helmet. Another puzzle. Why should our side be firing at us?

Of course, the knowledge of my mother's lack of origins did nothing for my ancestry, when added to my recent discoveries. There was I, masquerading as the convalescent editor of a respectable family newspaper, when all the time I was a mongrel mixture of Viking rapist and Norman conqueror, with a soupçon of French passion, a dash of Irish blarney, Welsh cunning and Gaelic temper, not to mention the instincts of a Border reiver, with God only knows what ingredient from an unknown grandfather. Though I have my suspicions when I consider the hereditary dark hair and wild natures of most of my Andersons.

Whatever the mixture, it has ensured the successful survival of all Andersons. They are to be found wherever men and women are found and in some strange colours and creeds. I have come across them from an African-American lift operator in the Empire State Building to a Buddhist monk in Thailand.

In fact, the Andersons are taking over the world, so prolific only the Chinese can stem the tide, and even with them, it's a fair guess there's not a few who bear the blood and even the name!

CHAPTER 5

I'll Never Forget Maggie's "Thingy"

I'm no expert on the sexual habits of the pygmy peoples of New Guinea. Nor do I want to know what goes on nowadays behind closed bungalow curtains in Nether Wallop. But I do accept that sex, whatever form it takes, is the only common factor to all of us, including Bill Anderson, and though brought up otherwise, I will not avoid the subject.

I approve of sex education in schools, if well-considered and with parental involvement. I have a tinge of envy at the sexual freedom which young people have nowadays. I disapprove of the permissiveness the "pill" has made possible, and I abhor the sexual aggression it has brought about in women. It is a time-honoured privilege of the middle-aged, married British male to fantasise about the blonde in the 8.17 am Blue Circle to the office. It becomes guilt-ridden reality if she suddenly leans over to him and whispers "How about it?", thus completely putting him off the *Times* crossword. You are free to substitute your favourite morning paper, sir. As long as you are honest and admit that, if Page Three suddenly came to life there on the train or bus and thrust herself on you, you would be the first to run a mile in case your wife found out.

This naturally reveals me as "a male chauvinist pig". It also points an accusing finger at my inhibited Scottish upbringing. Children of my generation, and before, knew little of the process by which we were conceived. I was a fair age, I can tell you, before I was quite sure a baby was not born through a lady's belly button. Or worse (which would have explained all that hot water to me). The

GOD BLESS MRS MCGINTY!

Reformation was 375 years old when I was born, and had birthed the Scotland of Calvin, Knox and the Band of Hope, as fierce a trio of inhibitors as ever put the fear of external damnation into any nation and its offspring.

A Protestant penis (there, I've used that word!) was only for the joyless begatting and begetting as prescribed in yards of the Old Testament. Yes, it was for more mundane purposes, but that came quite naturally and didn't have to be talked about. If it did have to be talked about, it was only by pointing vaguely in that direction or referring to it as "my willie". A vagina (I've done it again!) was no known part of a girl's anatomy, except in closed medical books, and there was no other known description for it in polite company other than "down there". True, there were dirty words for it in the factory and playground world of men and boys. But any good girl knew they were a filthy, brutish lot who were always after "down there" anyway.

Now, while something could be done to "bring a boy up properly" in order to sublimate his animal instincts, he was still an animal, so it was a girl's fault completely if she allowed his bestial nature to be roused. So from as early an age as possible, she was taught (though only each as was timely) the "Ten Commandments of Being A Good Girl And Dutiful Wife":

Thou shalt keep "down there" covered by thy raiment, even unto its use as a beast in the field, so that no evil eye may behold it, even thine own. Or thine physician, except then that it be that thy mother be present and thine physician be as ancient as Methuselah.

Thou shalt not let the wickedness of thine own finger hover "down there", nay not even in thine bath, verily even to ascertain that which thou harvest "down there". Unto this purpose thou shalt wash "down there" quickly with a sponge of Goliath size.

Thou shalt not let any male creature of any generation touch thee "down there", even though thou be clothed; nay, nor any other part of you; notwithstanding that which they call "the dance" when he shall place his hands away from sin behind thy back as ye stay one cubit apart from covertness.

Thou shalt preserve "down there" for thy lawful husband and none other. "Down there" shall be as a communion vessel into which none shall pour until the sacrament of holy wedlock be gold on thy third finger, left hand.

Thou shalt go to bed with thine marriage certificate below thine pillow that thou may knowest the act is legal and for the begetting of thine offspring, not thine enjoyment.

Thou shalt not raise thy flannel nightie further than be necessary for thine joyless sacrifice.

Thou shalt commune only in the hours of darkness, with blinds drawn, nor any candle, so that even thy husband shall not see the nakedness below thy nightie.

Thou shalt closet the door when you commune that thine own children shall not see that which they shouldst not see.

Thou shalt lie prone and lifeless in the missionary position, thine arms folded upon thy breast and with thine eyes closed, even in the darkness, that thou mayest concentrate on putting away wicked thoughts from thy mind.

Thou shalt commune no longer than be needed for thine husband's seed to be forthcoming.

So it came to pass that all good girls grew up on the myth of the gooseberry bush. "You're too young to know and when you're old enough you won't need to ask," fobbed off any question that fell outwith the Ten Commandments. Menstruation, I suspect, came to all too many girls as a sudden, savage and nasty shock – running tearfully to a mother in fear of bleeding to death, only to be handed a sanitary towel and directed to the toilet with a brief, embarrassed explanation and a dire threat that now "the curse" was on her she was even more untouchable until marriage.

For boys, it was the doctor's black bag that brought babies. "And if he shuts it too quick when he takes it out, it's a girl," someone would whisper as we talked about it up the tree hut in the golf course wood. And all those more knowing than we would giggle because they had seen their wee baby sister being bathed and knew that little girls did not have appendages like them.

But this, the first dirty joke I ever heard, made me set watch on Mrs McM, who was always having babies because she was a Catholic. The McMs were the only Catholics in the Crescent, because Catholics were only allowed to live beside us if they were definitely upper working class, with husbands in the council offices or teachers like Mr McM.

I can't speak with any authority about the sexual upbringing of Scottish Catholics, although I suspect that it was much like our own, except (as I soon learned in the streets) that every Protestant knew the Virgin Birth had to be a fraud and that, on top of making babies before they should, almost everything else they did was a mortal sin which condemned them to their own special hell called Purgatory – and that sounded too much like castor oil for my liking. They couldn't lie about their misdoings either, so they couldn't wait and hope their sins wouldn't find them out, but had to go through a special curtain in the chapel and tell the priest. I didn't have to tell the minister. It didn't sound much fun being a Catholic. But they did have one advantage over us Proddy boys. With so many brothers and sisters, usually crowded into a house that was too small for them, they learned the facts of life much faster and so, though you weren't really supposed to talk to them, it was quite handy to have a casual acquaintanceship with at least one Catholic boy so you could ask a guarded question or two.

Mrs McM was, by the Crescent's judgement, a "good" Catholic, which meant she was respectable, a fine mother who took her children to Mass regularly, which was good for them because they were Catholics after all, and never flaunted her religion in all those respectable Protestant faces. If she ever felt like a Jew in a pre-war Berlin suburb, she never let on and even baked scones for the whist drives run to raise funds to knit "comforts" for the troops.

"She's going to have another baby, you know," may have been a slight condemnation by Mrs Hislop when it was my mother's turn for the sewing bee which knitted those comforts. But it made her my woman of the year. Another baby. Mothers didn't go to hospitals or clinics in those days. Babies were born in the house where they should be. The doctor would bring them in his black bag.

I made every excuse I could think of to watch for him outside Mrs McM's house. Lingering on my way to school to bend down and tie my shoelace so I was hidden by the straggly hedge and would peep through holes in it. I lingered on my way home at lunch time, stopping my mates to talk about what we'd do that night, or quietly pointing to anything in the gutter that might have been a dropped coin, so I could have a quick look. I lingered on the way home after school, taking a book out as soon as I got off the bus so I could find a particularly interesting bit and pause, so absorbed I had to stop walking. That was a clever dodge because everybody in the Crescent knew I was a voracious reader.

I did glimpse the hurrying doctor. But his Gladstone bag never looked pregnant. Mrs McM was putting on weight but the sewing bee had explained that to me, "She always gets so big when she's eating for two."

I didn't cotton on even when there was an extraordinary general meeting of the bee for Mrs Barnard to announce "She's in labour. Mrs Moffat told me at the milkman." All the Catholics in Motherwell were in labour. I'd heard my father say so often enough. The doctor's black bag wrought its miracle that night. I was so angry. All that detecting stuff and all I'd found out through the McMs' window was that Catholics have a lot of crosses and pictures of Mary and the Infant Jesus on their walls. And that mothers get suddenly very fat when they start feeding for two. But at least I'd polished up the Sherlock Holmes play which I was to put to much use a year or two later when I fell in (unrequited) love with Fiona in the Avenue. Until her father came out and gave me a clip on the ear for hanging about. The swine knew I didn't have to go along the Avenue to get to the bus stop.

It is hardly surprising then that boys, only made more curious by second-hand knowledge, resorted to first hand. Masturbation was the only way they could find out how their willies worked, regardless of whether it did make you blind or deaf or both. Or worse. When the tale-teller boasted of a "quick grope wi' a lassie behind the school lav", he went on to confide that his big brother had told him that while a toss-off was some relief for such sexual arousement, when overdone it seriously impaired your willie's capacity to rise to the occasion and even led, when seriously over-done, to some dread affliction called "im-po-tence", which meant you could never make babies. I never got the chance to find out because the lassie seemed to give everybody a quick grope but me. And there was only one lassie like her in the school.

It was Sundays that conditioned our sexual education as much as anything. As cleanly close to godliness as a scrubbing brush could make a boy, we went off shining and pure to Sunday School, where the minister and teachers drove all wicked thoughts from us. And then we came home to read "Oor Wullie" in *The Sunday Post*. What a good example – the boy who could be naughty and needed a scolding from his mother or a slipper from his father, but never, ever, was dirty in word, thought or deed. The eternal member of the Cubs or Life Boys grew up drilled to perfect pure puberty in the Boys' Brigade or Boy Scouts, where a lot of discipline went a long way, too. *Mens sana incorpore sano*. Every hygienic, sanitary, sexless lesson was well laced with corporal punishment and traceable to some dictat in John Knox's *Book of Discipline* which gave more than a fair share of its doom and gloom to the subject of children and their erring ways. As I look around me at the permissiveness and promiscuity of the other extreme, I can't help feeling there's a happy medium.

The philosophy of it didn't concern me as a boy. Just the consequences. It may have been John Knox who made me feel guilty when a pal's sister enticed me into the rhododendron bushes behind the swings in the park. It was sexual curiosity that kept me there. And disappointment that drove me away when she only wanted to kiss.

And it was my mother who always started where the Sunday School, Life Boys and *Sunday Post* finished. That time in Draffen Street when Jimmy and I took all our clothes off on a hot summer's day the better to enjoy the warmth of the pavement as we lay outside his house licking up some sherbet we'd spilled from a penny sooker. Precious stuff and, if anything, the taste was made more tingling by the addition of cement dust. My mother was horrified but not by the pavement licking. Real dirt never did a growing laddie any harm. It was the nakedness. "Put your trousers on, William. You're a big boy now." I was five! Maybe willie was quite big for his age!

Nakedness was next to naughtiness. In winter, when my father worked the day-shift, he lit the fire before he left the house at 5 am and spread Mum's clothes on the chair to warm up. Come breakfast time, Mum would slip down from the Siberian bedroom in her "goonie", to dress in the warmth. I was never a sleeper and quite often heard her getting up. I would wait a bit, then go down after her. If the kettle had been long in boiling, or the fire needed attention first, she would not be dressed. At my step on the stair she would call out "Don't come in. I'm changing." I would huddle on the bottom step of the stairs, shivering and wondering. Changing into what? One of those big-breasted African ladies wearing beads and not much else that you could see in the old *National Geographics* at the dentist's? Or into Mrs Dracula? Or from the wanton woman of the darkened bedroom? It was the only place I ever heard her laugh! Whatever my fancy, she had always changed into my mother again when she let me in – my wee stout Mum, from her sensible black shoes to her permed hair, already peenied in her apron for another day of mothering. My fancies stopped when she forgot to take her corsets upstairs to the bedroom when she undressed one night. I was up first and there they were, sticking out from under the cushion of Dad's chair. Crikey! What a contraption. Acres of pink material, miles of lacing and yards of bits of whale bone. How did she ever get it on? But now I knew. She was changing from the fat, floppy-breasted, tired, lower working-class Draffen Street wife of the past into the respectable, well-upholstered, upper working-class Hillhead Crescent lady of the present. There was no more speculation after that.

It was an eye-opener to me when a country boy came to live in the town. After school, down by the Toddle burn, Eckie filled our appetites for colourful descriptions of what bulls did to cows and how lambs were born and, to a lad, we wanted to be farm boys. I could scarcely believe it. In and out through a lady's pee-hole. How could it be big enough?

Anyway, my mother would never have stood for anything as unsanitary as that. I scanned the discreet girdle ads in *The People's Friend*, trying to peer through the gussets. It was even more frustrating when Mum could afford *Woman's Own*. Those tantalising underwear ads in colour. What did they cover? As for the lingerie section of mail order catalogues, they inevitably drove a boy back to first-hand knowledge.

I joined the gang of peeping Tommies, Jimmies and Billies, who stuck their hands up to go to the toilet when the girls were at gym in the school hall. Or the playground in warm weather. Peeping through the bannister or railings at the sea of bouncing green, brown and navy blue Co-op knickers into which the girls tucked their blouses. There was always one in specs and pigtails, with a drippy nose, wearing the bloomers her big sister had grown out of which had a hole in the bottom where you could see a white flash of her bum. If only that cheap Woolworth's elastic would break while she was jumping for the netball. But it never did, and you always went back for two of the belt for "looking at the girls, you dirty little boy"! For you could be sure one of the girls, who were mightily embarrassed by our avid thirst for knowledge, would run red-faced to tell the teacher. We would wait for her after school to chant "Tell-tale tit, your granny canny knit. Your mammy canny go to bed without a dummy tit." Then, in unison until she ran out of sight "I saw your knickers. I saw your knickers."

Boys were vulgar and crude in sheer rebellion. "I'm going for a pish," I would shout to the others in defiance of the rather twee "stronering" which my mother insisted on her boys using. Every family had its own euphemisms. After stronering, we would go for a number two for which I had to take down my trousers. Both are more acceptable than the "Eh, eh" and "Wee wee!" which were the graphically phonetic words for the unspeakable functions which my own children were taught by their maternal Nana, much to my distaste. So, to the night I was a very naughty boy.

I must have been rising eleven at the time. It was another Sunday night *en famille* with the Andersons of Hillhead Crescent, in their comfortable council house, up on the hill at Jerviston. This put us a cut above the other council estates, mostly because two councillors lived there and made damn sure the only people who got houses there were "suitable" tenants, artisans of the upper working class such as my father, by virtue of being a top-grade steelworker, or professionals of the lower middle class such as teachers or Grade II civil servants. Yes, a nice class of people lived in Jerviston. No hint of scandal ever crossed our standard council-green doors (with your own choice of nameplate). If ever there was a scandal it was kept behind the closed door. What would the neighbours say! Mind you, even if they found out, which they always did, they kept quiet outside Jerviston, for what kind of people would the rest of the town think lived up in Jerviston if they found out that Jimmy had bilked the bowling club's annual outing fund. Or Jessie's daughter had been seen in the back balcony of the Odeon with a married man, and it was more than holding hands they were, and her only just out of school with a good job as a comptometer operator. No, best keep it to ourselves. Anyway, Jimmy's brother had put the money back. And Jessie would have words with her girl so that wouldn't happen again.

But ours was always a respectable house and such was the

gathering on that Sunday. Dad wasn't at work as it was a "break weekend". He'd finished the 2 pm to 10 pm back-shift on Saturday night and wouldn't go back to work until the day-shift (6 am to 2 pm) on Monday morning. Barclay, just home from the air force, had brought Maisie, the nice girl from the library. My mother liked her because she always helped with the dishes. Ian was seeking cultural relations at the time and had produced a buck-toothed prodigy in pigtails who spoke with a bool-in-the-mooth Edinburgh accent and played the piano rather more proudly and loudly than proficiently.

Some of my big brothers' friends always found their way to our house on Sunday night, too. Jimmy Nimmo, who always scoffed a plate or so of my mother's home-made scones with the overwhelming praise "By jove, these are no' bad, Mrs Anderson." And Dick Porteous who dived off a bridge into a river running with only inches of water and broke something badly, if it wasn't his neck. The company was completed by my sister Betty and her "friend", Bobby.

We scoffed the usual high tea of gargantuan proportions, from the tattie broth and crusty steak pie to home-baked pastries, cakes and biscuits from layers of tins in the pantry that still make my mouth water to think of them, especially that lemon meringue pie, hot from the oven and the war was over, so we could even put the black-market butter on the table without feeling that it might let Hitler win.

To put you fully in the picture, Ian was then a sensitive, pimply 17 year old full of his own importance. Barclay would be about 24, just back from the war and needing to settle down, seriously doing the rounds of eligible young ladies, looking more for their practicality as a wife than for any passion. Betty would be touching 22 and though Bobby was an "older" man, by all of six or seven years, which was old enough for her, his intentions were honourable. He wasn't just chasing her because she was a good dancer and one of the "fast" crowd of girls who went to the Salon de Danse on a Saturday night and liked a good time, even a kiss and a cuddle, as long as you didn't tell dirty stories in front of them or "try anything on" because they were from good families and wouldn't have any of that nonsense. It was marriage or nothing. Meantime, she hid her dancing shoes so Dad didn't know where she was going.

I was the clever brat of the family and a show-off who had to be put down, because children should be seen and not heard, especially children who knew just about every fact in Arthur Mee's *Children's Encyclopaedia* (all ten volumes, red Morocco bound) and was likely to contradict an elder who dared to make conversation about any subject from A–D, E–K, right through to W–Z (plus Index). Despite this, Mother was delighted and quick to point out "He's going to be dux of the school, you know," as some kind of proud excuse.

But I was indulged that night and allowed to stay up later mainly because my dad wanted to play Solo. Now my mother wasn't too keen on gambling, even for pennies when there were visitors, and Dad wouldn't lower himself to play such a skilful game as Solo for matchsticks so we settled for Stop the Bus, which was a child's card game though everybody liked it. So I was a good excuse for everyone to join in and play to keep William happy. Once they'd let me stay they could hardly refuse my constant plea for "just one more game", so I made the most of it. In the end, their patience failed to match my persistence and I was sent to bed. It had been an exciting night, with all those grown-ups to impress, and I'd won the last game.

Lying there in the dolly-blued white linen sheets, although I could hear the voices downstairs and wondered what they talked about once I went to bed – maybe even "that", though I doubted it, knowing my mother – I fell asleep, perchance to dream. I should have gone to the bathroom first! It was about an hour after I had gone to bed that it happened, I am told. The living-room door swung open and in walked a small figure in striped Co-operative pyjamas, eyes open but glazed with sleep. "What are you doing back down?" asked my mother – but too late.

To the utter astonishment of all ages and stages of sexual inhibitions or otherwise, the trance-like figure stopped where all could see, fumbled for the cord of aforesaid jammies and dropped the trousers clear to the ankles, where they lay like the corona on the moon. And there it was, the unsaid and unseen, a penis, too young to be an immediate threat to any female in the room, but palpably a prick on the verge of puberty, with the first faint flush of fair down fluffing up proudly on the pubis. What's more, it was all-too-obviously erect, flushed and firm, if not entirely with the marauding, pounding blood of manhood, certainly with the first stirrings of sexuality, undoubtedly assisted by the bursting pressure of a boy's bladder.

It was met by a pregnant hush.

I have had to piece together the various individual reactions from scraps of family conversation over the years. My father threw his head back with the pride of a stallion that has sired a well-hung colt.

Betty and Bobby exchanged knowing glances. Well, they were about to be married.

Barclay, good solid reliable Barclay, didn't bat an eyelid. He hadn't been winning the war in Burma for five years for nowt. His girl had the grace to blush and turn away.

Jimmy Nimmo asked for another scone and went on to be a confirmed bachelor who married late.

Ian's pimples exploded. The thought of what these girls in the room were seeing. Enough to drive an adolescent back to the boobs in *Health & Beauty*, even though he'd promised himself to skip this month's issue as a test of his willpower.

No memory, however jogged later, recorded the reactions of the buck-toothed piano player. I like to think she shouted "Geronimo!" and dashed to the ivories to pound out "Land of Hope and Glory" as she must have been about the right age for her first full frontal of a golden future.

Whatever sexual tensions were pounding in whomsoever's breast were soon defused. I wasn't finished.

In fact, I wasn't "expressing myself". I was simply bursting. I thought I was in the bathroom. So I took two steps forward, stepped out of my jammie trousers, carefully held the cause of all the consternation between my finger and thumb – I always was fastidious – and peed/piddled/stonered/pished/wee-wee'd/ widdled or any other euphemism which you find distasteful in a veritable flood of relief into the hearth of the fireplace, no doubt mistaking the cold tiles against my toes as the same sensation when against the toilet bowl. I then shook it to dispose of any drips, picked up my jammies and retired, leaving the minds of those behind to make of it as each must, according to his or her inclination.

My mother? Mortified! Black burning shame! To have demonstrated not only the unmentionable potential of a penis, but its rather more mundane usage, was, well, Jerviston must never hear about it. I'll tell you this. I never got to play Stop the Bus late on a Sunday night again.

Next morning, she did ask if I remembered what I'd done. I had no recollection and, even if I had had, I would never have admitted it, not to her. But for all my plea of not guilty, she still told me I'd been a naughty boy and not to do it again. When I didn't know what I'd done, that wasn't easy. But I wasn't worried about its impossibility. A cuff on the ear was often administered out of sheer exasperation on the basis that, if you weren't actually doing anything wrong at that moment, it wouldn't be long before you did, so the punishment wasn't wasted.

Consider it a warning, son.

Shortly after, an old, out-of-date copy of *Family Home Doctor* mysteriously appeared on top of the Bakelite™ case which held my font of all knowledge, the *Children's Encyclopaedia*. Nothing was ever said about it, but I have no doubt its purpose was twofold. It was the first of many intimations that my mother wanted me to be a doctor. It also held two full-page line prints of the male and female anatomy. My mother had realised I was no longer wee Willie Winkie!

I poured over those prints for hours. Dated 1929 as they were, the diagrammatic indications of the private parts left too much to my imagination. Still, I was learning, which – and you have been wondering when I would ever get to it – brings me to Maggie's "thingy".

Picture the scene a year or so later. A birthday party, in a similar council house. The boys scrubbed and shining, shyly self-conscious because they're hardly ever tidy, with brushed and Brylcreemed hair and still in short flannel trousers. The trousers were creased in front or at the side seams if your mother wasn't too hot at pressing them the proper way, but they were always just below the knee because you would grow into them, but never did, because you were out of them first.

As a matter of passing interest, I only wore my first pair of "longs" when I was 15 and going to a school dance where boys my age had grown so big they had a better case for long trousers, and the girls loved them and always picked them first for the Ladies' Choice quickstep. I wasn't going to be left out, so I sneaked a pair of Barclay's old blue air force uniform trousers out of his wardrobe and, because they were too long, hitched them up high on my chest, cinched the waist in with a snake-eye belt and hid the bit above the belt with my pullover. What a dash I cut – even if Blithe Dickson did pick someone else for the quickstep.

I took wee Betty home and she was so impressed with my trousers that she not only let me slip a nervous hand inside her blouse so she could prove she was wearing a bra, as much a test of womanhood for her as my trousers were for me, but also let my hand fall down from her waist, to her thigh and then, just for a second, press the flat of my hand on "that" place. Very respectably, of course, for it was all done outside her skirt and she only hesitated for a second before she brushed my hand away. But long enough to convince me that I was right about long trousers. Oh, Betty, if only you'd dared to look down at the pulsing bulge in my blues. Still, there was something to be said for short trousers – if only the handiness of hauling one leg of the trousers high to your haunch so you could pee without the bother of opening your fly, a not-to-be-sneered-at facility for boys in a hurry. Such as that night at Maggie's.

The girls were in pert party dresses, talcum powdered and fresh faced with only a hint of discreet lipstick, and we soon got down to the games. Kissing games! Postman's Knock. Bee Baw

The Anderson family, left to right: (back row) Bill, John (his dad), Barclay (eldest brother), Bobby (Betty's husband), Ian (brother); (front row): Bessie (Bill's mum), David (Betty's son), Sadie (Barclay's wife), Betty (sister).

The Sunday Post was not Bill's first editorship. Pictured here is the Magazine Committee of Dalziel High School. W Anderson was Editor.

The young Bill wrote in his final Editorial in the school magazine:

"After six short, happy years, the time comes when I must make my way forth through the portals of our renowned school only to return there perhaps as a Former Pupil. I shall not say I am reluctant to leave school, for everyone feels an urge, some time or other, to find out what the Fates are spinning for him in the World outside the sheltered and enjoyable life of scholastic endeavour."

The full committee: W Anderson, E Barnsley, K Yuill, J Elliot, M Findlay, M Shaw, S Gibb, A Anderson, F Elder. (With staff credited: Mr Paterson and Mr Cossar).

Army Days – Oswestry July, 1953.

"E" 121 (Field Troop). "E" Battery – Mons Officer Cadet School, December 1953.

After officer training, 432418 Second Lieutenant William Anderson, RA (Royal Artillery) went on service overseas – assigned to the Nominal Roll of 13 (Martinique 1809) Battery, Royal Artillery, one of the 14th Field Regiment's batteries in Hong Kong.

A Smashing Holiday — And Doesn't Cost A Bean !

LAST week I told you how I'd been " dared " to do a week's holiday in the Highlands on nothing.

Well, I'm still alive to tell the tale!

It began at dawn on Monday. I stood in front of Inverness Town Hall, wondering which way to go.

I couldn't toss up. I hadn't any money. But all the books say " Go West, young man "— so I went East!

It was a lovely morning. The rain had brought on the gr...

If ever a window was built for a view, it was the one in this house. It was as big as four normal windows, one huge sheet of glass, with no cross bars.

I went up to the Nissen hut that stood beside the house and knocked. And that's how I met Alec Clyne

BY A SUNDAY POST REPORTER

But right in the middle of all this a grand piano! Yes, there it stood, with a bo...

Melver took over Mealmore only six months ago. They came here...

He Starts From Inverness At Dawn Tomorrow

By A " Sunday Post " Reporter

WELL, I asked for it!

It all started when the editor showed me the letter.

" You lads on ' The Post ' are always talking about grand ways to have a holiday. Well, I'd like to put on a bet with you. I'll bet you can't have a week's holiday on nothing!"

I should have kept my big mouth shut. But I didn't. I said, " Huh! Nothing to it!" And that was that.

So tomorrow morning I'll set out from Inverness. On my back will be the bare necessities of life. On my feet will be the stoutest shoes I can lay feet on.

In my pocket will be a clean hankie—and NO MONEY.

I'm blinkin' well going to win that bet. I'm going to have a first-class week's holiday on nothing!

I won't use hostels (I'm not in the S.Y.H.A. anyway). Any travelling I do will be either on foot or in lifts I can get.

And any bed I sleep in will have to be earned—the hard way. If I can saw logs, or serve in a bar, or mind a bairn, or milk a cow, I'll expect a bed or a meal in return. I may not get it—but that's my worry!

I'm going to meet a lot of folk I've never met before. I hope they'll be kind! And if I don't come back with a packful of stories, I'll eat my typewriter ribbon!

I don't know where I'll end up. It may be John o' Groats.

But I'm not kidding myself. It could be tough. Maybe nobody will want to entrust his cow (or his logs) to a bloke who's sharpened his teeth on a typewriter. I can easily end up finding out how soft an Inverness-shire hedge is. We'll see.

But if you should happen to see a weary-looking fellow trudging up the road from Invernees—you'll give him a lift, won't you!

Wish me luck!

I hope to tell you of my adventures next Sunday.

HON JAUNTS

1957.

September 29	HON as Onion Johnny.
October 13.	HON makes a hit with the wandering minstrels.
October 20.	HON in judo class.
October 27.	HON as an ambulance man at Hampden Park.
November 3.	HON as a cinema usher.
November 10.	HON tries to pawn his gold medal.
November 17.	HON at the turkish baths.
November 24.	HON investigates the night life in Glasgow.
December 1.	HON as an auctioneer.
December 8.	HON is sawn in half.
December 15.	HON in Sauchiehall Street giving away fivers.
December 22.	HON as a barrow boy.
December 29.	HON at Calderpark Zoo.
1958.	
January 5.	HON in pantomine at the Pavilion.
January 12.	HON is tigers cage at Kelvin Hall Circus.
January 19.	HON sparring Peter Keenan !

The HON Man was always ready for a physical challenge. Whether it was football, judo, country dancing or sparring with Peter Keenan – the 1950s Scottish bantamweight – or fighting legendary boxer Dick McTaggart.

HON at the opening of the Forth Road
Bridge, September 4th 1964, signing "specially
autographed souvenir pictures of the bridge".

HON with the Harlem
Globetrotters
(June 4, 1961).

The HON Man was no stranger to the stage, or the film set – whether performing in a ballet or as a detective, making a film test, or playing the role of Dick Whittington, a stunt man, or being in pantomime at The Pavilion, or doing a BBC audition.

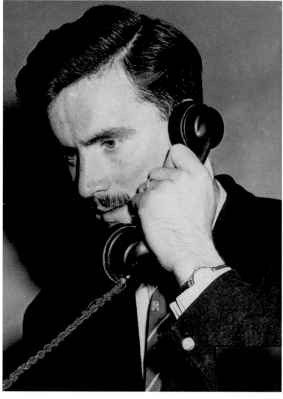

Just one of the many HON Man escapades – "disguised" as a door-to-door salesman.

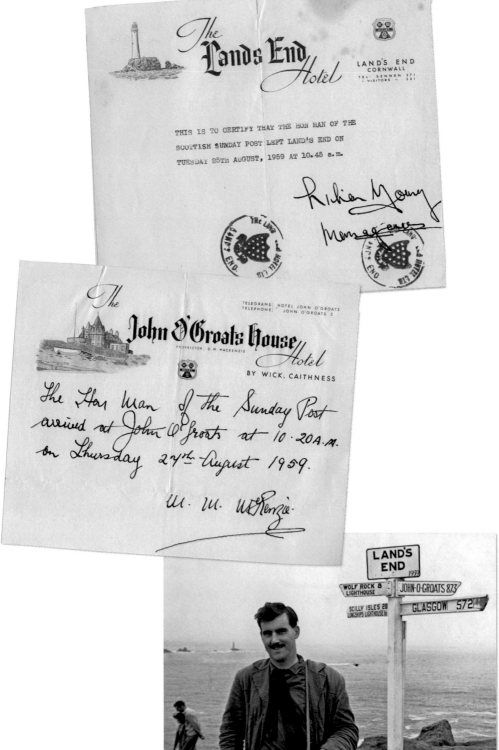

THE Lands End Hotel

LAND'S END
CORNWALL
TEL. SENNEN 271
" VISITORS " 321

THIS IS TO CERTIFY THAT THE HON MAN OF THE
SCOTTISH SUNDAY POST LEFT LAND'S END ON
TUESDAY 25TH AUGUST, 1959 AT 10.45 a.m.

Lilian Young
Manageress

The John O'Groats House Hotel
PROPRIETOR D. M. MACKENZIE
BY WICK, CAITHNESS

TELEGRAMS: HOTEL JOHN O'GROATS
TELEPHONE: JOHN O'GROATS 3

The Hon Man Of the Sunday Post
arrived at John O'Groats at 10·20A.M.
on Thursday 27th August 1959.

M. M. McKenzie.

LAND'S END

WOLF ROCK 8 LIGHTHOUSE
SCILLY ISLES 28 LONGSHIPS LIGHTHOUSE 1¼
JOHN-O-GROATS 873
GLASGOW 572½

HON's Land's End to
John o' Groats adventure
August 25–7, 1959.

The Forces were a regular HON target. He joined The Guards for one story; the Territorial Army for another. Here, he is in the Libyan Desert with the Paratroopers (October 1960).

The HON Man appearing in *Emergency Ward 10*, for the article
December 18, 1960 (pictures copyright © Associated TeleVision).

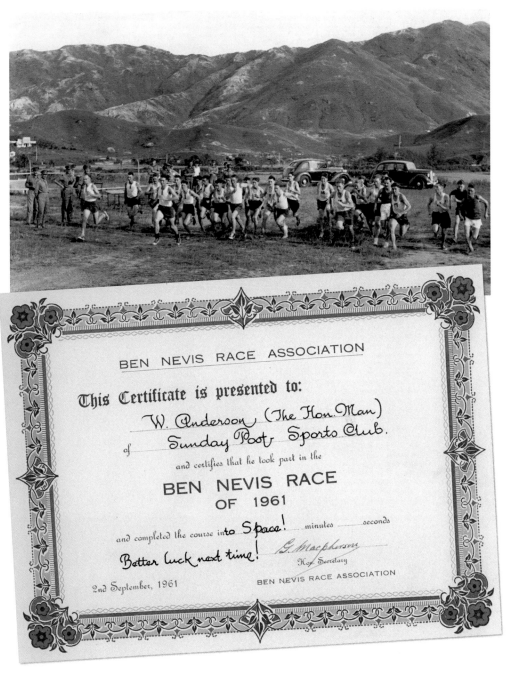

The HON Man in the Ben Nevis Race, September 10, 1961.

The HON Man enjoyed a broad spectrum of work experience – as an onion johnny, ambulance man, cinema usher, auctioneer, pavement artist, chimney sweep, dustbinman, flower seller, rag man, debt collector, magician, sheep shearer, and many others.

Pictured below: HON as a busker, entertaining the queue waiting to see Frank Sinatra in *Come Blow Your Horn* (1963).

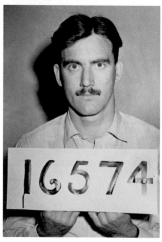

Babbity. Or sometimes we were lucky and parents who didn't know any better let us put the lights out and then we would play the daring orgy of Stations, where, by a system I can't recall, the girls shunted round in the dark, in a tantalising swish of dresses and delicious delicate whiffs of eau de cologne. You got any girl on any knee and might even risk a tentative tip of a tongue between her lips – if she was particularly acquiescent and safe from you telling any tales about her – which was the way the French made love, didn't you know?

Whatever the game was, I found myself out in the hallway with Johnnie Hislop, one of the Templeton boys, Billy or Jimmy, Albert, who was Maggie's brother and Maggie sitting on the stairs.

That's when Albert announced a new game – Dares. That we had certainly played before. They call it Chicken nowadays. "Would you like to see Maggie's thingy?" he asked. Would we? Would she? For we all knew what he meant and eyes swivelled to Maggie, happy, laughing Maggie, of the long gangly legs. The tomboy who played the boys' games better than the boys and could run away as fast as anybody when we kicked old Cameron's door. She even joined us behind the air-raid shelter where we hid to smoke cinnamon sticks and insisted on having a puff too. Frankly, I'd never thought of her before as even having a thingy but looking at her there, in her pretty party dress, the faint bulge of breasts budding through a bra, eyes twinkling with mischief, and her knees just ever so little apart, hinting at all the dark mysteries up there, beneath her skirt, I was seeing her for the first time. Not Maggie, but a girl, a woman-to-be.

My revelation was interrupted by Albert. "You'll have to pay me thruppence each." At which you might guess that Albert's vocation in life was to live on immoral earnings, though truth will out and he became a policeman, much respected in the community.

We produced our threepenny bits with incautious haste. Maggie's eyes flashed. Ours pleaded. "Shares," said Albert. She hesitated. "Remember, it's a dare," he went on. "You can't refuse a dare." It was too much of a challenge for Maggie. The boyish aggression in her won over any thoughts of maidenly modesty. "OK," she said.

"But if it's a dare, one of you must show yours, too." That was different, but we needed to see. We could sort that out later, after we'd seen. We all nodded agreement. The dare was on.

With the speed of accustomed usage, Maggie put her hands up under her skirt and, still sitting on the stairs, eased her buttocks up enough to quickly slip her knickers down to her ankles. There they lay, pristine, virgin white, elasticated Co-operative knickers. Maybe even Marks and Spencer's. For a second, she paused. We craned forward anxiously. Was she going to quit on us? Perhaps it was the excitement of the party, or sheer devilment. But she didn't. Gently, but quickly, she lifted up her skirt.

Oh, my God, there it was. Her thingy. For once I was glad I was the smallest boy in the street. She was sitting a few steps up so I was looking up at it. I had the best view. What a thruppence worth and I drank it all in. The surprising flat white spread of flesh above the mound of darkening fuzz with, yes, crikey, a parting in the middle almost like the one in my own short back and sides. But that wasn't the cleft. It couldn't be. That had to be lower down there somewhere in the tight triangle, where the hair already threatened to grow longer, between the dark smudges of the tops of her inner-most thighs. But where? Where exactly? Too late. It was all over. The curtain had fallen. But I had seen it. Her thingy. There were mysteries to fathom. The tingling yearning in me. I was growing up.

"C'mon then, who's it going to be?" Maggie was standing now, knickers up, hands on hips, a high point of red on each of her cheeks, but smiling the dare back to us. We'd all forgotten her terms. Our turn, yes, but whose turn? Without a word, we turned and looked at Master Templeton. We knew, whether we were younger than him or older, that he had the biggest, a whopper, of which we were secretly green with envy, but consoled ourselves that it was just the luck of the draw or because his father had a big one, too. It had to be him. How could we dare to show Maggie anything smaller after that? Or, if someone smaller accepted the dare, the chance of Albert telling her later. We pushed Master Templeton forward, but he grabbed the hat stand to hold himself back. He didn't want to.

The biggest, and he didn't want to. We'd as much to learn about ourselves as boys as we ever would about girls.

"What's going on out there?" Master Templeton was saved. It was Maggie's mother, a plump motherly lady who I always liked. Did she know, just looking at me? Red and shame on my face that I had seen her fair daughter's thingy. Perhaps not. Mothers do know when parties are too quiet. We were marshalled back into the living room, chattering excitedly to cover our guilt, and Maggie, brave Maggie, would have to wait for another day.

We never mentioned the dare again and Maggie went back to being her old self. She blossomed into a bonny lass, and, as far as I know, married happily and lives in glorious and undisputed respectability. It was only a game after all. But I can only hope she'll pardon me when I say I'll never forget Maggie's thingy, and I'll always be grateful to it. I went home whistling a popular ditty of the day, with the words to a dirtier version running through my head:

I wish I was a diamond ring
On Betty Grable's hand,
Then every time she took a bath
I'd see the Promised Land.

Added to the prints from the *Family Home Doctor*, and the garnishings of gossip of my peer group, I was slowly putting it all together, as near the facts of life as you could get, in Jerviston, anyway.

I had seen the "Promised Land". From then on, I grew up quite normally, only occasionally on the way home having the good fortune to find myself behind a lady climbing up the stairs on a double-decker bus ahead of me and despite myself, hanging back, hoping for a glimpse of white thigh, twisted stocking top and suspender belt, so forcing me home to have a quick, guilty, wash behind the locked door of the bathroom. My time would come …

CHAPTER 6

When Did You Last See Your Father?

When I first came across WF Yeames' picture of the Cavalier boy standing proudly, but with downcast head, on the stool before the table of Roundhead inquisitors, I felt an immediate empathy with him.

When did I ever see my father? Shift work, golf, garden and my mother saw to that. Her obsession to overcome the social stigma of that secret of the blue picnic case meant the clever boy from Jerviston had to be sheltered at all costs from any taint of Draffen Street or before, even his father. The father was husband and provider. But the boy was the passport to unassailable respectability. You can't call a doctor's mother a bastard.

So I saw my father by appointment only. If I kept very quiet, and as still as a frightened church mouse, I could climb on his knee for five minutes if I was up when he came home from work and slept the sleep of the exhausted in his big chair. There I lay, head against his grey flannel work shirt, holding my breath. Drinking in the smell of him from the sweat to the flux of molten steel, furnace fumes and mill grease that made his black worsted trousers as shiny as a helter-skelter. He was a man, my father, and I worshipped him. But if I wakened him, I was hauled away to his cry of anger, "Can a man no' get some peace in his ain hame, Bessie?" If he awoke himself, I was put down more gently and told to "Go and play, son, there's a good boy," while he went and got "shifted" – washed and dressed – whether it be for bed or golf. He was mighty proud of those plus-fours and that tweed bunnet in which he peacocked before my mother to ask "Do I look all right, Bessie?" before he went out, transformed from the dirt and weariness of work into one of the best amateur golfers in the west of Scotland. As Captain of his club and as "Anderson, one of-your-best-men, y'know", he earned the privilege of playing a round with the bosses at the club, which the selfsame Colville's had provided as part of their "good work" for the community. He was on the way up, was my father, as long as he didn't get ideas above his station and tipped his bunnet to them when they met on the first tee; and as long as he kept producing the record tonnage year after year during the war at a fixed wage of £15 a week, agreed by Iron, Steel and Kindred Trades Federation, as the union was then called.

I was a late child. He was over 40 when I was born and already he was getting old with the sheer hard graft of the steel mill. His wild young days were behind him when he was banned from every public house in Lanark, where he courted my mother, a mill girl – a charge hand, mind you – in the heady days of Robert Owen's Social Revolution at New Lanark, where the workers' welfare was made a patriarchal duty of the enlightened employer.

My father was a tough, stubborn man, tempered by the steel he made, proud of "getting on" from stock boy to roller. Proud indeed that he was top dog in No 4 Bar Mill where, in the days before computerised technology, it was skill, experience and a man's eye that counted. My father could tell from across the room when a picture was hanging 1/16th of an inch out of square, and his steel tape, callipers and plumb could be produced to prove it – if any dared bet on it. An eye that was needed to judge the passes of ingot steel through the ever-decreasing rolls that reduced them from ingot to the bars that made railway tracks or bridge girders, or otherwise. He had the courage to stand as a red hot bar was whipped by hydraulics inches from his toes, to calliper it for size, knowing that the wrong pass at the wrong temperature would turn it into a whip-lashing monster, snaking up and across the mill and cutting down anyone or anything in its path. The secret notes of figures and diagrams of the roller's black "Pass" book were as closely guarded as a Masonic degree.

His hands were so hard, he could pluck a boiled egg with his fingers from boiling water without taking the pan off the cooker. His nails were misshapen from fingers trapped in mill gear wheels. He always had a "black" nail which he would cautiously scrape with a razor blade until he had made a hole in it to release the bruised blood.

And yet, they were an artist's hands. That's what he'd really wanted to be. But a cissy wish like that was no job for a hammer-man's son. So he sublimated it into his spare time – drawing skilful and humorous cartoons for the works magazine; painting delicate crinoline ladies on the three dimples of a Haig's whisky bottle to turn it into a bedside lamp; brushing the most intricate patterns and scenes onto delicate china to be fired into vivid colour for posterity. As I write, I glance up to a plaque on my wall. He did it especially for me. A wash of russet brown and Lincoln green as background, with the outline of a bearded, helmeted Roman centurion cut out with a palette knife. And signed on the back "J Anderson, 1956". And it is a work of art. It is a talent my middle son has inherited, passing me, of which I am quite envious.

So a hard man, yet a sensitive man. Never a loving man, yet a thinking man with an intelligence far beyond his limited school-ing. A true Scot of his generation, he had a deep respect for formal education, yet stood in awe of it, even in his own children. A philo-sopher, who could discuss the timeless questions of the universe with my elder brother better educated and further travelled, far into the night. A theologian who had a fatal attraction for the min-ister, who would come to cross swords once again, only to retreat in confusion for all he was a Doctor of Divinity, before the logic of the steelworker. My father believed in that essential good of man, with all his weakness, which is the essence of Robert Burns, but none of that nonsense about heaven and hell. He worked in hell! Having said that, he accepted the religious conventions demanded by my mother, for the sake of appearances. And though his smile to the family pew was wry, there was no prouder man than John Anderson, in full swallow-tail coat and striped trousers, stamping noisily down the aisle.

I was to know him this way only for 15 years, and at a distance, before the accident that destroyed him as a man, and turned him inwards on himself, and away from me, from all of us, forever.

So it was my mother who brought me up, pulling me along behind her as she laboured on her thick ankles and aching feet (she always had circulation trouble) with a string of pearl beads at her neck and a brooch on the lapel of her very sensible dark coat, to the store for the messages or the church for Sunday School or the doctor's to get "something for nits" – the head lice which raged in Scottish schools but not one of which, by way of doctor's potion, fine comb and carbolic could be allowed to rest on the head of the clever boy who was "going to be somebody and show them all". If her lips tightened, I knew I had done something that wasn't taking me another step forward to my golden future and her rightful place in society.

She wasn't a woman who showed love and was embarrassed by it in others. No hugging or kissing of her, by her or anybody else of somebody else. When the older boys were encouraged to bring their young ladies for Sunday tea, it was a brave young miss who sat on a knee. "There are chairs for everyone in this house," my mother would announce as she laid out yet another groaning table.

Her emotions lay too deep for laughter or tears. She had never known much love as a child. She had never learned it is what we all need and seek, none more than herself, and should give and take freely. On the occasion she did allow herself the luxury of a laugh, or could not stop a telling tear, we were delighted and she was confused.

Once I came home from primary school with an essay, yet again given top marks by my teacher, Nannie Jacks, who lived not far away in Hillhead Drive and with whom my mother plotted the future of their star pupil. I gave it to my mother to read, expecting not even a pat on the head but the usual "Yes, William. Very good, son. You can have a chocolate biscuit for being top boy. Now do your lessons before you go out to play." Little did I know that it was love so fierce, pride so intense, and ambition so driven, that she dare not show it for fear of revealing herself to the world; the bastard mill lass starved of so much and wanting so much for her family that she had never known. But this time she stopped at a line in my essay. I had been writing about the children sent away from the cities to "foster" homes in the country to escape the war. "I know my mother loves me because she calls me her evacuee for fun," I had written. She read it out loud, ever so slowly. "Oh, William," was all she said, then I saw my mother, to my utter amazement, both laughing and crying at the same time. For whom, I'm still not sure. Herself, the evacuee from her past or myself, the boy who had been given as a gift of hope. But I found myself laughing and crying, too. She was to recall that essay many a time and, for the last, when we held hands on her deathbed and both of us for only the second time in our lives, cried together and would have laughed had we been able.

I suspect it is the core of that inner emotion which only a mother can truly understand.

She used to joke that she had only gone to the "raggit" school – the parish charity school for the poorest outcasts. It was only when I was on the other side of the world for some years that I came to realise how "many a true word is spoken in jest", another of her favourite sayings. My brothers had the experience when Barclay went to war in Burma and Ian, after the war, to seek his fortune in Australia. She would pester my father to write to us, and eventually, he would, reluctantly, true, for he was a man who did not waste words, but when he used them did so well and his rare letters were little masterpieces. But sometimes he dug in his heels. "It's his turn to write," he would say, and my mother knew she wouldn't move him until the airmail arrived from whichever one of us it was. But she might have something on her mind that was too important, that couldn't wait, in case she might forget. So it would arrive: a letter from my mother, in a laboured child-like scrawl; absent of any punctuation; one sentence running into another and, when she

remembered there should be a full stop and a capital letter somewhere, putting them at the very next word, whether in the middle
of a sentence or not, which gave it the strange look of an ancient
Biblical script that had to be deciphered.

For me, the important news was always of how well Sam Barnard
and David Murray were doing. Somewhere after the titbits of local
news, the writing would become bolder and more certain. "Sam
Barnard has been made head English teacher at the high school."
"David Murray has won the Lorimer Gold Medal for Biochemistry
at university." Followed by the usual, that she still had faith in me,
that I was going to make her proud of me.

Sam and David, did they but know it, were the bane of my
life, ever held up to me as the shining examples. Sam, a Hillhead
Crescent boy, was the much older son of mother's best friend Mary
Barnard. He'd done well at school, gone off to war to win the DFC,
the hero of several bombing missions; came home to street banners; became a scratch golfer; shot through university to a degree;
took up teaching and became the well-respected headmaster of a
Strathclyde senior secondary school. Sam was the perfect son. He
had never been known to be a naughty boy.

David, though my mother didn't know it, had never been anything else but naughty. He was my best friend at secondary school;
the naturally brilliant son of a Chief Constable, or it may have been
Deputy Chief, who walked through any school subject with a photographic memory; topped the Bursary exams for all Scotland; took
every prize there was on a double degree medical course at university and became a very learned Professor of Pathology in Canada.

Between them they were all my mother wanted me to be, but I
never could be. I forgive them now – but in my youth there were
times I would willingly have choked them by stuffing my mother's
letters down their throats. And a jury of those who had ever suffered
from shining examples would have found me "Not Guilty".

But I was being shaped for fame and fortune long before that,
mostly by those old Scottish truisms which passed for conversation
with my mother. I have already told you of her favourite "Be sure

your sins will find you out." For any embarrassing question about herself, or her family, from her family, friends or anyone else, she always gave a little shrug of her head and declared stoutly, "Ask me no questions, and I'll tell you no lies."

The sewing bee, a hotbed of rumour and gossip, was especially subject to some of my mother's best axioms:

"Never speak ill of the absent or dead."
"Dogs bark as they are bred."
"It's no loss what a friend gets."
"It's a long road that has no turning."
"The devil's aye good to his own."

The devil figured largely in many of her sayings, delivered in her native tongue, and losing something in my more BBC translation. But they were endless:

"Be always the man you would be called."
"Strike me, strike my family."
"The man who pays the piper calls the tune."
"You can't put an old head on young shoulders."
"A crooked man throws a crooked shadow."
"Vice costs more than virtue."
"The devil aye finds mischief for idle hands."
"I'll never be spared to see that day."
"Wishing won't feed the weans."

If you overheard two women of similar ilk having a conversation it was like listening to *Patriarchs and Prophets*, from which many of them had been handed down, mother to daughter. First, the discussion of whatever or whoever it was:

"I hear Mrs Campbell's man has got a rise and they're going to Weston-Super-Mare for their holidays."
"And her wanting a fur stole for her silver wedding."

Then the proverbs:

"Never the one who didn't suffer for getting too big for her shoes."
"Aye, pride goes before the fall."

End of conversation.

Many of these proverbial conversational clichés were, as you might expect, warnings of what would befall if you did get above yourself. The Scottish character is to deflate such ambitions, in the working class most of all, and I have already mentioned some of the divisions. They were more divisive and rigid than in any other class.

The lowest-of-the-low working class lived in rented, crowded squalor, doing midnight flits by begged or borrowed horse and cart to dodge the landlord and the man who knocked seven times – a formality required of the Sheriff Officer who came and still does with the warrant to sell off all worldly goods, bar the bed, to pay off debts.

The lower working class lived in better rented accommodation in tenements, proud people who all scrubbed their doorsteps and paid the rent whenever employment allowed, but might steal if times were hard. They were the most close-knit community of all.

The middle working class always paid the rent in their rows of Coronation Street villas because they were the ones with a "steady wage" and saving to go up in the world to the upper working class, which lived in the pre-war council estates, like Jerviston, and were respectable, honest citizens, one and all. It was always easier to move down than up.

The uniting factor of the women from all these classes was that their highly stylised conversation and use of truisms was, though they'd never have admitted it, a common language.

A lower working-class person who did a Billy Connolly in public would pass it off with a crude "Better oot ye than in ye." That self-same tenet by the time it reached the upper working class might be the rather more polite "Better an empty house than a bad tenant."

But they knew what the other meant. They'd both farted.

My mother never did. Not in public. But she was as full of the "betters" as the next woman:

"Better buy than borrow."
"Better late than never."
"Better alone than in bad company."
"Better bend than break."
"Better half a loaf than no bread."
"Better keep the devil outside the door."
"Better let that flea stick to the wall."

As you might expect, many of them were not entirely proverbs, but handed down sets of instructions directed at keeping children on the straight and narrow and raising them in that image of manhood and womanhood as laid down by Mr Knox:

"Sit still. You're like a hen on a hot girdle."
"Hold your tongue to cool your porridge."
"Don't be a bubbly jock."
"Has the devil got your tongue?"
"Stop dreaming. Your minds are chasing mice."
"If you could only see yourself. "
"Too ill for school, not well enough for dainties."
"Your face'll fix like that one day."
"Stop bothering me. You'll be a man before your mother."

When there was a fad for autograph books, it was the opportunity bar none to set them down and, if you want a laugh, get that old one out of the attic and browse through it. They're all there, in varying disguises.

Even my mother couldn't always resist the family putting down all their favourites with a flourish of a signature. She practised two until she could write them quickly and sign "E Anderson" with a firm hand, and without licking her pencil. Either it was:

"Sticks and stones may break my bones, but names will never hurt me."

Or, depending on her mood, the more cryptic:

"They say – what say they – let them say."

Freud might have made much of those autographed expressions of my mother's philosophy. In pursuit of it, she cut me off not only from my father but my brothers and sister until I'm quite sure they could have grabbed the smart Alec and cuffed his ear to Kingdom come.

The coarser branches of the family were ostracised, too. Even poor Auntie Jean, fatter even than my mother, a coarse LWC woman of Irish extraction (or so my mother told me) with whiskers. Yes, whiskers and a hint of a moustache; smoked like a chimney; cursed like a fishwife; had a heart of gold and was much loved by mild, meek, droll Uncle Jimmy, who worked beside my dad, but lower down the pecking order. They lived up a close not far from the Co-op and though it would have been a castor-oil-lie offence if my mother found out and I had to deny it, when I went for the messages, if I met Auntie Jean in her baffies, out for another packet of Woodbine, I would always stop to chat and she would give me a dusty boiling from her apron pocket and say "Here, Wullie, that's for bein' a guid boy tae yer maw." We would exchange the knowing smiles of those who have a cross to bear and go our separate ways, me chuckling at the thought of Mum hearing my Auntie Jean calling me "Wullie" instead of "William". Or, come to think of it, "Gumsy" by my pals after I lost all my front teeth, top and bottom, to an abscess and went without for a year until they grew again. Or when they were restored, "Winkie" by the girls who had become such a source of interest to my inquiring mind. It was always William to my mother until I was a grown man, when even she realised Bill wasn't all that bad.

Perhaps because William was a name precious to her as one of the only happy memories of her past. The Williamsons were the

Lanark family who gave her a home and a name. I don't know if she was the daughter of a Williamson, or what. But she lived with them until she was married. There were three Williamson brothers who went to the First World War and never came back home. She had been very fond of William Williamson and, in one of the few references to her past, would tell me I'd been named after a brave soldier, though she never made him a relative by saying he was my uncle, or any other kin. I liked that. Named after one of the tragic heroes who gave their yesterday for our tomorrow ... I wonder what they'd make of our today?

My father had a different story, equally romantic and sad. According to him I had been named after his youngest brother, William, who died young. He never elaborated. But in the Fry's Chocolate box that had belonged to my Auntie Nan, I found William's story, or most of it, in a faded newspaper cutting.

It reported the funeral of William Anderson, youngest son of Alexander Anderson, born 21st December 1895. Died of septicaemia 3rd March 1910. Only 14 years old. It went on to describe how the hearse was preceded by the bugler of St Andrew's Troop Boy Scouts, followed by the Scouts of affiliated troops. While on either side of the hearse marched the boys of No 9 Motherwell & Wishaw Troop of which the deceased was the popular troop leader. Septicaemia. Blood poisoning. There was a lot of it still about then in childhood and childbirth. Even a boil could lead to it. Or a cut finger. And fatal, because it was 1910. The very year a Scots farmer's son called Alexander Fleming had passed his final medical examinations and won the Gold Medal at London University. But 18 years before he discovered penicillin. So I lost an uncle and gained a name. Such are the curious twists of life.

Incidentally, the practical side of the Scot, which can grieve while it counts the cost and wonders about the will, showed in the funeral bill attached to the cutting:

To cost of funeral, not including superior landaulette motor car to seat five – £4 19s 6d.

Another funeral bill showed that when William's father, my grandfather, died 20 years later, the funeral cost £12 15s. So they had inflation, too. Even if it looks peanuts by comparison. It probably wasn't compared with the average wage at the time.

I had my choice then – the soldier hero or the tragic popular Boy Scout leader. I would not choose between them. It's not much of a choice, really – death by loss of blood on the battlefield. Or death by poison in the blood in bed. Compared to life by intensive care!

I envy people with an instant recall of every moment of childhood. Mine is fragmented; patches of vivid colourful material, but not lovingly stitched together in the complete, cherished quilt.

Those very early days in LWC Draffen Street, a two-room, kitchenette and scullery with toilet outside the back door. A hall to the front door straight onto the pavement. Two hole-in-the-wall beds. And a bed in the front room. So where did we all sleep? Me in my pram or cot, I suppose. But how did Betty get the privacy that my mother would insist on?

The Friday scrubbing of everything from the doorstep in, including me, sitting up on the wooden sink in my semmit, feet in the basin. If my dad and the others did bath in the tin bin in front of the fire, I can't recall it.

Handed to the woman over the fence, Mrs Campbell, my second mother, to be spoiled while Ian, who had a "funny" leg, was hauled off to Yorkhill Children's Hospital in far-off Glasgow for yet another plaster, or splints or manipulation. Wondering why Ian, gammy leg and all, could half-hop, half-run, faster than me, so I was always the one that got Mum's cuff on the ear.

Flitting to Jerviston in winter snow, when I was five, up the hill, hauling bits and pieces on a big sledge to the better life. Only, and it seemed such folly to me, to have to come back down the hill to start in the Calder Primary School in, yes, Draffen Street, just across the road from our old home and where I was to fulfil my mother's early hopes by becoming Dux Boy, thanks to her, Nannie Jack and Arthur Mee.

Fridays, after the scrubbing, when Betty sometimes took me to

Band of Hope meetings, where a flickering lantern flitted the evils of alcohol across a less than white portable screen.

Saturday night when, because there was nowt else to do with me, if the shifts were right, and the golf, I went with Mum and Dad to the first house of the pictures. My dad stopping at the town cross just to "slip across the road for the Saturday paper, Bessie" – the football results edition which was an alibi to slip into the Railway Tavern for a smartish half-and-half-pint and still have time to catch up with us before Moscardini's. Or joined us there after the football match, sucking a peppermint. We always "sat down" to a fish tea with bread and butter. Not like those common folk who rushed out with their fish suppers wrapped in *Sunday Posts*! And always the Odeon, because it never showed anything but family pictures fit for young eyes and Mum could be sure of the Hays Office censorship even of American movies! The Saturday night outing was a habit that continued for the many years before television reached into our living rooms and turned us into square-eyed zombies – the opium of the people. You cannot have a sit-down tea at Moscardini's dressed in your Saturday best if you're going to watch *The Generation Game*. And there's an apt title for it all!

Being pushed off in the bus to my Auntie Nan's on Sundays, after church, where Uncle Wull loved to play Stop the Bus until Granny knocked through the wall with the walking stick she kept at the foot of the bed because she knew we were "dealing with the devil's handmaiden" which seemed rather an exaggeration for the grimy playing cards.

Loud-voiced, gentle Auntie Nan, six feet tall, with the biggest box of buttons any boy's imagination ever made into armies on the carpet, who spoiled me by making puff candy which I stuffed until I was as puffed as the candy. The polio-afflicted Uncle Wull whose twisted body frightened every other boy but me, and who left me his American Waltham gold pocket watch in gratitude. And Granny Anderson. Yes, that selfsame Janet Anderson from the roots of the family who, after Alexander died, worn out with the years, and bedevilled by that Colvin streak in her which should have made her a lady, suddenly announced she was taking to her bed and did so, in her dutiful daughter's home, for 14 years, where she was waited on hand and foot. Where she died and was my first sight of death in a coffin – that fine parchment yellow face, surely made of delicate bone china and the lace Juliet cap she had always worn. In death, looking like a lady.

On holiday to Lanark, which seemed far enough to me on the top front seat of the No 242 double-decker bus. Exciting enough, too, with the cattle market and statue of William Wallace round which whirled the wild frolics of the annual Lanimer Day. To see my other Auntie Nan, the daft one, and Uncle Jake, a council roadman whose every word was an oath, and who died horribly, little by little, as the gangrene rose in his legs until he lost both, but still wasn't saved.

Lanark, for a holiday in the house with the foghorn wind-up gramophone and His Master's Voice™ record of Gracie Fields singing "The Biggest Aspidistra in the World", which we played until the spring broke, and fell about laughing, simply because there was the biggest aspidistra in the world on the window seat of the house.

Lanark, to meet the joyful, laughing Williamsons, Toyes, Mochries and Corneliuses who were the ask-no-questions part of my mother's clouded ancestry; including Uncle "Pie Lee" Williamson, who did own a tiny bakery in which he made mutton pies and had so many missing fingers nasty rumours flew about their contents.

Yes, there are many fragments; yet so many missing pieces of the jigsaw of my childhood; the childhood that ended so suddenly at 7 am one morning in 1950 with an urgent rap on the front door.

My father should have been home at the back of 6 am, to potter in the garden, unwinding from work, until we woke. He wasn't. And the knock was my Uncle Jimmy to say why. "There's been an accident, Bessie."

I was 16. I had not seen my mother's face so ashen since Barclay was near to death with diphtheria, then a 50-50 chance disease. She hurried to answer the door, so dreading it might be what she feared that she'd even forgotten her old dressing gown and stood there, stunned, in her goonie. She knew it was serious. The steel mill had claimed too many lives and limbs for it not to be.

It was. Uncle Jimmy explained quickly, but calmly. I have expanded what he said to make it clearer. The hydraulic rollers had jammed. Their job was to ram-roll the steel bars into the different "passes" through the mill, gradually reducing the bars in size. My father could not stand back and see another record tonnage slip away. He stepped in to see why the engineers couldn't find the fault. His foot went down into the machinery and was trapped, crushed. For four hours he was trapped, in agony, but refusing morphine because the pain kept him alive. As they worked to free him, some of the steel plates that formed the floor of the mill were removed. For reasons that still remain obscure, this freed some of the machinery of the mill, and drove a hydraulic ram against my father's leg, crushing it up to just below the knee. An accident within an accident.

After that, he was freed quite quickly. My Uncle Jimmy had been fetched from his job elsewhere in the works and had stayed with my father all the time, until Dad was taken away in the ambulance. He then came to Jerviston to break the news to my mother. He was as quick in the telling as my mother was in her reaction. First shock over, we all dressed and went, by bus, to Law Hospital. He was still being given the immediate life-saving emergency treatment. My mother was allowed in to see him, briefly. When she came out, she was biting her lip to put on a brave face. But we knew by her eyes, it was bad.

I could see it for myself when, suddenly, the doors burst open and my father was wheeled out on a trolley table into the corridor where we sat, on his way to the operating theatre. His face was all I could see in the paraphernalia. It was shrunken into a little old man's with strange grey and purple patches where it wasn't deathly white; his thinning hair plastered to his head by the sweat of pain. His eyes were closed and sunk deep into his head.

He was hours in the operating theatre. His leg was so badly mangled, it had to be amputated, boot, trouser leg and all, and then they had to work feverishly to make some kind of stump of it, in a body that had lost too much blood and was deep in the coma of shock. His family waited, on endless cups of tea, reassuring one another. Not Dad. He's as tough as the steel he makes. He'll hang on, this bull of a man. This 57-year-old bull of a man, who'd toiled and fought for 43 years, draining himself, to give his wife the respectability she wanted and his family the opportunities he had wanted for them as much as her.

He survived. He made it through the ten anxious days, ten painful weeks and ten operations to give him a stump which could bear an artificial leg. He survived to walk into the limb-fitting centre on his crutches, to walk the parallel bars with his new leg until the stump was raw, the limb fitters limp, and walk out on it, without the crutches, on the same day. He survived to enjoy a game of bowls instead of golf, adjusting the mechanics of the leg himself so it would lock in a special way to let him half kneel down to throw the bowl – and won a few competitions to prove it worked. He survived to swallow his pride and go back to a kind of work, first as a store man in my brother-in-law's plumber's business, then as a store man in a small mill that could use not him, but his knowledge and the stored experience in that black "Pass" book. He was happy to be working with steel again. He survived another 19 years.

But he was never the same man. The toll had been too great. A succession of hernias, strokes and other afflictions of the worn-out body first laid him low in bed. Then hospital, then back home and for spells between them for 15 of those 19 years and the last of them almost entirely in hospital, until cancer, too, finally reduced him to a shell of illnesses in which only an invincible spirit and a heart like a steel mill kept him going for months more than the most optimistic prediction.

A phone call on that last day brought me dashing 80 miles by car. I was only just in time. His heart was still so stubborn, fighting the fatal pneumonia in that ravaged body, that the hospital had decided he had to be helped over the final hurdle. He looked up when I went in to join my brothers, both fighting tears at his bedside. He searched right inside me with his eyes, still alive with the memories, if nothing else.

"Oh, it's Willie. What are you here for? I'm no' dead yet, you know."

Then this man, who loved me as I loved him, but neither of us could be first to admit it; this man who announced loudly every Sunday morning so the whole geriatric ward could hear, that someone had better bring him his son's paper soon, so he could read it, but would tell only my mother how proud he was of me; this man took Barclay's hand, gulped up the great gouts of black blood and, still defying death, died. I didn't wait. There is no dignity in the end of the strongest and bravest. I drove from the hospital to my sister's house by the country road and on the way pulled into a quiet lay-by where I sat, a man as hard as my father, and cried until there were no tears left in me for him or myself.

That man in the lay-by was a lot older than the teenager who went home from hospital the day my father was declared out of danger. But I had to face the fact he might never work again in any other than the lightest of jobs. I was struggling with myself – with the first decision I ever had to make for myself. I was in my sixth year at Dalziel High School. Despite popular mythology, they had not all been the happiest of years.

My mother's conviction that I was different had made me different. Her constant persuasion that I was superior to everyone else had persuaded me to feel superior. Her belief that I should be kept apart from family and friends had made me a bit of a loner. The fact that I was a late child, always in the company of adults, had given me a preference for their company, rather than my peers. More than just being at ease in their company I felt a need to earn their approval, as my mother had dinned into me. Oh, I wasn't a snob or a pig or a swot. Far from it. I could tell a dirty joke with the best of them. I got up to more mischief than most. If anyone ever wonders who nipped Elsie Murdoch's bottom in the school hall at morning prayers, it was me. Thereby adding a new high note to "Onward Christian Soldiers".

If anyone wonders who nailed down Gummy Walker's desk lid so he wouldn't get the belt out, it was me. I had to retaliate after this eccentric mathematics teacher lined up 57 boys in the corridor, late from school lunch after a snow fight, and, totally unaided, belted every one. If anyone doesn't know who lowered a dead mouse on a string through the hole in the roof of the science lab, thus giving Pogo Drummond apoplexy, it was me. (And if any Dalziel High boy with a bent for the dramatic would like to know the secret route from the tower, just write to me.)

It was I who was lined up outside the Rector's room waiting for Doc Gibb to administer six of the best, double-handed, gown flying as he flapped up and down to get some steam up. Well, Nina Dounes' mother had pointed out clothing was still on coupons – and me playing noughts and crosses with chalk on the back of Nina's black serge coat had ruined it. Worse, she would not go on the school bus as long as that awful Anderson boy was also on it. A right clever Dick he thought he was.

'Twas I who experimented with phosphorus. 'Twas I who traced a cross on Leslie Robinson's forehead with a finger dipped in silver nitrate, thereby blackening the tip of my finger and marking Leslie as a minister's son for the week that it took for the chemical to fade. This Papal blessing also marked him for life as he went on to become a Methodist medical missionary.

And in everything, aided and abetted by that paragon of virtue, David Murray, whose ingenious mind usually devised the *modus operandi* which the devil in me was delighted to execute. He, like me, was a boy apart. With David, it was his genius which set him so. We were twin souls – much like Leopold and Loeb – though we never got round to stuffing small boys into culverts.

I tell you this not boastfully but to show there was more Hairy Breeks in me than my mother could ever belt out of me. I rolled through school like a tidal wave, my restless mind always seeking new outlets to test my talents. I played rugby hard and well. I was a dab hand at snooker in the "free period" allotted to the Miners' Welfare Social Club. Editor of the school magazine wasn't enough, so I started the school's first newspaper, *The Dalziel Domino*, which slandered everybody, pupils and teachers alike. It also had a popular and very bloody horror serial, written with dripping pen by, guess who – David "Doctor Death" Murray. I starred in the Debating Society. I was the first pupil on the Parent-Teacher Committee of the Cleland Memorial Committee (which raised money to buy playing fields in memory of the school's war dead).

I won the mock general election as an unpopular Conservative candidate by the promise of a half-day to all who voted for me. The Rector refused to give it on the grounds that (a) I had no right to offer it, (b) it was not on the local authority calendar of half-hols, and (c) the sooner young people learned politicians never keep promises the better for them. So he gave the new MP for Dalziel High a belting to show the school he thought I was a bit of a con man, too. Hurt by this injustice, I threatened to withdraw my voice from the role of Nanki Poo in *The Mikado*. Doc Gibb was a devotee of not only Gilbert and Sullivan, but discipline. The school opera survived with yours truly relegated to the chorus!

I can see now I treated school as a giant circus, with myself on the high wire and pupils and teachers alike only the supporting acts. There, way above them, all my pent-up energies and desires would burst into glorious flower. While they saw me as a weed! Looking back, I can only agree with them. I must have been absolutely insufferable.

I suffered for it, of course, in all the subtle, sadistic ways that schoolchildren everywhere can find to burst a balloon. They pricked and squeezed it; punched it surreptitiously in the softest part; burned it with cigarette ends; pushed it against hot radiators; spilled a drop of acid on it in chemistry class; rummaged it roughly around the playground; banged it against the side of school buses; even, at an extra-mural school camp, collapsed a tent on it while assorted feet jumped all over it. But the balloon, whatever it felt inside, refused to burst and went bouncing on until it was beyond their hands and feet and minds.

Mainly thanks to one James K Scobbie, the gentle red-faced giant with the shabby mince-stained tweed waistcoat of his equally crumpled tweed suit, then the head English master and later to be the Rector, whose broad Scots voice belied the keen shrewd intellect and the classical scholar's grasp of language, but betrayed the working-class origins which gave him such an understanding of his boys.

He was a born teacher.

If my mother made me what I was, Jamie Scobbie made me what I am, opening up my imagination to the wonderful world of words and their expression and to the minds of those who wrote them. I had read every book I could lay my hands on as a child (and *Swiss Family Robinson* 11 times for I ticked the fly leaf to keep count).

Now I ravaged every book Jamie could give me from his own library, with his tight, neat little notes on the margins. Chaucer, Shakespeare, John Donne, Milton, Tennyson, Keats, Shelley. And Burns, of whom Jamie was classically critical but inordinately proud of his insight.

Food for the gods. And savoured the nectar, sipping at the following lines from Milton's poem, "Lycidas", word by word, for the nose, bouquet, the flavour and the texture.

> Fame is the spur that the clear spirit doth raise
> (That last infirmity of noble mind)
> To scorn delights and live laborious days;
> But the fair guerdon when we hope to find,
> And think to burst out into sudden blaze,
> Comes the blind Fury with the abhorrèd shears
> And slits the thin-spun life.

These have always been my favourite lines. The fatalist's life in one Waterford crystal goblet in glorious rich red claret.

Palgrave's *Golden Treasury*, for they were all in it, became my missionary's Bible, always in my hand, to be read and read again, quoted (and misquoted if it suited my argument), until I knew it backwards. So much so I was one of the few presented for the third of the English papers available at the University Entrance Bursary Examination because it consisted only of quotations and a discussion question about each. You had to choose six. You "spot" the quotation by naming author, book, play or poem and its exact place in the work, then discuss the question in the context of the work. Perhaps three lines from all of Shakespeare. Or two from *Childe Harold's Pilgrimage*. Or one from *The Old Curiosity Shop* (Dickens fortunately writing long sentences). And I revelled in it.

But there was more to Jamie than words and their beauty. I never could stand the grammar of it. Never mind the width, feel the quality. That it was a substantive clause bothered me not a whit. That it qualified some pronoun left me quite cold. That it was in iambic pentameter did not make it an epic. If it rolled off the tongue and reverberated round your mind, that was the stuff of which dreams were made. Give me a clever 18th-century epigram every time.

I could have loved and lost
And been unhurt
By manner cost
Disdainful eyes; Goddess who will not bend not only lost a
lover
But a friend

And I wrote that myself at 15.

Jamie understood that, as he understood all the weakness and failings in his boys. He was a boys' man. Away from the school, when he would take us youth hostelling over the hills to test our bodies as well as our minds, there were always little bits of cigarette paper stuck to his bottom lip, where a cigarette had been forgotten as he talked until the long ash fell off to add to the detritus on that waistcoat, and only the heat warned him to pull the fag end off his lip before it burned him. He wanted us to be rough and wild on the Lammermuirs because it burned off the physical energy left long after he had spurred our mental energies to their last. If you cringed a tackle at rugby, Jamie would be first to shout from the touch line "For God's sake, Willie, what's the matter with you? The bigger they are, the harder they fall. Get stuck in." Then, as you left the field, he'd take a moment by your side quietly to say "Remember what Byron said about courage?" And you would shower the more quickly to get home to find out. He never married. He was wed to his vocation. He was a Scottish dominie of the old school. A marvellous man. A father, teacher, confessor in the finest tradition of what was, despite the sneers at it from the confused comprehensive school of thought, the best education system in the world. Ask Adam Smith, James Watt, Alexander Fleming, David Livingstone, Kelvin, Macadam, Logie-Baird and the rest.

Why we should mock this system today, I do not know. It gave the Scots an insatiable appetite for learning, for finding out and for building that sent them out into the world and all over it with a reputation that made a Scot wanted by the world as no other man. Ask the world!

But what did that world want of the 16-year-old whose father lay in hospital?

CHAPTER 7

All The Virgins Go To University

I saw the advert in *The Glasgow Herald*, in the reference room of the Carnegie "Let There Be Light" public library, where often I spent an hour after school keeping in touch with the current affairs so essential to any young man of letters – though most of those affairs were Bill and Blithe or Dick and Jean or David and Kathie, behind the high shelves of the aptly named "Human Biology" section. It was the only corner hidden from the librarian and so as much frequented by courting couples as pimply, flushed youths seeking further information on "Human Biology". I could have told them there was little under "Intercourse", even less under "Onset of Menstruation in The Puberal Female" and nothing at all under "Contraceptives", but as many upper working-class and lower middle-class marriages were first contracted in "Human Biology" as in The Palais dance hall or Chico's cafe.

There was another reason for *The Glasgow Herald*. Inside it was hidden my favourite volume of *Just William* which I had sneaked through under my blazer from the children's section of the library; hidden so that no pal could see young Shakespeare seeking inspiration in his predicament from a nostalgic glance through the boy who never grew up in years or was anything else but in trouble.

Alas, Richmal Compton was solidly middle class herself and neither the respectable Mr Brown nor any of her fathers ever lost a leg in a common steel mill.

So the invitation leaped out of the small ads, third down in Sits. Vac: "Cook-Steward wanted for motor vessel cruising Western Isles. £4.10/- per week. All found. Phone Airdrie 123456."

That was the answer. Get a job. Any job. That job. For many reasons.

I hadn't been brought up unaware of the harsh facts of economic life. My father out of work for who knows how long. No job. No wage. No pay packet every Friday to be handed unopened to my mother. We never went short. Far from it. Anything we ever needed, and sometimes only wanted, from bicycles to bagpipes, somehow came our way, later, or sooner if we saved towards them ourselves. But that is not to say there was ever money to spare. Every penny went to preserving our Jerviston status. Where was the money to come from to keep our heads high – and see me through six years of university? I was the leak in the budget. Betty was busy building a business with her husband. Barclay had hauled himself up from tradesman joiner to under-deputy manager of the council direct labour department – another victory for Bessie! And Ian had just finished a five-year slog to put AHICS after his name, and was already wondering how Australia would welcome a chartered surveyor to a land that was growing and crying out for his diploma. All three were later to go on to build successful businesses of their own. (So I am still the leak in the budget.)

So went my reasoning. First, financial; second, selfish. I didn't want to be a doctor. I had the Certificate of Fitness to University which my six Highers had earned me. The application forms, overseen by my mother, were away to the medical schools of Glasgow, Edinburgh and St Andrews, in that order of preference. I had already had my interview with the august professors of Glasgow, putting my best foot forward, as the school had coached, to show the lad o' pairts eager to save humanity. "Don't forget to mention rugby and the debating society. They like an all-round candidate." It was now fast accepted by all that I would go off and learn to be a doctor with, and in the shadow of, my friend David. But I wasn't in the least eager to pledge myself to Hippocrates. I wanted to read and write about humanity, not stick rubber clad fingers up its, well, I'm sure you've got the drift of it. I had the Science subjects only by dint of endless nights sweating over them. Words were my delight. A three-year MA to learn more about them, then consider what to do with them, perhaps even teach them though the latter path had the shadow of Sam Barnard across it. I would have to go one better than him. But it was the pen not the scalpel my hands wanted to wield. Third, the blood of Hairy Breeks. What was over the horizon?

I got the job, told the Headmaster I was leaving school, and got Jamie Scobbie's conditional approval for my plans before I told my mother.

Got the job? Oh, yes. That was the easiest part of it. What about the cooking? Nae bother. My butter sponge, though bearing my mother's name, was the lightest of the sewing bee's offering to the Kirk Bring-and-Buy. As she had taught us all the virtues, so standing on your own feet was one of them. I could cook, sew, darn, purl and plain, scrub and polish with the best of them. I never thought twice about it. Boys or not, we all had to be able to do it. If it did nothing else, it would make us better husbands than Mum already thought any wives deserved. As long as it was only a relaxing hobby for me, she was delighted when I turned out to be a born chef – and revelled in the astonishment of family and friends when I converted the most complicated recipes into a feast of delight. When the visitors had eaten, and the women started showering Mum with congratulations, there was always the jealous one who gushed "You'll have to give me the recipe for that, Mrs Anderson." When she would say "Oh, you'll have to ask William, he made it you know, he made it all." Then she would sit back in triumph at their confusion. If her son could do that, what hope would they have against his teacher?

It is a talent I have always nourished and it was to find professional expression in the à la carte menu for my family's restaurant venture. Modesty forbids me to go into detail. Just ask anyone who has ever enjoyed my cooking. The fact that I should have stayed an amateur is neither here nor there. Though I am delighted it is hereditary and my youngest son is a chef.

So cooking was no problem. And stewarding was only the good housekeeping my mother taught me, but with a fancy title and uniform. There is nothing quite like the brash confidence of youth!

At any rate, it impressed a certain Colonel Duce, the fixer for a building company called Matthew Thorn & Co Ltd, who were big in the new dust-free, germ-free wall surface they were plastering inside buildings all over the country, mostly in hospitals – Gyproc, if my memory serves me right. Their vessel it was, used for selling wall surfaces to clients who didn't mind a little pleasure mixed in. This, happily, also made it a tax dodge. Colonel Duce was as military a man as I've ever met. His interview was like a question-and-answer briefing for the Second World War.

Frankly, I didn't think I had any real chance of a job. In many ways, it was a boyish romantic gesture. I'd make them all take back their feathers! Especially that gang who bullied me at school. Up yours, Cags Johnstone, I've run away to sea. But my hopes did rise when I saw the motley bunch of scruffy sea cooks waiting in the anteroom, washed ashore on a tide of whisky and prostitutes. Even Para Handy wouldn't have touched them with a barge pole.

So it turned out. Although Colonel Duce was apprehensive of my age, it has never been a bar to life at sea, has it? Just think of the boy on the burning deck. I looked respectable, sounded honest, declared myself willing to work all the hours God sent. The fact the others all asked for more money did have some bearing on the decision. Above all, my nails were clean and my hands well washed, which was more than could be said for the others, whose fingers would have clouded any consommé beyond redemption by white of egg.

I went home in the bus with a week's wages in advance and a railway warrant to Oban; surprised, excited and afraid. When my mother was really angry, she would turn away, tight-lipped, and would simply not say a word to the offender for days on end, as if that person had vanished off the face of the earth. She was afraid of her own temper. It took time to allow herself to disgorge and then it took just as long to get it out of her system, on and off, as the offender came and went. I was too big for that belt, so it would be the silence before the storm.

It was not. It was the last reaction I expected. She stood in the kitchen, saying not a word, icing Empire biscuits. I stuck on the cherries, one by one, very carefully, as I tested her out. "Dad … no money … why not a job … just for summer … leave school … don't worry …"

There was no reaction. Just more icing. More cherries. "Matter of fact … have a job … left school … away from home … Oban … warrant … here's my first wage." The icing knife paused and continued to the end of the last biscuit and the last cherry.

I couldn't begin to hazard a guess as to what was going through her mind in those long moments. But then it was made up. She pushed the money back across the table. "Well, if that's the way it is, keep the money, son. You're going to need it." It was a yes. A definite yes, I knew, for she'd called me son instead of William. Who can fathom a mother's mind? Maybe the clincher was that I hadn't mentioned about not wanting to be a doctor. I had only loosened those apron strings.

That was on a Tuesday. The following Monday morning I was on my way to Oban, in the double-breasted navy blue uniform suit of the previous CS. Small as he'd been, he was still a size too big for me. But it left plenty of room for my seafarer's swagger as I fought a force ten gale through St Enoch's Station to the train, knocking a few pirates aside with my swinging seabag – brother Barclay's air force duffle bag, pressed into service to carry my cook's issue and all the other worldly possessions I would need for the great adventure.

In the compartment, I casually threw aside the double breasts and stuck out my chest as far as a youthly chest can stick, so everyone could see the satin-stitched white letters on my navy wool seaman's jersey (which was new and did fit):

MV *MARILYN ABBOTT*

Aarh! Jim, lad. Hand the black patch to that bifocal-specked bloke in the other corner, so busy reading his *Titbits*, he hasn't seen the young seadog who could tell him a yarn or two that would curl his toupee. "If he gives thee any snash lad, send for Long John and I'll silver-plate his slit gizzard for treasure trove before thee can say 'Pieces of eight' or 'Buckets of blood', boy." Yes, it was a magic journey. Those worthy reasons for it forgotten in the adventure of it all. Freedom is a high trip for those who have never been free.

He was waiting for me at the end of the platform. The McAllister. And if it near as dammit rhymes with The Talisker, it is by God's design, for he was a walking bottle of malt. A chisel-faced, red-eyed, black-thin-haired, unshaven sot, hewn from the miserable rock of his Hebridean home Eriskay, and if there was the Gaelic lilt to his tongue, there was no love in his heart for any man or beast. He was the dourest, meanest, most spiteful man I have ever met – and I've met them all. A painter's labourer with Thorn & Co in winter and when the vessel was laid up, and her Captain Bligh when she was at sea. Yet so devoutly Catholic that he would think nothing of going to early-morning Sunday mass still reeking of the excesses of the night before and, though it was alleged that in the seven years he'd worked for the company, he only went back to Eriskay for two weeks every year, he had sired seven children. I was a Protestant and a clever chap who, Colonel Duce had informed him, would probably be going to university after the season. It was oil and water. Fire and brimstone. He hated me before he even met me. I hated him the moment I clapped eyes on him. And feared him.

His first words to me were: "F – ing boy. Send me a f – ing boy to do a man's job," and he tugged his greasy skipper cap lower over his eyes, turned and hurried away, leaving me to follow him or not.

It was as well we saw little of each other. He ate, slept, drank and did what skippers do alone in his stink-hole of a tiny cabin, emerging only to go ashore to the pub, to cook up a deal with a chandler or two or, if he did happen to meet me, to snarl some Gaelic gibberish at me. At sea, when he had to come out of his cabin to command the vessel from a flying bridge, he told the engineer to tell me I was forbidden to go up there, on pain of castration. When I delivered his meals, a gnarled hand would grab them through a part-opened door with a Gaelic grunt. When he had to pay me my wages, he would throw them on the galley sink – the nearest to four pounds and one ten bob note he could find in the "float" that the company sent him every week for running expenses which, since I often bought the bottle, included his whisky. How I hated him. More so because, in the physical make up that lay beneath the damage of the years, and the layers of Highland mistrust, poverty and repression, he was physically not unlike my father. How could he. How dare he. How I hated him. Peter the engineer was a more kindly, younger, inshore fisherman from Mallaig. He became my intermediary and intercessor with The McAllister. Angus the deck-hand was an Outer Islander, too. Cheerier, not all that much older than me, but showing early symptoms of a McAllister in the making and the pair of them were as thick as thieves.

The education in life that I had lacked I soon learned from that crew. If my mother had known half of it, she would have sent the International Red Cross and the US Cavalry to rescue me. But I do not propose to dwell on it, for much of it was coarse, crude and foul-mouthed – the knowledge that is the stock-in-trade of bilge scum from Benbecula to Bilbao, Liverpool to Lisbon and Singapore to San Francisco. And I loved looking and listening to every new word and deed of it as much as I hated The McAllister. It is not for the ears and eyes of those who are not of the brotherhood.

And there was a bright side. The *Marilyn Abbott* herself. A sleek 72-foot wartime motor torpedo boat (MTB) that had been con-verted for comfort, she was fast from her twin 72-horse Perkins' petrol engines and as manoeuvrable as an MTB had to be in those desperate days when they played a deadly game of Tig or Hide and Seek with the German U-boats. Just as well. I once saw The McAllister, drunk as a lord, taking her through the tricky passage north out of Oban harbour to meet a MacBrayne's steamer coming in. MacBrayne's, though their lifeline, were red rags to the wilder Highland bulls and, rules of the road at sea or not, McAllister was not giving way. "F – ing MacBrayne's," he bawled, as he glared at her with glazed eyes. "Layte agayin. Late ass f – ing usual." Knowing the accent helps the feeling of that sentence considerably. He then gave five short blasts of the MV's horn which is the mariner's warning that another vessel is steaming into danger and had better do something about altering her course. To which MacBrayne's replied with two toots ("I am altering my course to port") which would be his normal turning to pass the inner channel buoy, and in the situation pertaining was, in essence, telling McAllister to think again about the signal on the steamer's jackstay which meant she was manoeuvring in a narrow channel, and could not give way. It was fully intended to put McAllister in his place.

"That f – ing maan from Glaassgow," snorted McAllister, thus explaining all about the steamer skipper's character and antecedents and pushing the throttle forward as he said it in order to race the MTB in a zigzag twice across the other's path before, knowing his boat's capabilities, he side-streamed her to pass properly on the steamer's port side, thereby setting the bells of hell ringing on the steamer, giving her skipper heart failure and all the passengers apoplexy but avoiding any nasty Board of Trade questions about his seamanship. He then mouthed Gaelic oaths for quite half the passage to Tobermory. That night was the drunkest I'd ever seen him. When he staggered back aboard at dawn, he looked and smelled as if he'd slept in a ditch – the peat bog stank that runs behind the Islay Mist distillery.

We carried a party of six passengers, with maybe a couple of children, on trips of anything from a long weekend to the full fortnight tour through the Inner and Outer Hebrides, across to Ireland and sometimes down to the Isle of Man, if they wanted a change from the magic of misty purple islands with the certainty of rain to kiss-me-quick and candy floss with the probability of sunshine.

I soon got my recipe book knocked into a routine. I'd take the tender to Sawyer's ponds on Kerrera from where they despatched seafood to world-wide customers and provisioned the *Queen* of the Cunard line as well as the cook-steward of the *Marilyn Abbott*. I'd buy half-a-dozen lobsters and a stone of herring. The herring went to the fo'c'sle with "tatties and convoyance", boiled potatoes and beef dripping to mash into them. The lobster went to the saloon in various guises on the menu from Thermidor a la Ganavan (a sandy beach that served as a local beauty and bathing spot) to Long Island

Clam Chowder (in which I used left-over cold lobster, disguised with crab meat and rock cod). The left-over consommé of one day became the stock of the Tomato Ardennes of the next. (Just add a tin of tomato puree and a large chunk of rough pâté, ladies, and if you haven't fresh, a scoop of long-life cream on top. It's superb.)

So, with ingenuity, makeshift and an adaptable recipe book, I learned the kitchen tricks that others are taught. Nothing was wasted. Left-over veg, for example, was simply mashed, slightly curried, scooped into scallop shapes on an oven tray, to become Legumen Madras on my menu. I made up the names to suit the dishes after I'd cooked them from what I had. The one and only disaster was Yorkshire pudding for a Yorkshire man. He was so pleased at getting the freedom of my galley to show me how to do it properly (and I was shrewd enough to congratulate him on his unsweetened, singed doughnuts without a hole) that, when he left, otherwise overwhelmed by the unusual gastronomic delights of his trip, he pulled a wad of rolled fivers from his pocket and peeled off two for me as a tip. McAllister told the engineer to tell me I had better share it but as he never shared more than a passing smell of his evil breath with me I told the engineer to tell McAllister he was too late. I had sent it home to my mother and if he thought he could take the candy off a kid he had better think again or I would tell Colonel Duce how much the so-called new tender really cost.

The kid was learning fast but I had never seen so much money, or held as much in my hand. The *nouvelle cuisine* this forced upon me earned twice as much in tips as my all-found wage.

In the coffin of the galley I cooked up more novelties, threw off my chef's cap and apron, donned my steward's monkey jacket over my chequered blue trousers and dashed through to serve, bowing and scraping and smiling, with a "Yes, modom, certainly, sir." As the Uriah Heep of *haute cuisine* who knew where his next tip was coming from, I learned to take my fresh air on deck, as is every sea cook's inalienable right, just as the passengers were gathering to disembark. Let McAllister glower as he pleased. If any had forgotten the usual custom, my smiling presence was there to

115

remind them. I would try to look just a little wan and worn from my work which was always worth another quid. So I passed from innocence to cupidity.

I also fell in love. Mad, pining, passionate, poetry-writing, unrequited love. She was the dark-haired daughter of the cheery Italian who had a cafe on the pier. A Madonna. A Mona Lisa. But with a mother who soon tagged me for a lecherous seaman and chaperoned every moment we were together. When I plucked up courage to ask her out, mama always had something else for her to do. Plump, jolly, but determined as only an Italian mama can be that her daughter was untouchable, especially where sailors were concerned. Even young salts, far from the care of their own mother and who might be going to university. This winning appeal to her maternal instincts and ambitions did not move her. So we loved from afar, as far apart as her behind the counter and me at the table behind the door, exchanging undying devotion only with our eyes and the rare tingling of our fingers as she dared, no, willed me to touch them when she cleared my cup away. I always gave her a pound note if I could, so I could squeeze her hand when she handed me the change. And the day she returned it was the day I knew I was in love.

So the lad brought up on a cup of tea for every occasion learned to love espresso coffee. That was all that came of it. We parted, both as virginal as we had met. This became a matter of grave concern to the engineer in whom I stupidly confided. Thereafter, it became his mission in life that I should "lose my cherry". "That girl's ripe for it," he avowed in his direct way. "You know what Italians are like." He suggested various ways of diverting mama. I refused because he was pouring cold water on my high passion. That my Madonna might be like that! Also, I knew mama was not as easily diverted as he thought.

Just as well. I went back to Oban many years later, went into the cafe, knowing I wouldn't be recognised, and there was mama. "My God, she hasn't changed a bit," I thought. "I wonder what her daughter's like." Then I looked closer and realised it was the daughter. It was only when I was shaving next day that it dawned on me, "My God, and you look like your father!" I have a sneaking suspicion that if Romeo and Juliet had survived their passion to middle age, it would have been a much different story!

The summer was passing. The shadow of Staffa was longer in the water each time we passed it to show another part of Fingal's Cave with its strange asphalt columns.

The first time I was as moved as Mendelssohn. Thereafter to me it began to look more like one of Wimpey's less imaginative multistoreys. But there is a magic about the Western Isles that has pulled me back again and again. Little I saw of them then through a steamed-up galley porthole, trying to turn a crêpe suzette as my coffin heaved in the face of a March gale on the passage to the Outer Hebrides, listening to every weather forecast with the ear of a steward who knows seasick paying passengers expect someone else to clean up their puke. There was one certainty. Whatever life held for me it could never be lower than mopping up someone else's vomit from a cabin floor to pump it down a sea-cocked yacht loo with a stubborn handle. As I knelt there to get a better grip of the pumping handle, I raised prayers of gratitude to old Hairy Breeks that I had a strong, seafaring Viking stomach. He never let me down.

One day the telegram arrived. Everyone in Oban knew who everyone else was and I had been around long enough by then. So as I tied up the tender to the fishing boat and crossed her to the pier ladder, the postie was passing. "There's a telegram for you," he said. Our mail was held "Poste Restante" at the post office. There are no daily deliveries to vessels at sea. I didn't want a telegram. It could only be bad news. My father, maybe, or some other tragedy. I walked to the office, collected it, but couldn't bring myself to open it. I folded it up unopened and stuck it in my trouser pocket. Then I went for the "fresh store" supplies – meat, vegetables and bread – and packed them in a box to carry to the tender. When I reached the end of the promenade wall I laid the box down for a rest before I went out on the pier. The telegram was burning a hole in my pocket. I took it out, opened it, slipped out the message, threw the envelope away, picked up the stores and, still holding the box balanced on my arms in front of me, wiggled the telegram with my hand until I could read it.

It was a disaster of unpredictable proportions.

CONGRATULATIONS. ACCEPTED FOR UNIVERSITY.
COME HOME IMMEDIATELY. MOTHER.

I couldn't phone. We didn't have one at home. I couldn't write. She would not wait for a letter. A telegram couldn't say it. I would have to go home and face it.

These thoughts were going through my mind as I walked on staring at the words. Yes, I was excited by the thought of university. It was common knowledge all the virgins went to uni – and might be as anxious as I was not to stand out in a crowd. No, I didn't want to be a doctor. Yes, I was enjoying my freedom. No, I did not want to go home. Not yet.

At which point I walked straight off the edge and plunged ten feet down into the narrow band of water between pier and dinghy – steak mince, shoulder steak, carrots, turnips, sliced pan loaves, cardboard box, telegram and all!

I surfaced, grabbed the step ladder and climbed back up onto the pier. There I stood, dripping, watching the slices of bread and bits of butcher's brown and waxed white wrapping paper bobbing out to sea on the ebb tide, along with assorted floating vegetables and my sodden telegram. That sodding telegram. The seagulls swooped and one, greedier than the others, mistaking the pulp of buff paper for bread, beaked it up, then dropped it as quickly when it wasn't Mother's Pride after all. But I am, greedy bird, I am. And I am stuck with it. Then I cast my bread upon the water.

I was still wringing wet when I got back to the *Marilyn Abbott*. McAllister's lurking eyes immediately suspected the worst and sent the engineer to ask me if I'd damaged the dinghy and if so, I'd pay for it. You will note his concern for any damage to me. So I told the engineer to tell McAllister, no, I hadn't swamped the tender in a flat, calm sea. I had received a telegram to say my father was ill and I had to go home, if not immediately, as soon as duty permitted, and it was such a shock I fell off the pier.

I think he was so chuffed at my downfall that he said yes to Peter, without thinking and Peter translated that as meaning I could go off the following day, Thursday, as long as I was back before the next party arrived on Monday.

I sat in the train, marshalling all my arguments. Dad was still in hospital. I could look after myself. I thought I'd be best away from home for a bit. University – well, I had thought about doing an MA degree, maybe after a couple of years to see the world. I knew I could get a job with a shipping line now.

It was all signed, sealed and delivered before I got a foot though the door. Mum appreciated what I'd done. But it was all settled. I had my place in the medical faculty of Glasgow University. She had sent my acceptance. The money was arranged. £100 in a savings bank book to cover the books, lab coats, instruments I'd need. The university had sent me a list and, "Since you weren't here, I opened it in case it was important. I knew you'd understand." She had priced the list to find out how much I'd need. The grant of £42 would cover my class fees.

"But that's only the first year," I started to say. I couldn't get a word in edgeways. That was arranged, too. The union said Dad would get compensation. Thousands, more than enough. In fact, after a long battle, and without much union help, he finally settled through a lawyer for £3000. On the same day the cheque was collected, Mother arranged for the lawyer to draw up a new will for Dad, with his agreement, to set £2000 of it "in trust for my son, William, to be used for all fees, and other expenses necessary for him to qualify as a doctor at Glasgow University." What a woman!

Then she said she had a surprise for me. She went out and came back with it, on a coat hanger. A beautiful black flannel blazer. None of your Co-operative divvy merchandise. Forsyth's of Glasgow no less, the best. There, already stitched in place on the breast pocket, the gold-braided badge of Glasgow University, the fish, the book and the burning bush.

"Put it on, William. Let me see you in it."

How could I refuse? I put it on.

She hugged me. She came forward and threw her arms round me. My mother, Bessie Anderson.

"You'll do it," she said, her eyes glistening with tears she wouldn't shed. "Do it for me. Do it for your dad. You should do it and I know you can do it." It must have been one of the longest speeches she ever made.

It would have saved us both a lot of heartbreak if I had stood my ground. But I couldn't. I would go to university and be a doctor. My mother knew I would. She had always known, from the beginning. There were no exclamations of joy or celebrations. What was to be, would be.

She was a little surprised when I said I would have to go back to Oban. She thought I would stay at home now it was all settled. I told her I couldn't let the company down. I'd given my word. She saw that. So I went back to The McAllister. For just a moment, he forgot himself and made to come forward to greet me when I climbed the aft steps onto the deck. The bugger had missed me, if only to sharpen his Gaelic insults on. He might even be human.

We put on a couple of short business-come-pleasure trips as end-of-season perks for some of the company's clients. The business was mostly whisky; the pleasure mostly end-of-season hotel waitresses, with large breasts and sore feet.

Then there was a family party, a big client, who didn't fancy the first week of shorter days and the longer rain of the September islands. So we took them to the Isle of Man, and it was raining there, too. They decided to fly to Ireland to the ancestral stately home, leaving us with four days before we had to be back in Oban. Peter was still worried about the pristine state of my manhood. The Isle of Man was too good a chance to miss. According to the engineer, it held 100,000 women, to suit every taste and every one "asking for it". I only needed one. He persuaded McAllister one engine was acting up and it would be safer to fix it before the passage back. McAllister nodded and disappeared for two days.

I "borrowed" McAllister's best cap and Peter and I went ashore, singing "The Ball of Kirriemuir" with gusto, giggling like schoolboys at the great plan. He was to be the skipper. I was to put on my posh accent and be Sir William Dalkeith, youngest son of the Earl of Jedburgh, with pots of money and a luxury yacht tied up in Douglas harbour.

If that didn't pull me a willing bird, nothing would.

It was my first binge and the heir to an earldom could drink no less than gin and tonic so I don't remember much about it. I do know our double act went down a bomb in every hostelry in Douglas, and we ended up with so many willing birds at a party, we didn't dare take them back aboard. Peter's achievements that night are between him and whatever bedpost he laid his head, if he did. I returned from it *virgo intacta*.

I stood at the end of Douglas pier, urinating and singing "The Ball of Kirriemuir" at the top of my voice. The last act of defiance, with full chorus and all the verses I could remember, before even the seagulls got fed up with me and rose from the moonlit water to scream back.

We decommissioned the *Marilyn Abbott* to winter quarters in Hunter's Yard at Gourock. It was the first week in September and already there was a chill in the air ...

CHAPTER 8

Ah Youse Animals Aff Fur The Zoo

So I went to university, where I lost my virginity, learned to play bridge and to look at women's high heels for a character reference. I went with the growing awareness that not only did I not want to be a doctor but there was no way I could ever become one.

But what high hopes rested on the blazered shoulders of that restless youth who walked into Hunter Hall on that first morning to matriculate, following the distinguished footsteps across that marbled hall of William Cullen, William Hunter, Tobias Smollett, Joseph Black, Joseph Lister, Murdoch Cameron, Sir William MacEwan and John Glaister.

Which of those bright-eyed, bushy-tailed newcomers would be the one to discover a cure for cancer which could be popped into your mouth before or after, like "the pill"? Would it be my friend, David, at my side, the brilliant mind in the mildly lecherous body, or the acned swot with the steel-rimmed specs, hand in his pocket nervously fumbling with his testicles, or maybe the tall, serious girl in sober suit, wan-faced below the mannish hair and already deep in *Gray's Anatomy*, all 1372 pages of it?

Perhaps it would be one William Anderson, washed ashore from the life raft on which he was paddling to freedom to face the reality of long molecule enzymes and the innards of a dissected rat? Unlikely. See how his eye was caught, not by the various medical societies hawking their wares from stalls around the hall (memberships of which were much approved by the professional honorary chairmen of such when it came to marking papers) but by the other delights on offer, such as:

Learn to Play Bridge by Culbertson
Join the Best Debating Club in the World
Naturism and Man (That had to be nude women, too!)
Are You a Rugby Player?
Sexual Freedom for the Single Student.

I still have my green-bound Matriculation Book, the one that was supposed to record my progress from coarse ex-sea cook to learned Bachelor of Medicine and Chirurgery (which we immediately translated to Surgery when friends asked in case they thought we were studying for six years to become chiropodists). It records, in the archaic language of halls of learning, that I entered the curriculum of the Faculty of Medicine at an inclusive fee of £44 and 2 shillings for the first academic year, on the Eighteenth Day of July, 1951. My Matriculation Number was 1487 and receipt of the prepaid examination fee of 10 guineas was duly acknowledged.

Note the different values of money. Already the bureaucracy of the budding NHS was accounting in pounds and shillings, whereas the Senatus Academicians who set the exams still demanded their fee in guineas. My "doomsday book" also preserves for posterity that I failed the first year science subjects of Botany, Zoology, Medical Chemistry and Medical Physics at the first attempt – yes, all four – but passed them at the re-sits in September, and was then entered into the "Second Professional Course of Anatomy, Physiology and Biochemistry".

There my medical history tails off into obscurity, whereby hangs my tale. But it is an oddity that I could go back to Glasgow University tomorrow, present my green Matriculation Book and demand re-entry into the "Second Professional Course" and, despite all, end my days examining piles and worse.

On matriculation, there was even an oath to sign. It was in yon fractured Latin much beloved of those who wanted you to sign something you didn't really understand. However, Latin was then a required language for entry into medicine, so I had just enough recall of it to read the *Sponsio Academica*, even if there hadn't been an English translation at the foot of the page for those clever enough to have needed a dead language to write prescriptions. Have you ever looked at a doctor's prescription? It could be written in Sanskrit for all you can make of the abbreviated, feverish, illegible scrawl.

Nevertheless, I think the oath – the high principles of which had to guide the next six testing years – worth repeating here:

> "As a student in the University of Glasgow, I solemnly prom-
> ise that I will fulfil the requirements and regulations of the
> Senatus Academicians and will conform to its discipline;
> That I will not wilfully damage the fabric or furnishings of
> the University and will make good, to the satisfaction of the
> Senatus, any damage caused by me; and that, for the rest of
> my life, so far as in me lies, I will maintain the honour and
> welfare of the University."

It's a hoot, isn't it? So very Scottish. Despite the lofty phrasing, it sounded just like my mother. No call to glory, this. No trumpets or banners. No inspiration to save suffering humanity. No remonstrance to make the most of yourself and your opportunity. Not a vestal virgin in sight. Just be a good boy, behave yourself, do as you're told, pay for any damage and don't let the Senate down. They really did believe we were unthinking dumdums. Even their priorities were from that blasted Book of Discipline. Obedience. Restitution. Honour. I wonder if students still have to sign it?

As we all do with the humdrum, I soon fell into the habits of my new life. Up at 7.30 am for the bus to the station for the 8.10 am train to Glasgow Central and the 9.15 am "caur", one of those happy, hopeless, shoogly Glasgow trams in red, yellow and green, that rattled their way across the city on tracks fizzing blue sparks from the contact pole with the overhead wires. It trundled up Renfield Street along Sauchiehall Street, jarring across the Charing Cross junction to the tree-lined run out to the Gilmorehill Terminus at the University. And every trip a delight of new faces. The cheery workman "What's the time, son?" "It's ten to nine." "Oh, ma Goad." A glance at my scarf. "Ah see yer a student. Well, if ah'm late fur work again the day ah'll be gettin' ma jotters tae."

And away he hurried, laughing at his joke, a dialect pun on the ruled exercise book students called jotters – the same name employees gave to the "insurance cards" they would be handed when they were sacked. The trams were as much part of Glasgow as Ibrox, Parkhead or The People's Palace, shunting that quick-witted, quick-tempered, suspicious, argumentative, kindly soul who is the Glaswegian. "A yoong student. Awa' an' work." "There's only wan thing wrang wi' you students. Yir mooths are as big as yir heids." Great deflators, the Glaswegians, as most Scots are. But the tram was a classless meeting place of minds and ideas. Everybody used them, from bowler hats to bunnets, peenies to parasols. There is no equal today. Try talking to someone on a commuter train! The tram was to provide one of the more embarrassing moments in my continuing quest for the facts of life.

I was in the toilet of the Men's Union when I suddenly realised I had left it late to catch the tram from the terminus. If I missed the train I'd another hour to wait. I grabbed my books and ran for it. The tram was just trundling away. They were never fast. I could catch it. I ran on and was reaching out to grab the pole and jump onto the open platform when the conductress standing there started pointing at me and laughing. She was one of those peroxide blonde, gum-chewing, "C'moangeraff", Glasgow caur custodians of which myths were made. She kept stabbing her finger at me, laughing with the throaty chuckle of a working girl who's seen everything. And she had! The dawning cold in a certain part of my anatomy was making me aware of it even before she cupped her hand to her mouth and shouted "Dinna bring ony mair oot son or ah'll faint wi' fright." I glanced down. My chilling feeling was confirmed. I'd forgotten to close my flies and as I ran ...

I stopped running and dropped my books to cover myself. As I turned to "adjust my dress", I could hear her voice enjoying every minute of it.

"Haw, Flash. Whit's yer phone number? Ah hvna seen the like since the wean peeled a banana."

Salt of the earth, those Glasgow conductresses. I miss them – just as I missed my train that day. My favourite was Big Bertha, whose massive bosom almost burst the brass buttons of her uniform. Her ticket machine bounced helplessly about on it with every bump, which made me ponder what would happen to any head laid on it.

She was as timeless as tea was Bertha, the same unknown age and origin for the "twenty years on these bluidy caurs an' not a thank you yet" she would shout at every new load of passengers. Every morning it was the same joke at Gilmorehill: "T-e-r-r-minus. Ah youse animals aff fur the zoo." She wasn't over fond of students. Or the University. Nor would you be if you'd been on the same run for twenty years.

Into the Union then for a cup-of-tea-and-a-Paris-bun breakfast and so to the classes. Despite the many distractions, I did go to a few for the requisite count of lectures attended. Enough to get the "class ticket" needed for exams. The system was simple. Every seat in the lecture hall was numbered. Every student had a number. The lecture room door was locked sharp on the hour in the timetable. As the lecture started, a lab "boy" (who could be eighty if he was a day) or some other assistant would scan the serried ranks. If your number was exposed, you were marked absent. The "boys" were wise to every dodge, including spreading six out to make seven, for they counted the rows, too, and wagged a finger to warn your friends they couldn't cover up. So they had to shuffle their bottoms back to cover their own numbers properly, and so reveal yours. The lecturer ignored any such manoeuvrings. He had an hour to fill. That was his number.

From the lectures to the laboratories. Zoology – to make a frog's leg jump with an electric shock; or reveal the prolific ovaries of a rat. Botany – to draw the dead leaves and name the parts of the belladonna flower which for the life of me I couldn't see had much to do with modern medicine, since the days of using belladonna were long gone. Medical physics – in which we played with blocks of wood and string to prove your head won't fall off if it's held in place with string. Medical Chemistry – where you needed Davie Murray's photographic memory just to remember the lecture headings. Those endless chains of letters and numbers. I could never remember whether $C12H2204$ was blood sugar or pancreatic carbonate of soda, if such even exists. My old failing. That combination of impatience and imagination. Never mind what the bricks are made of, let's get on with the building. Just like English grammar. Did it matter if it was a past participle if it made you laugh or cry? Did it matter if it was a $C12H2204$ or a $C4H12022$ if it cured you?

Anyway, that was my alibi in that first year to cover the guilt of skipping classes to enjoy all those other more pleasurable diversions university life had to offer. I became a bridge fanatic, spending hours in the card room of the Men's Union, where some of the greats played, hovering behind their hands to see how they'd bed that singleton or take that tricky finesse. Card sense I had, from contract whist, Solo, Newmarket, Nap and all my generation's other cardboard substitutes for TV and squash. I picked up Culbertson, Acol, Ben Cohen and John Reese, the bridge experts. I learned by my mistakes until I could hold up my hands with the best of them.

The total concentration of a double-squeeze end play for a slam with two aces missing, thanks to a misunderstood new Italian convention, was so absorbing there was room for nothing else in my mind. Bridge has all the cut and thrust of battle, but not a drop of blood is spilled. So it filled my need to feel my adrenalin flowing and gave me the funk-hole I needed to hide from myself, my mother and the imminent June examinations at the end of first year.

They were a waste of time, as I knew they would be. I flunked all four subjects. The moment I saw my name was missing from the lists on the notice board – and A for Anderson didn't take long – I went home, packed the duffle bag and took the train to Oban and my contacts in "the shipping business". I never thought of it as running away to sea. It was far less romantic. Oban was the only place I knew, far enough from the accusations of home, where I had a chance of getting a job quickly, even if it was only as a deck-hand cook on a seine-netter.

I left the traditional note on the sideboard, propped against the Westminster chiming clock my father had won at golf. He had wanted to be an artist, and they sent him to a steel mill. They sent me to university, and I didn't want to be a doctor. There is a lesson in it for all theys. Find the mould that fits the child!

The note was a straight steal from *The Boys Own Paper*: "Failed exams. Will get a job. Don't try to find me. Bill."

My second dash for freedom lasted twenty-four hours – the time it took Barclay, my eldest brother, to guess where I'd gone. It didn't take much guessing, if you think about it.

My contact, the kindly Highlander who was the *Marilyn Abbott* shore agent, had told me that the inshore fishing boat crews often arrived on the Glasgow train after a weekend at their homes. There was always the chance they'd be one short. A crisis at home. Or in a police cell. Or still drunk. The station was next to the fish pier, as you might expect in a fishing port. So if I met the train, I had a hundred yards to ply my wares. "Anybody short of crew? I'm strong and I can cook." And off to the herring, where even a cook on a one eighth share of the catch could come ashore with a wallet filled to overflowing from the silver-blue bonanza. Although at the top it was a closed shop within families, many of the menials were Glesca keelies, as was I now, in the roughest clothes and roughest tongue I could find for my new role.

I stood at the platform barrier, watching for the incongruous unmistakable going-home dress of the fishermen: dark blue suit, with brown shoes, Fair Isle pullover of loving design by wife or girlfriend, a bunnet for the skipper and Sunny Jim caps for the crew; rolling as they walked, their wind-beaten faces dour and unsmiling at the thought of what lay ahead, with a weather eye open for any devil's servant of a black cat or Holy Willie of a minister who might cross their path before they got to the boat. Either was an evil omen.

A superstitious lot are Scots fishermen. No inshore boat ever put to sea between midnight Saturday and midnight Sunday in those God-and-Devil fearing days.

And there they came. Three crews, at a quick count, but fifteen of them, so no shortage. Never mind. There was always another day.

Or so I thought, until I saw Barclay, my big brother Barclay, striding down the platform, too. Sensible, dependable Barclay who married sensible, dependable Sadie, had two sensible, dependable girls and built up a sensible, dependable business, and has every ounce of respectability and respect that my mother could ever have wished. My brother and I are like chalk and cheese but I worshipped him when he was out there in Burma, at the Armarda Road jungle airstrip, winning the war. The sensible, dependable ACI (Fitter) was still a hero to me. I loved him then, and I still do. But I knew my mother knew Barclay could be depended on to handle the situation sensibly. So my goose was cooked. Any emotional display of defiance would be wasted on Barclay. He would just wait quietly until it was all over then offer a sensible solution. He was the Uncle Jimmy of our family, as Jimmy had been to my father's harum-scarum lot, who were always wanting to be artists or running away (as Big Uncle Alex did, to Australia) while Uncle Jimmy worked away for 50 years in the steel mill, enjoying a game of bowls and married to my fat Auntie Jean, whose coarse failings he quietly tolerated with another puff of his pipe.

I could not storm Castle Barclay, any more than anyone could ever breach Fort James. "Where are you staying?" was big brother's first question and we walked back to the cheap hotel, to a room so small there was no more than a bed in it, and we sat on it to talk.

I told him all that I could never tell my mother. He sympathised and soothed. He put his arm round me as I cried it out. We went for a pint, a shrewd pint that acknowledged we were talking man-to-man for the first time together. Then he sprung his sensible solution: "Nobody ever solved anything by running away from it. Come home. Talk it over. Then, whatever you decide, I'll back it all the way." It was a reasonable compromise. Not one a reasonable man who'd just had a pint with his brother could refuse. So I went home.

To stormy tears, recriminations, accusation and counter-accusation. First the excuses for me. "You're just tired. It's the worry." Or, "You must have got into bad company." My only company was Davie Murray (and he must look to his own conscience!). Then the cold logic. "What's wrong with being a doctor?" My father, whatever he felt about it, had washed his hands of it and said little other than "It's up to him. It's his life." And even that was a firm stand for him. My mother had done her homework again. She'd talked to the Bursar. I didn't have to leave university. I could re-sit all the first-year exams in September and, if I passed, go on to the Second Professional Course as if nothing had happened. Did I want to be branded a failure all my life?

That got me, right between the ribs. I could pass those exams standing on my head, blood sugars, wood blocks, rats, belladonna and all, if I wanted to. I just didn't want to. To hell with what the neighbours will say. Tell them I've been overworking and need a long holiday. Tell them I've had a nervous breakdown. Tell them I've failed. I don't care.

I did, desperately, but I could bear the brand of disgrace.

Then came the clichés. "William, what we want in life and what we have to do are entirely different things. None of us is free to do as we please." All the wisdom of the working-class ages. She had brought me up to be different. Now my mother was telling me I had no right to be different. If I have made my mother seem a Tartar in all this, it was not my intent. She was not an unkind woman. She was not as selfish or self-centred as she may sound at times. It was just that she had a single-minded obsession that we should all succeed. By her definition of success, of course. That definition had nothing to do with wealth or possessions. It was burned into her by her own beginnings and our Scottish background. It was respectability. Hear no evil. See no evil. Speak no evil. Do no evil.

It was too powerful a will for me to resist. I have never been able to say "No". Not for long, anyway. So I took the easier way out and said "Yes". I would go back to the University if only to prove to myself that I could stroll through their silly exams.

I was a hermit in my room that summer, cramming into two months what I had failed to learn in eight. The light in the downstairs smallest bedroom of 16 Hillhead Crescent burned to all hours. My zeal made my mother as happy as she'd been for long enough. Bringing in my tray meals. Making sure I went for a walk to get fresh air. Taking *Gray's Anatomy* from my hand when it had fallen on the bed when my eyes refused to stay open any longer. Tucking me in, as though I were a bairn, and switching off the light with a whispered "Good night". "Good night. Sleep tight. Don't let the bugs bite. If they bite. Squeeze them tight. They'll no' bite another night." How many working-class weans were soothed to sleep with that?

I emerged only on Sunday nights to go to the Dicksons, and the longest running game of Solo in the world. Every Sunday night the young bucks of Motherwell met there, and not just to satisfy Tam Dickson's love for this card game. He also had two daughters, Mae and Blithe, both beauties; the one classical, the other sensual and let me not say which was which, for that would be telling. All of us had been in love with one or other, or both, at one time or other. Now the posse of suitors, though tried and rejected, used Sunday nights to worship from the card table, much to Tam's annoyance, if you made the wrong lead at Misere. He did forgive me, however, that Hogmanay when I got roarin' fu' for the first time in my life – well, even a hermit has to let off steam – and, ignoring the front gate, walked clean through his new hedge to collapse on the pavement and be put to sleep among a pile of visitors' coats on the bed until I was recovered enough to be sent home. Only two interruptions were permitted to the Sunday session. The girls with tea and plates of Mrs Dickson's home-baking. And fifteen minutes of Semprini's piano playing on the radio, first at 6.45 pm, then when the maestro was switched to 10.45 pm.

Semprini, Solo and sexy daughters. Strange are the reasons for remembering some of the people who page our life, for I have no doubt there was more, much more, to Tam Dickson than Sunday nights.

Resits passed, for ten weeks of the Second Professional Course, I scarcely ate, thanks to anatomy, every day, for two hours, before lunch. If I did eat, I would dash to the loo and be sick. Consider the scene on that first day of the course: he-who-did-not-want-to-be-a-doctor in pristine white laboratory coat (all too soon to be blooded); clutching in one hand a small wooden box with hinged lid containing an assortment of scalpels, lances, probes, tweezers and other fiendish stainless steel instruments, and in the other hand the blue Book I of *Systematic Anatomy (Arm and Leg)* with Full Coloured Illustrations.

In the Second Professional Course, there were 73 of us – and 42 of them. The cadavers. The bodies. The "subjects". Once living and breathing. Now the withered or bloated parchment replicas were steeped in formaldehyde baths to preserve them; injected with blue and red dyes to feign some semblance of a bloodstream; and waxed to simulate what had once been supple. The bodies that lay, row upon row, on stainless steel anatomical tables with drains at each corner, were the products of the ghastly charnel house next door that made them ready for our unskilled, unfeeling instruments. Mostly, as though it mattered, they were imported from France. All shapes and sizes, mostly old. Four of the 73 students promptly fainted, three of them never to return, and all of the remaining 69 went every shade of white and green. Ten managed to make it out the door to be sick. Two didn't. And me. Turning away to retch, without actually being sick. There is a most descriptive old Scottish word for this particular ailment. It is called "boking". It was like Dante's *Inferno*; not with hellfire and brimstone, but all the more disturbing for being so cold and clean.

It was deliberate, that mass-confrontation. The first test of that clinical detachment that is a must for the medical profession if they are not to go mad. Some failed the first hurdle. Others struggled on for a week or two before disappearing quietly. I lasted ten weeks.

After the survivors had been reassembled, we were given the mandatory lecture on the dignity of the "subject" – both the cadaver and the anatomy of it we were to learn by dissection – with a severe warning as to conduct. There was to be no repetition of the disgraceful shenanigans of the previous year when certain students had been rusticated for one term for an April Fool's Day prank. Daffodils had been stuck and ribbons tied where they should not have been. Not to mention each and every cadaver sporting a university scarf. Think on this. That tried and trusted GP of yours may have been one of those sports!

Then we were assigned, four to a corpse. Our first term was arms. Thrift was in evidence. A senior pair of ghouls could be working on a brain and at the same time supervising and demonstrating to the more junior Burke and Hare on an arm. Thus maximising use of the cadaver and saving on the number of paid "demonstrators" needed to walk from table to table, questioning, discussing and themselves dissecting to tidy up your mess and reveal that the piece of string in the dehydrated stewing steak was indeed the anterior aspect of the sciatic nerve. Or the trickier feat of cutting out the string to reveal the posterior aspect without reducing the string to unidentifiable shreds and the meat to stringy mince.

For me, it was as awful as I've pictured it. By the time we had finished with these bodies, they wouldn't have made a decent cadaver broth for starving cannibals. "Cut firmly but carefully through the skin," said the demonstrator as my scalpel hovered over my first arm. "No, along the line of the muscle," as my shaking hand scarred across the gluteus maximus. But whose skin? Whose muscle? Whose arm? I looked at the desiccated face of a mightily old female subject. Wrinkled far beyond redemption by Pond's. Sunken cheeks that would never blush again even with rouge. Pock-marked from pox. Yellow skin of the neck in such grotesque folds her chin was hidden even with her head in the anatomical position. The silver streaks of childbirth on her belly, if you could call it such, showed she had been somebody's mother. And girlfriend, wife and lover of some man.

"Not so deep. Watch what you're doing." The voice of the demonstrator called me back to the scalpel, slicing the mother's flesh. "Excuse me," I said, and fled. This time I was sick. Violently, vomiting up the despair and guilt and knowledge that even if I had wanted to be, I never could be, a doctor. Even when that dried up dead flesh lived and spilled blood, the nightmare would be the same, only in glorious Technicolor™.

Thereafter, I survived anatomy by escaping into fantasising about any distinguishing mark on any cadaver that made them individuals and not subjects. With a nose like that he must have been a circus clown. And I would be off on Barnum and Bailey's French tour, flying the trapeze as he made them laugh. The clown with the big nose and the tragic secret he was going to die a pauper and end up a poor subject for the knife. Or the younger woman with the long legs and the mole on her cheek who was a chorus girl from La Moulin Rouge, who had loved a French count, but committed suicide when he threw her aside for a seamstress; bound for an unmarked suicide's grave until diverted to Glasgow University. Why else did her lungs show the signs of drowning?

David, as you might expect, could do the dissections and draw them one-handed with half his mind and do the *Glasgow Herald* crossword on his knee under the table with the other hand – with the clues from memory! I could have killed him.

Instead, I went out and lost my virginity, which was every bit as satisfying if a little amateurish. It was Charities Week – the seven-day orgy in which university students got rid of their high spirits in much the same manner as that which runs football hooligans the risk of arrest. A week in which all honest citizens barricaded their homes, and locked up their wives with such daughters as hadn't matriculated for the festive rites. And all in the name of charity. It was a pagan performance which, with only minor variations, took place in every college of learning. It was traditionally ended by a 24-hour fancy dress Breakfast Ball, which speaks for itself.

I had become involved in the running of Glasgow University's charities week. There is a story, purely apocryphal, that it was the same year the University newspaper ran a banner headline that read "CHARITIES WEEK EXPENSES REACH ALL TIME HIGH", alongside a cunning juxtaposition of a subheading which said more discreetly "Collecting Can Convener Buys New Car".

I was a deputy assistant cans convener, living for the week (my mother approved of the charities which would benefit that year) in the empty office in Blythswood Square which had been "donated" as a headquarters for the fund-gathering. Nobody bought a new car. We lived rough in sleeping bags on bare floorboards. We did steal two bob (two shillings) from the full collecting tins which were gathered there to pay for the snack-bar pie and beans on which we lived.

We did sell Exemption Posters – which shops paid for to put on their door to keep collecting students away from their customers – in Trongate pubs, not for charity but for bottles of booze, including five bottles of Canadian Club whisky. I was no connoisseur. It was whisky, and late into the night, after the labours of the day, we would binge on talk and raw rye, which we called "Redeye" or "Gutrot" in celebration of its two most telling effects. Blythswood Tongue, a complaint marked by rawness from the long late discussions in which we set the world to rights and redness from the rye, became common in both sexes. I was a Bohemian, and revelling in another new role. My mother would have put it rather more unromantically, as "keeping bad company".

I couldn't be bothered with the fancy dress that went with the Breakfast Ball, so I went to the Queen Margaret Union's all-nighter in a blazer and flannels. All the virgins went to university and Queen Margaret's was their union, their club. They were all there, those sex-starved young middle-class ladies, getting tipsy, too, as their inhibitions slipped away and another of the Ten Commandments dimmed in the depths of another Bloody Mary.

I had Canadian Club in my blood and Hairy Breeks in my heart.

No more false alarms, like the night before, with the intellectual Viona, who had asked me to share her sleeping bag on the Blythswood floor, raising my hopes considerably, and embarrassingly at such close quarters, only to reveal she wanted to discuss her self-imposed Lent of a month's abstinence of "any of that" to prove the power of mind over matter. I was tempted to test her theory. Yes, Viona, and my mind's on your matter. But no matter how my mind sought the soft whisperings that would break her fast, by breakfast, it was still talk-not-touch. I'll take a bet she's now the left-wing games mistress of a private school, going off on Trafalgar Square demonstrations between hockey matches.

No, tonight's the night.

There is a destiny that shapes our virginity, rough hew it as we will. It was walking towards me. As unsaintly a Margaret as ever graced the Union. Bold, smiling, daring eyes peeping out from long blonde hair worn in the style of Veronica Lake. My love was Doris Day, but it was no time to be choosy. She was swigging a gin and tonic and if any further confirmation was needed that here was a free spirit, her flimsy dress of a Roman lady had slipped and her left breast had popped out over it, bare of any modest 34 C-cup Marks and Spencer's bra – a siren to my desire.

I wasted no time. I was the virgin. I homed in on the fair maid and hid her before a more experienced lecher could spot the Belisha beacon and cross the room. "Smashing isn't it," she said, and I knew by her tiddly giggle that I was going to take advantage of that fact.

"You look as if you could do with some fresh air," I said, deepening my broken baritone to sound more like a man-of-the-world.

She nodded. I threw my blazer round her, not as a gentleman, but as a bootlegger hiding booze from a rival raid, and smuggled her out of the Union and into the grounds of the University Chapel, which was the nearest darkness, and the porch of which was the nearest hidden corner, making small talk all the time.

"Stop talking," she commanded, and became soft and compliant in my arms, leaning there against the door of God's house. I could hear my mother "Treat every girl as you would your own sister and you won't go wrong." I could hear God "What do you think you're doing in my doorway?" Neither castor oil nor eternal damnation could stop me now. She was willing and I could feel it in every soft press of her body against my hardness.

I pulled her out of the porch and onto the grass, and we lay down in the even darker shadow of some monument, safe from any prying eyes in University Avenue.

I had a twinge of suspicion at the almost-too-easy way her dress slipped back to her waist as she raised her knees and opened them; revealing not the flimsies of a Roman lady, but the girdle, suspender belt and white knickers of a very proper young lady. What did I do about those? I could hardly run out into the street and ask the first passer-by. Take it one step at a time, lad. I knelt down between her legs and lay on her. I had prepared for resistance. I had boned up on the answers.

"My mother wouldn't like this?"
"Your mother isn't here."
"I want to wait for marriage."
"You'll have to if you don't hurry up."

None was needed. She was melting beneath me, from the heat flushing me. She made no move to help or hinder. This was it. I fumbled for me and for her. That's when she said it. "I want to, but I can't." Hell's bells! How could she want to and not be able to? How could she stop now? How could I stop now, with Hairy Breeks and Canadian Club raging inside me?

She put her hand up to my cheek. "I've … you see … it's not …" Then, deciding there was no other way to explain, she said, "I'm wearing Tampax™."

As a blood-chilling douche, it was more effective than a cold shower. My passion subsided in the same second. The John Knox in me was scandalised. It was all dirty and Sunday School again. She knew. She could see it in my guilt-stricken eyes. Or sense it in my rigid body. She pulled me down and kissed me, a sisterly kiss. "C'mon, worse things happen in church," she said. "You better take me home."

We stood up and adjusted ourselves and, suddenly, we were both as sober as we had been drunk, holding hands as we walked to the underground station and in the train which took us to the district where she lived; to the tenement flat which she shared with two other girls. They had gone home, away from Charities Week. She had not wanted to go home. She didn't like home. As she made me a cup of tea in the tiny kitchen, I saw her in the light for the first time. She was several years older and wiser. But she liked me. And I liked her. And love was for fools who read picture papers. We were kindred souls, she and I, and we went to bed.

We stayed there for three days and I did lose my virginity. I cannot speak for her. But it was a private joy which I will not share. Nor would I tell you her name, even if I knew it. For neither of us asked the other. There was no necessity for names in our needs.

I saw her only once again, thanks to David, my practical friend, when I confided in him some weeks later about my lost weekend.

"Did you use anything?" he asked.

It dawned quickly. I hadn't. Again I couldn't speak for her. But I had to find out. I hung about outside the Queen Margaret Union for a week before I spotted her. We were as shy as strangers. "How are you?" "Fine." "You're looking well." "Thank you. So are you." "Eh?" "No, I'm not pregnant." "That's good. I was worried about you." "Thanks … I'll have to hurry. My class …"

'Twas there that we parted in Queen Margaret Drive, passing ships that had sheltered from the storm in the same harbour – a storm that blew itself out in three days and nights.

There was one minor repercussion. My exploits in the Chapel grounds had blazoned my grey flannels with a pair of grass-green knees. I didn't play cricket, so that took some explaining to my mother. I don't think she really believed me that it was the result of the boisterous horseplay among the lads that marks every Charities Week.

That weekend was my last lesson in anatomy. Let them live with the horror of the charnel house (a building used to store bones) and the "vivas" and "tutorials" on the epidermis of a dissected arm. My skin had suffered enough flagellation. I laid my plans carefully. No Oban this time. I wrote to the Ministry of Labour and National Service and cancelled my deferment. This was the licence which allowed students to complete their studies before serving the two years of compulsory training in the armed forces that others had to do at the age of eighteen.

Their reply brought my "call-up" papers, but warned it would be six months at least before I had to report, when I would be sent a railway warrant to the appointed training regiment.

I recalled a medical society excursion to Gartnavel Mental Hospital, where we had seen the man who thought he was King of the Jews and an assortment of other manic depressives, schizophrenics and paranoids. One of the lecturers had been the medical superintendent of a similar institution who had mentioned there was always a shortage of male nurses for mental hospitals.

I phoned him, explained my situation and heard him saying, "Yes, you can start next Monday if it suits you." They weren't short. They were desperate.

When all was arranged, I went home to face the music. My father was baffled. My mother made one last try to "make me see sense". But it was a *fait accompli*. I said my goodbyes, packed the duffle – and went into a mental hospital!

CHAPTER 9

These Are The Keys To Hell – Don't Lose Them

Hartwood Mental Hospital (long since closed) was such an institution, and it was to Hartwood that I was assigned. My months there only confirmed what that horrendous movie, *The Snake Pit*, put on celluloid to shock the balcony and make the back stalls cling tighter together.

It was hidden away in one of the few patches of countryside in industrial Strathclyde, built like a stately mansion to disguise its purpose from any stranger who glimpsed it as they passed by, or to be pointed at with a hushed whisper by those who knew it. "That's Hartwood" was explanation enough to send a shiver down the spine. It was built in the country to set it apart so that few would have to see it, and for all its gracious lines was a fortress where security came before succour.

The status of its staff in society and their pay and conditions in the Health Service were commensurate. The lowest of the low. It was not their fault. They did try. They did make token gestures towards treatment. But the system made them as much outcasts as the inmates.

For the simple reason that sheer physical restraint was as much a part of the system as any medical regime, the nurses in the men's wards were all male. A few were caring and qualified. Most were not.

I arrived on my first day, a failed doctor, looking for any job, with two other new "attendants". One was a bruiser who had been sacked as a cinema doorman for demonstrating his pugilistic abilities with two Saturday night drunks. He had a mental age not much older than those he would "nurse" and a curious habit of pinching his cauliflower nostrils then sucking his thumb. The other was an out-of-work school-leaver who had failed the Army and police entrance exams and chosen this vocation because he wanted to wear a uniform. Such was the desperate shortage of staff, we three were welcomed with open arms. Somebody might get a day off now.

There was no training. We got a ten-minute lecture. The first part explained why we should tell the outside world that we were no longer called "attendants" but "male nurses", to make the rose sound sweeter-scented, though the thorns remained. That didn't take long. The rest was devoted to key security. We would be given two keys. One to the ward in which we worked. The other to the corridors that led to the hospital facilities. They were to be worn at all times on a chain attached to a stout belt round the waist. Any door that was unlocked had to be locked again behind you immediately. Failure to obey this rule could mean instant dismissal. The loss of your keys was an emergency alarm. Alarm bells were placed at every strategic point in the building. "These are the keys to hell – don't lose them" was the last admonition and the last perceptive statement about Hartwood or its inmates that I heard in six months.

The stately front housed administration and the communal dining halls used by those well enough. Behind that lay two wings, one male, one female. Each wing had three wards with a long connecting corridor. The wards were prosaically called Lower, Middle and Upper, but apt. As a soul can rise through the degrees of purgatory, so the most violent and untreatable entered hell in Lower and "progressed" through Middle to Upper. Or descended as they "deteriorated".

In practice, this classification was made more on the grounds of co-operation with the staff than mental health. The Upper ward housed comparatively harmless zombies, so was where new staff were started. The really hopeless cases. Whereas, many an inmate of the Lower was only a mildly insane man raging against his illness and constraint. It was Catch 22. Any sign of sanity was insanity.

Indeed, the sanest man in Hartwood was a patient in Lower. As teachers become childish, policemen become suspicious of their own families and journalists become cynics, so the staff of mental homes eventually become eccentric to a minor or major degree. Is there any way a punch-drunk, nearly mentally defective cinema doorman would do other in the constant company of madmen?

"Auld Bob", as we called him, was one of those unfortunates of the 1920s who had been classified as what was then called mentally defective (MD) for playing truant and other mischief, and as a boy, clapped in a mental home and kept there until there was no way he could face the outside world again, and didn't want to, for Hartwood was his home, and its denizens, mad or staff, or both, his family and friends. The Lower had the only individual rooms in the wing. They were, in fact, restraint rooms, for violent patients; dark rooms where scissors stabbed into forgetful nurses and ties that could choke were never worn.

Auld Bob had never been known to be violent. Quite the opposite. He was a quiet, gentle soul. But he had reached such a position of privilege in the curious hierarchy of the hospital that he was permitted to take up permanent residence in a restraint room. To make it his home. And daft Bob was not. For this was also convenient for the administration building, thus cutting the risk of the staff being seen pushing their betting slips under his door. He was the hospital bookmaker! From the top office down, they bet with "Honest" Bob. Entrusting their tanner trebles or bob Yankees to the old mental defective who carried his book in his head, for he wasn't a "runner" who sent the bets to an outside bookmaker. There was no way he could. He ran all the risks, stood all the losses and pocketed all the profits. He always sat on his bed, a small, stout man with legs like the Pillars of Hercules fixing him firmly to the floor by his slippered feet. He always wore the same dark suit, with an open waistcoat. The jacket pockets held the loot. The waistcoat pockets filed the betting slips. Nor was it his only business.

He also had a large battered leather suitcase positioned below his bed in such a way that he could bend down, grunting over his belly, pull it out and open the lid to reveal his cigarette, tobacco, stationery and haberdashery businesses. The shops were far away in the village. The hospital shop had fixed hours. So Bob was the ever-open (or ever-closed, depending on how you look at it) source of a quick packet of Woodbine, or an envelope for the fixed odds pools coupon, or a comb. Strictly cash. No credit. He never smiled. He never spoke much. But I was fascinated by this man who had survived hell in a world within a world. Next door, three male nurses could be fighting to put the jacket on a manic elative man in an apoplexy of violence, while Bob was quietly contemplating the latest *Dandy* or *Beano*, for it was only picture comics and betting slips he could read.

Remember the W Somerset Maugham short story "The Verger" about a verger who is sacked because he can't read or write and goes on to make a fortune with a string of tobacconist shops? The doyen of yarn spinners must have smiled quietly to himself when he gets the banker to ask the verger, "Good God, man, what would you be now if you had been able to [read and write]?" And the verger answers, "I can tell you that sir, I'd be verger of St Peter's, Neville Square." But fact is stranger than any fiction. Where would Bob have been if he hadn't been a mental defective?

He told everyone that when he died, those who found him should help themselves to whatever was in his pockets or the suitcase. He was found dead in bed one morning – of completely natural causes, I hasten to add. Not even a betting slip was found when his body went to the mortuary. As to who claimed his body or the wealth tucked away in some bank account, I cannot tell you.

Routine was the oil in the machinery of the mental hospital. The lid on the pressure cooker. Condition them to absolute monotonous unbreakable routine. The patient who asked to go to the toilet after ablutions was a minor crisis that involved unlocking and locking the day ward door to get to the toilets, needing a nurse all to himself to "supervise" him in the open cubicle, then unlocking and locking the door again. Let him go and stand in the corner, wringing his despairing hands in the turmoil of his mad mind. He can wait till

144

the next toilet call. If he soils himself, just log it in the ward book as another symptom of his insanity. Or the major crisis of a patient who wouldn't put his clothes on for a visitor. Two of us spring into action and haul on his hospital handouts. He can tear at them as much as he likes. Just log it – and remember to give him a quick sedative before the visitors arrived. Nobody breaks routine. Not even the staff.

My first shift was the 4 pm to 10 pm, when newcomers saw least until they were broken in to be unshockable. I would "lock in" and report to the charge nurse. On my first day, I was put in complete charge of the day room with 40-odd inmates flying about their cuckoo's nest. It was a large, rectangular airless room, with one good chair for the nurse, a few other assorted armchairs, soft and unweapon-like, and rarely used. Plus what had been a billiard table in an enlightened attempt at rehabilitation. It caused too many arguments which threatened routine. And the nurse who turned his back once too often and was laid low with a cue when a zombie he had teased once too often had struck back in a tormented semblance of dignity. Only the eyes in the observation window of the charge nurse's room had saved the nurse from having the pink rammed into his malicious mouth. He had gone back to being a bus conductor.

Now the billiard baize was faded and torn, a platform for a few ancient unread magazines and an ashtray for supervised smoking periods, with cigarettes or pipes lit by the nurse from a few matches counted into the box. And as something to lean against.

At 4.30 sharp those who could walk would be lined up, locked out of the ward into the ward corridor, counted and locked out into the long corridor and led in an aimless shambles to be locked into the dining room where, having been fed, the process was reversed.

The food? The good news is there was plenty of it. The mentally ill either eat voraciously, like animals, peck like birds or eat nothing at all. The number eating varied arbitrarily depending on who was fit to go. There was no way to plan. So almost always there was too much food.

The kitchen staff did their best with a starvation budget and out-of-date equipment. But it wasn't the Royal Hilton. Nor had it to be. Those who ate with the appetites of wolves cared not what was on their plates but slopped it up heedlessly and uncaringly. For those who hardly ate, it didn't matter. If a few had appetites and did make a fuss, they were told to "Eat it up, like a good boy" or spoon-fed with such force as was necessary to make them realise that eating, too, was a routine. The force depended on the kindness or otherwise of the nurse concerned.

The potatoes told the whole story of the cuisine. The staff canteen ran to greasy chips. The patients' dining room, never. Not ever. Whatever came between the make-do soup and lumpy custard always had the same potatoes, washed but not peeled, cut into quarters and steamed in cauldrons, then dumped onto the plate in a soggy heap. They ranged from tolerable in the new season to the disgusting old potatoes of the previous winter, which ran to some greyish flesh among the eyes, skin and black bruises.

After tea, it was recreation and "comforts". There was no TV or radio to prevent any disturbing news infiltrating from the outside world. A few were trusted with harmless newspapers such as the *Daily* or *Sunday Mirror* but never the *News of the World*, to raise uncontrollable urges and desires.

The patients' recreation consisted of a few old jigsaws, some comics and a picture book or two; and draughts, which even the most childish of men could grasp, though it usually ended with the board flying across the day room. The "comforts" were those brought by visitors or purchased with money from visitors – chocolate, cigarettes, fruit, new comics, painting books, puzzle toys like the Chinese links (which drove them even dafter, so we always tried to "lose" them). These were rationed out to patients. Now it would be wrong to say there was not dedication, kindness and honesty in the staff. But most of them were men defeated by the system and conditions, as much inmates as those they guarded. And a few thought the patients' "comforts" were a perk for them.

This would lead to the grotesque sight of a suspected nurse doling out the Woodbine from a packet of ten to a suspicious Down's

Syndrome inmate who would not be satisfied until the remainder was counted and that number marked on the outside of the packet before it was returned to the locked "comforts" cupboard in the charge room. It never dawned on the patient that any theft could easily be concealed by crossing out that number and substituting the new figure, for the poor soul could barely remember his own name, let alone what had happened in the previous smoking period. The impecunious cinema doorman thought it was very clever to steal a Woodbine this way and would laugh at his victim's baffled face when he was told his cigarettes had run out and his mother would have to bring more.

Those evenings were the closest there was to treatment. A doctor came round once a day for a brief look at the ward notes, a prescription or two and away. But in six months in the hospital I never saw a psychiatrist in the ward; nor did I ever take one patient from the ward to a psychiatrist. It must have happened; surely it must have happened. But if it did, this humble servant of the NHS never saw it.

So we were the psychiatrists, the failed medical student, the cinema doorman, the flasher, the former bus conductor and the uniform fetishist. But only at recreation and according to our conscience.

I can see that day room now. Myself, in black uniform trousers, white open neck shirt and white butcher's apron, barely out of boyhood, sitting on my hard-backed cane-bottomed chair just inside the locked day room door. To my right, the glow of bright light from the observation window where the nurse in charge would be reading his Hank Janson paperback. In the ward, the dimmed light of 60-watt bulbs was bright enough to see the weird world of which I was sole dictator.

Though full of mentally ill or challenged individuals, it was well-ordered, for each patient had his own undisputed "territory" for recreation. However, any encroachment could mean a sudden, savage explosion and most of the staff carried the bruises to prove it.

Is it not an ironic comment on how sadly humanity has failed to find peace, let alone tolerance and understanding one of the other, that the most basic expression of the territorial greed which makes nations go to war can be found in the day room of a loony bin? The inmate who had delusions he was the son of Jack the Ripper would always sit on the relic of an easy chair with the lacquered occasional table in front and lay out the draught board for the arrival of the monomaniac who would kneel to play. The delusional inmate would always win, sometimes before a tantrum of mania would scatter the board and pieces, whereupon the eternal loser would stalk off into the only empty corner (left empty, by a curious common consent, for any who had to find safe refuge).

There he would stand facing the wall, in a childish huff, until he remembered he had, despite himself, saved it, the last surviving page of his wife's letter, to savour it before indulging his fetish by tearing it into the tiniest pieces possible, frenziedly smaller even than confetti. No piece of paper was safe from him. He even had to be wiped by the nurse when he went to the toilet.

As this drama played out, the demented alcoholic with delirium tremens would be crossing the room, back and forth, counting steps to himself until, with mathematical precision, he had rediscovered the exact spot where he had stood a thousand times before, trembling, head down, until someone or something disturbed his shaky equilibrium and off he would go again. And in that unfathomable way that the mentally ill can make allowance for others, his spot was a safe distance from the paranoiac who squatted on his hunkers, arms hugging his knees, eyes flicking until he could no longer stand the celestial rays searing him from the light bulb above or the sound waves resonating in his mind from the ether. He would jump up, wild-eyed, frantically waving off his terrors, before sinking back into a stupor until the next attack by "them".

His wildness was alarming but harmless. But we knew to always keep one eye on the big sullen brooder who stalked round and round in a tight circle, muttering to himself, or arguing loudly to ten thousand spectres, thinking himself persecuted by tinker and tailor. If his hysteria broke through the surface of his derangement, it was all hands on deck and back to the Middle to walk himself into less dangerous circles or to the Lower if one of us was hurt.

I would do my best, honestly! Hopeless as it was, I would walk round them trying to do some nursing. True, always with my back to one wall where I could take in the rest of the room at a glance. But I would give a little time to each, however hopeless the case; even the sergeant-major, as I called him, who would, for days on end, stand or sit to attention quite content in his near-nakedness. The same man who would almost calmly tear to shreds any clothes put on him to rid himself of the screaming demons they concealed. His "bad time" would last two or three days. For the rest of the time he was content to be fully clothed as he barked orders to the moon. It was no surprise to learn from his file that he was an ex-soldier who had been decorated for bravery.

It was a revelation to discover my charges included not only the defective discards of the working class, but a teacher, works manager and an alcoholic bank accountant. Another lesson in life. Mental illness is no respecter of importance, which may be obvious now but was a considerable shock to me then. To think that the gibbering drooling patient who thought he was the Crown of Thorns and who tried to pierce himself with any sharp object that came his way, had once been a minister!

But I found it impossible to make any contact with those unhappy minds. There was a reason other than their afflictions. Routine! To ensure the least possible disturbance to the smooth running of hell, what was left of their minds was doped and drugged until they were as near to automatons as madness would permit. The day shift saw to that. It came on at 6 am.

By then, the night-shift would already have the inmates stumbling down from their locked dormitory. Those who could, washed themselves. Those who could be trusted were even issued with a safety razor, the blade checked on return for even a small piece missing from one edge. Those who couldn't were stripped of their sodden pyjamas and (shivering in winter if the heating boiler had broken down) were herded, naked, into the showers and toilet cubicles where their excrement was wiped or washed from them and their day clothes put on them from the big wicker laundry baskets or their lockers. The only scene I have ever seen like it was of the Belsen gas chambers.

If it is any excuse, there were so many of them and so few of us. And there was so little time until the medication line-up before breakfast and after, depending on the placing of the meal in their prescription. They were lined up at the panel that opened in the charge room window. Through the window, the charge nurse passed out the pills and potions. Rarely did a chart have to be consulted. Some had been on the same drugs for twenty years or more. Inside, the day-room nurse made sure the medicine was taken. This carried a heavy responsibility. There is none so cunning as a maniac who doesn't want to take medicine. (Remember, it may be, to his mind, the cause of his insanity.)

The biggest problem was the commonest sedative – paraldehyde. A central nervous system depressant, paraldehyde is still used today to treat certain convulsive disorders. It also has been used in the treatment of alcoholism and in the treatment of nervous and mental conditions to calm or relax patients who are nervous or tense and to produce sleep. It was cheap and effective, but at that time it had to be taken orally in bulk. This meant, for those on it, a medicine bottle of it every morning and sometimes at night, too. A pall of paraldehyde hung in the hospital, for it had a sickly-sweet, yet pungent, odour. It reminded me of the castor oil of my childhood! I could feel myself retching as I took the cork off, upended the bottle and, holding the patient's nose, poured it quickly down his reluctant throat. Speed was not cruel, but essential, so it was downed in one huge swallow before the patient could gag and throw it back at the nurse. It was a job I hated. Few took it willingly. Some reluctantly. Some forcibly. Only the most insane swigged it down like whisky and wiped their lips with satisfaction.

The rest of the morning was administration. Lunch much like tea. And in the afternoon, visitors. Never in the day room. Too danger-ous. And too open to prying eyes. Those who never got visitors, and that was most, plus those who could not be permitted visitors, were left locked in the day room.

Doctors' orders banned some visitors. The mother who had caused the psychosis. The wife who constantly badgered her husband into discharging himself because he was a voluntary patient and it was all too much for her. Most patients were committed by law. The few who were voluntary could theoretically discharge themselves but only through a Medical Board, and Catch 22 laid down that arguing you were sane before the MB only proved your insanity. Few escaped by that door.

The lesser class of trusties was allowed into the short corridor joining the day room and access corridor, but still between locked doors, where they could have a brief word with their visitors. It was usually as brief as it took to mouth a scrap of family news, such as "You're looking better today", and hand over the "comforts" before leaving. There isn't much else you can say to the insane, however deep the hurt to be seen in the more compassionate visitors' eyes.

The best-behaved, the MDs and those with milder forms of behaviour, were allowed out to the long corridor with their visitors, where seats had been set along the wall. They could sit and talk, or walk, or mingle. It was the nearest the hospital came to normality. It was where you saw the kindness and caring of those who had to bear the cross of a "daftie" in the family. On their guarantee "not to let him out of your sight" some visitors were allowed to take a son, brother, father or friend to the shop or canteen, locked out and in by a nurse, of course. To see a mother hug her thirty-year-old mountainous beaming-faced Down's Syndrome son, with a mental age of seven, always brought a lump to my throat, however often I saw it, for it spoke volumes for the love, and hurt, that only a mother can feel.

Occasionally, as a diversion for visitors who could find nothing to talk about, we would give the paper-tearer a *Daily Record* and turn him loose in the outside corridor where he would tear a paper trail. It wasn't meant to be cruel; he enjoyed an audience and it let the visitors "ooh" and point and whisper, saying "There but for the grace of God" and be glad their own was not as daft as that. But it *was* cruel.

The visitors saw the patients at their best; carefully chosen and even more carefully prepared, sedated if need be, so that everyone could see they were getting the best treatment possible and could go home with a clear conscience.

No visitor ever saw the night dormitory upstairs. The same size as the day room, but with a bed for every patient. They were only far enough apart to let a nurse slip in sideways. That shift was a nightmare that lasted eight hours from 10 pm to 6 am. It was a battle to get the disturbed to bed. It was a battle to get them to settle down. It was a battle to keep them in bed. The earlier shift had to cope with undressing them, getting them into pyjamas and upstairs. Then the night-shift took over. I cannot and will not go into the more sordid details of packing 40 deranged men into their sardine tin of a dormitory but, somewhere between 10 pm and 11 pm, it would be accomplished and the lights switched to a dim blue glow.

Then it would begin – the terrors of the night. Screams and groans. Moans and the mouthings of the language of Old Testament tongues. If our nightmares can leave us in a shivering cold sweat, think of theirs. Think of the two nurses, padding silently along between the rows of beds, wide awake in the middle of forty nightmares, pausing here to restrain a restless one, bringing the sleep walker back from the window or ushering another to the night soil buckets which coped with the calls of nature that couldn't wait. Only two kinds of nurse could cope. Those with infinite compassion and those with no imagination. The dedicated and the dull. The hardest bargaining that went on over swapping shifts centred round those dreadful hours of darkness. Dawn was a blessed relief because our terrors faded with theirs and there were only the ablutions to face before staggering utterly exhausted to the male nurses' residence and the oblivion of bed.

My months in Upper ended when I strained my back heaving the big brooder over to dress the bed sores his sheer weight had caused. After four days on my back, I was transferred to the Reception Hospital (RH).

This was day after night. It was a separate building behind the main block in which there was real nursing. Even the charge was an SRN, one of the first men in Scotland to achieve these honoured letters, as I recall. It was called the Reception Hospital because it was here that admissions were first held for classification. There were psychiatrists. There was treatment to be seen. True, it was in a segregated, locked section with doors that bore cryptic letters like ECT, to which I never gained entry. I was in the medical section – the hospital for the hospital, where patients were treated for the physical illnesses that we never think of happening to the mentally ill, but do. All those with which "The Doc" of *The Sunday Post* has such a sane touch – from mumps to hernia, appendicitis to prostate.

The more serious were sent to a general hospital, to come back quickly after their op for convalescence before return to their wards. Those that could be were cured. Those that couldn't, stayed to die. My new duties were in that terminal ward.

It could be quick, as it was with the old man. I was sent with the ambulance to bring in a "committed" patient. His committal forms said "senile dementia, with dangerous delusions." He shrank in a chair in the living room, clinging to the skirt of the dutiful daughter who had given him a home for 17 years, endlessly repeating his plea to her. "Don't let them take me away, Mary." She was in tears. Her husband stood apart, endlessly repeating "It's for his own good, Mary." The old man's will was all but broken before we carried him into RH. He made some resistance by refusing to stay in bed until his frail arms were bruised all over even by the gentlest restraint in putting him back to bed. But then the will went, and the spirit, and he was dead within three weeks of being admitted, and you could see him doing it to himself. Yes, it was quick with some.

It was a lot longer with others – the ones in the tertiary stage of syphilis. It could take 30 years for that youthful indiscretion to catch up with them because they had been too ashamed to go for treatment – to the stage where they had paralysis, numbness, blindness and dementia. They took a long time to die. There were three in the terminal ward. Nursing them put a fear of syphilis in me that has kept me far more faithful to my wife than any marriage vows or John Knox for that matter.

On a death, the nurse on duty had to fetch the death trolley – a wicker basket coffin on wheels – from the mortuary. Then wash the corpse and take it to the mortuary. There were the inevitable NHS forms to fill in and other formalities. Sometimes even an order to attend the post mortem. I had to attend one. It was a patient with a rare disease not unlike Parkinson's but far more serious. It meant the patient's nervous and muscular systems were "out of phase", even in such everyday functions as bowel movement. The post mortem showed the reason for his years of mad, miserable existence before terminal illness had sprung from a part of his brain that had atrophied, probably from syphilis. So much for the cause. But when the young pathologist imported from the general hospital (ten guineas and a free lunch) opened the abdomen, one of the effects was also revealed, for his bowel bulged and rose up above him like a string of colourless party balloons tied together. I was utterly convinced by the effect of that grotesque sight on me that the best decision I ever made was not to be a doctor.

When asked why I didn't speak out about Hartwood, I can only offer the lame excuse "Who would have listened?" Anyway, I was in for my own rude shock. About half a mile away from the main hospital, in its own grounds, lay Hartwoodhill.

It held a strange mixture of geriatrics, long-term but mild-mannered mental defectives able to look after themselves, sufferers of nervous breakdowns and shorter-term itinerants, usually older people with vague, harmless delusions, who came and went as need be. Though a joint institution it was not "closed" like Hartwood.

I was out for a walk in the fresh air, a daily need, and took the paved path up towards Hartwoodhill. I stopped and shut my eyes to hear the countryside, breathing deeply, the better to smell it. When I opened my eyes, a sparrow of a woman was hopping down the path towards me, chirping to herself, her head bobbing like a bird. I did not need a second look. The tangled relations of my family reached even to Hartwoodhill. It was my Wee Auntie Nan, wife of Wild Jake from Lanark to whom I was fostered for holidays. As opposed to my Big Auntie Nan to whom I was fostered for Sundays only. Not my father's sister but one of my mother's vaguer relations. And a temporary inmate of Hartwoodhill. Not for the first time or the last. I didn't know that. But she knew me. "Oh, Willie. It's you. What are you doing here? Your mother was in to see me just last week."

My first thought was purely selfish. Me a nurse and my auntie a patient. If it ever got out … but I had always had a soft spot for "Nannie Goon", as she was known in the family. We chatted about this and that, then she said she had to get back, leaving me with another family puzzle. My first reaction was fear. I had been so close to madness, I was getting as neurotic as the other nurses. If Nannie Goon was mad, had I inherited some strain of madness from my mother? My second reaction was puzzlement. Why had my mother visited her and not me when I was working only half a mile away?

It puzzled me for years until I had all the pieces to put together. First, Wee Auntie Nan was far from daft. When life in Lanark and Jake's excesses of the English language got the better of her, she would throw a few minor eccentricities at her family and neighbours, go to the doctor's and "get a wee holiday in Hartwoodhill", where her presence was tolerated because they could see her "wee holidays" were all that prevented her stepping over the edge. A fair and sensible arrangement all round, except for Nannie Goon's family who were mortified. However, they have survived what they saw as their shame to become very respectable, even to a minister's wife.

My mother was very fond of this amazing little woman, and when Nannie went "on holiday" my mother would visit her, but secretly, for Wee Auntie Nan was part of that life from which my mother tried so hard to escape. She had not visited me at the same time because she wanted to keep us in separate compartments of her life and also because I had declared my independence and she had decided to respect it "until I had sorted myself out". Yes, a remarkable woman, my mother, with her fierce ambition for those in her present life yet her compassion for those in her past.

The Hartwood chapter of my life was closing and the next chapter was already opening in the shape of a long, buff OHMS envelope my mother had forwarded to me at Hartwood. Inside was a railway warrant and my instructions for joining 67/68 Training Regiments, Royal Regiment of Artillery at Oswestry. Where the hell was Oswestry?

CHAPTER TEN

If I Say Your Neck's Dirty, It's Dirty

I have the wound but no medals to show for my three-and-a-half years in Her Majesty's Service. My only mention in dispatches was for slugging a naval petty officer on the field of rugby, which somehow got to the Brigadier who reckoned it "just wasn't done" and gave me a rocket for "unsportsmanlike behaviour". My only distinction is that I was once the only pair of eyes guarding the free world from invasion by 600 million Chinese and, since the colony of Hong Kong could have been over-run by a dozen Chelsea pensioners with pikes, it's not much of a claim to fame.

So I do not intend to dwell on those six weeks that turned an ex-sea cook, medical student and mental nurse into "22881263 Gunner Anderson W, sir". It has all been told by better pens than mine. Indeed Leslie Thomas built a career on *The Virgin Soldiers*. There is no man more boring than the ex-soldier recounting tales of his square-bashing, boot-hulling, bullshitting, Naafi-girl-banging, floor-bumping, head-baring, boot camp training at the hands of a bawling coarse-mouthed brutal sergeant who screamed at him to salute anything that moved and polish anything that didn't.

For those who went through it, there is no need to enlarge on it. For those who didn't, there is no way of explaining the means by which the Army makes a man of you. But it does and to prove it I have a fading photograph showing all the gormless rawness of the recruit who has learned to do-as-I-say-not-as-I-do, but has still to "get some in". The regulation rake of that still new black beret makes me look like an effeminate French *poilu* suddenly snapped to attention.

National Service was compulsory for two years, and brought the princely sum of 7s 6d a week. Signing on for the minimum period of 3 years for the "regular" Army (there were the other alternatives of 7, 14 and the full 21 years) immediately doubled it to 15 bob. As I was young, short of bobs and had nothing better to do, I signed on for three. This immediately made me the gaffer of my hut with brutal bullying powers over my fellow unfortunates, which I used to the full. "Simpson, I'm nipping down to the Naf for char and wad. Give my boots a bull for parade and I'll forget your name for Fatigues." "Guard duty? Oh, that's up to the Lance-Bombardier, but I'll put in a word for you."

By such means did Adolf Hitler rise to power. Only, if our Little Corporal, called "Bombardier" in the Royal Artillery, found out about my blackmail, he wanted his cut. "Get a fag for me, too, or I'll have you by the balls on inspection." This was a perfectly fair system since, whatever drill sergeants or any other instructors tried to do, it ensured that any bucko who wanted to get on always did exactly what was requested by the rank immediately superior to them.

This system was really what made the most senior non-commissioned rank of Regimental Sergeant Major (RSM) akin to God. How many pints did he command in the Sergeants' Mess? There was such a gap in our blackmailing powers, he could make a Hut Senior Gunner like me crawl across the parade ground on hands and knees and eat from the pig's midden. And he would, if I didn't observe proper channels by letting the Lance Bombardier let the Bombardier let the Sergeant let the Colour Sergeant let the Battery Sergeant Major let the RSM know that the chinless wonder in Hut 22 was no National Serviceman but a colonel's son who wanted to be incognito to see if he could become a soldier the hard way without his father's help. Knowing full well that by letting it slip the RSM would make sure he had a nice cushy number. For if the RSM is God, any colonel is God Almighty and generals are so high on the military Olympus they are only ever seen safe from any mortal danger as saluting bases at passing-out parades.

From which you'll gather I took to soldiering like a Pathan rebel to a long-barrelled rifle. The Army was made for me. The routine to end all routines, thereby relieving me of any responsibility for myself or my immediate future. The perfect cop-out to let me find myself and what I wanted to do. I was not unintelligent and could say "No, sir. Yes, sir. Three bags full, sir" with a ringing conviction that took me to top recruit before you could write the report that said "A bright boy from the right background who will make a fine soldier and is the material of a good NCO." This may mark me as a crawler. I prefer to think of myself as a realist who quickly cottoned on that the Sergeant meant it when he said "You play the game with me, and I'll play the game with you."

There was also the unquestionable fact that, by and large, the Scot does make a good soldier. Never forget he is brought up on *The Book of Discipline* which was only an early religious version of Queen's Regulations. I was happy being a soldier. I loved banging my nailed boots down as hard as I could on the parade ground. It was just a grown-up version of the Draffen Street game of sliding along the pavement to make the sparks fly from the new studs hammered into the heels of our boots to make them last longer. I loved getting dressed up for Guard Parade, chest out to show every button was shining, latest of the thin red line. Housewifery was no mystery to me. I could darn a sock as neatly as an intricate tapestry and not leave it in lumps that made big blisters on route marches. My mother had taught me well. I could look after myself, the very quality most in demand in armies after discipline. But then I never had to go to war. I missed two by the skin of my teeth.

I did have one brush with the brutal sergeant who thought I was getting just too big for my boots – he insisted loudly on morning parade that my neck was dirty when he knew darn well it wasn't. I marched with red burning shame in my neck and black burning hate in my heart. But, as he knew it would, this taught me to temper arrogance with humility, both of which are vital to the tight upper lip of the British military man. "Yes, sir. Only the three of us. We did manage to knock out all 45 Panzers, but I did have a bit of luck with the wadi that gave me dead ground cover." What was his name in *The Hotspur*? The fearless sergeant who was always knocking out German Panzer battalions with two mates and a bit of humility?

From basic training, I went for six weeks to the classification regiment that converted the trained soldier to 22881263 Gunner Anderson W, TARA (I). I could not have been prouder of those letters after my name in Regimental Orders. Keep your Dux Medal, your MA, stuff your MBChB, Bill Anderson is now a TARA. And I had achieved it all on my own. A TARA, as called in usage, was a Technical Assistant Royal Artillery. Be you a lance bombardier or general you cannot fire a gun and guarantee to hit the target without one. He is the bloke who with compass, measuring tape, rules and map and an instrument not unlike a theodolite, can tell you the exact point on earth where the gun happens to be and so makes it possible to know where to point it, the range and all the other gubbins to hit the target. And a Grade I Tara was the best of them! For the first time in my life, I was fully trained to do something. Even that modest accomplishment was a good feeling after failure. If my brother could boast he was an ARICS I could always boast I was a TARA.

I was so good, there was talk of me being kept on as a trainee instructor. This may not have been entirely unconnected with the fact that the Regiment had a good rugby team and I let it drop to the Bombardier who let it drop to the ... but it got up to the Adjutant that I had played for the Dalziel High FP team who had won the Wigtonshire Sevens, which was next door to the Border Sevens and anyone who knew anything about rugby knew of Gala and Hawick and the other Border breeding grounds of the best Scottish rugby players.

Even better, the Colonel was there at the first game I played as substitute for the regular loose head wing forward and liked what he saw. "Good show, Anderson. Jolly good show," he said as he

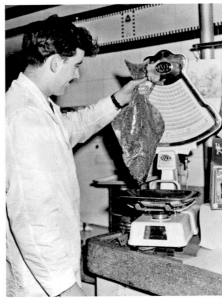

Above: HON as a fishmonger (March 2, 1958).

Above: HON as Gypsy Jim, the fortune teller
(April 20, 1958).

"It's a terrible job but somebody has to do it." The HON Man judges a beauty contest.

The HON Man could be seen in Sauchiehall Street, Glasgow, on more than one occasion giving away five pound notes (December 1957, and again in 1958, and 1960), or selling pound notes for half price (1959), and, (pictured left) even pound notes for a penny.

Edward Heath, Prime Minister from 1970 to 1974 and leader of the
Conservative Party from 1965 to 1975, with Bill in *The Sunday Post* office.

Bill with Margaret Thatcher. This picture was taken before the 1979
General Election that saw her become Prime Minister.

The duties of The Editor of *The Sunday Post* are many and varied – a reflection of the paper itself. Left: judging *The Sunday Post* "Clootie Dumpling Contest"; below: at *The Sunday Post* Falklands Memorial, Edinburgh, November 28, 1982.

The "Oor Wullie Special" locomotive naming ceremony, December 14, 1985.

"Oor Wullie", a *Sunday Post* regular since 1936, often played a part in marking special occasions.

Pictured below, when HMS *Fife* visited Dundee in 1985, is its Commander Jonathan Tod (who went on to become Vice Admiral Sir Jonathan James Tod KCB CBE), receiving a unique Order of the Bath.

Why does The Sunday Post sell so well?

That's a question I'm often asked. I always tell the story of the Fleet Street newspaper group who sent some top executives up to Scotland to find out exactly the answer to that question. The story goes that they locked themselves in a room with the Editors of their Scottish publications and several back copies of The Sunday Post. Three days later they emerged looking a bit wan and wabbit. Their top man said, "Well, we still don't know the secret but I can tell you we'll all place a regular order for The Sunday Post."

[Joking apart] I don't think there's much doubt we did forge a unique link with our readers over the two World Wars when The Sunday Post was a breath of home, a link with home in a world where there was little radio, and no TV, and a newspaper really was the only way in which the vast majority of people could stay in touch.

~~The reader~~ people preferred The Sunday Post ~~because~~ *the way* it kept them in touch.

for circulation as well and The Post spread in England as well. Particularly of course ... East, where I suppose the very character ... *very close relationship* ... feel of The Sunday Post and ~~what we have tried~~

96 Albert Road,
Gourock
10th June 1979

Dear Sir,

while staying recently with my nephew and his family in Guayaquil, Ecuador, he drew my attention to the enclosed cutting from a Sunday edition of the newspaper "El Universo", regarding the record-breaking circulation of the "Sunday Post".

I thought you might be interested.

I may say that the "Sunday Post" is air-mailed out to my nephew weekly and he gets it on the Thursday of the issue week. Need I add that it is greatly appreciated by them.

Yours faithfully,

Ada M. Blackwood

(Miss) Ada M. Blackwood.

The Editor,
"Sunday Post",
DUNDEE

Left: A clipping tucked away in Bill's desk – sent to him by a *Sunday Post* reader June 10, 1979 – seen in the *El Universe* newspaper in Ecuador, regarding the "record-breaking circulation of *The Sunday Post*."

The Sunday Post magazine, *First Sunday*, was launched on September 2, 1988. Pictured here, left to right (back row): Sheena Miller, Mike Filmer, Editor Maggie Dun (later to become Maggie Anderson!), Bill; (front row): artists John Timmons and Karen Cockburn.

Bill, on his appointment as Managing Editor, DC Thomson & Co Ltd, November 26, 1990.

Bill pictured looking over the city from the parapet of the Vista Room of the DC Thomson building, Meadowside, Dundee.

Bank of Scotland Press Awards, May 24, 1991. The "Special Award" was presented to Bill by Sir Thomas Risk, Governor, Bank of Scotland.

Bill and Meg pictured at Buckingham Palace, 1991, on the occasion of the award of CBE for his contribution to journalism. In the same year he became the first Scottish member of the Press Complaints Commission.

If the cap fits … away from work, Bill enjoyed fishing and sailing.

The SUNDAY POST

Death of former Sunday Post Editor

■ **Bill Anderson.**

BILL ANDERSON, former managing editor of The Sunday Post, died on Friday aged 77.

Bill retired in 1999 after a career at the paper spanning five decades, including 22 years as editor.

He started his career at the Post in Glasgow as the paper's "HON Man", with the challenge of Holidaying On Nothing.

The role saw him travel the world, becoming one of the first Western tourists to venture behind the Iron Curtain to Communist Russia.

The quality of his writing saw him rise rapidly to be made Sunday Post editor aged just 34.

Under his stewardship, the paper became the biggest selling in Scotland with a circulation of over a million.

The achievement earned a place in the Guinness Book of Records as the newspaper with the highest per capita readership in the world.

Born in Motherwell, the son of a steel worker, Bill was fiercely proud of his working class roots.

In 1991, his achievements in journalism saw him awarded the CBE — which his domino partners claimed stood for "chapping both ends".

The same year he was awarded the Bank of Scotland Special Press Award for "a lifetime's outstanding contribution to Scottish journalism."

Bill attended Dalziel High School, before studying medicine at Glasgow University. After two years he decided a medical career wasn't for him and left to join the army.

Commissioned in the Royal Artillery, Bill served for three years, including a posting to Hong Kong where he did some writing for the South China Morning Post.

He joined The Sunday Post on return to civilian life. In 1990 he left the editor's post to become managing editor.

He said his proudest moment in charge of the paper was when, as a result of a Sunday Post campaign on "dirty milk", Scotland was declared the first brucellosis-free country in Europe.

He also took a major interest in Scotland On Line, the internet company jointly owned by Scottish Telecom and D. C. Thomson.

Scotland on Line developed into and became brightsolid, DC Thomson's successful family history internet and data hosting company .

His retirement after 42 years with DC Thomson in 1999 gave him more time to enjoy his pastimes of sailing and angling.

Mr Anderson, who lived in Broughty Ferry, is survived by his second wife Maggie, three sons and eight grandchildren. His first wife Meg died in 1993.

"Bill set the benchmark for all of us at The Sunday Post," said current editor Donald Martin. "Every week we strive to produce a paper that he would be proud of and builds on his great legacy."

Mr Andrew F Thomson, chairman of DC Thomson, said: "Bill Anderson was an outstanding journalist and one of the great editors. He made an enormous contribution to The Sunday Post and to the firm in general."

swung his swagger stick to call me to him after the match. There I stood, dripping mud and blood, at full regimental attention. "Thank you, sir. I did my best. The lads played well." Note the right touch of humility and team spirit.

I had been noticed. The next Regimental Orders (ROs) promoted me to Acting Lance Bombardier. If that stripe was confirmed, I was on the gravy train. A cushy berth as a Non-Commissioned Officer (NCO) in a training regiment – with lots of time, the best of food, opportunities to travel and play rugby. I could feel the Field Marshal's baton in my hand.

Then the other RO caught my eye. Short Service Commission. Any trained soldier with A-Levels, Scottish Leaving Certificate or equivalent, with the CO's approval, could apply to the WOSB with a view to commissioning as a regular Army officer.

"What is WOSB?" I asked the Adjutant's clerk. War Office Selection Board: three days of interviews, character tests and general jumping about with a number on your chest and back, where they decided if you had the makings of an officer and a gentleman.

That surely wasn't for an ex-sea cook sweat like me. I had the education. I'd been to university. I could play rugby. I was no fool (if that helped). But an officer? A working-class Jock like me with a Lanarkshire accent that still had traces of a glottal stop? Officers all had posh accents. But look at the pay – 35s a week. And a uniform allowance. What did I have to lose? It was always a few days off other duties. I tested the water with the Bombardier who tested the water with … and the Colonel's message came back. It might be a loss to the rugby team, but he would approve my application to the WOSB. Thus did my patriotism, pride and thirst for glory take me off to Aldershot. And the promise of 35 bob a week, of course.

It was a dawdle. Before I went, I did some uni-style boning, spotting the questions and writing out the right answers until I had them pat. I devoured *The Daily Telegraph* for current affairs. Pored into Army manuals in the regimental training library for "Qualities of Leadership" and "How To Conduct An Interview", which gave me the reverse role. I said nothing to my family but did ask if Barclay could send me some of the literature he had been given at a Civil Defence (CD) course at some castle or other. It was the time of the cold war when CD seemed a good idea and middle-management civil servants and local authority management staff like Barclay were being sent on courses to send them back into their own backyard as instructors. The piece of literature I remembered was in the bundle he sent. I was quietly confident. When it came to the all-action leadership tests, I made sure No 5 was evident, but not over evident. I led when asked to lead and played willing team member when someone else had to work out how to cross a mine field with two planks, a barrel and a piece of rope. If he got stuck, I would modestly suggest the obvious solution. It was the same games we had played in Carfin Hall woods many a time – a stay concealed from the enemy park keeper!

I had two worries: that accent and a working-class background. They had to show up in the three interviews that interspersed all the activities. But Hairy Breeks was up there rooting for me with the gods of war. At my first interview the officer spoke with a cultured, but unmistakably Scottish accent and had an aunt who lived in Hamilton. It was on the posh side of the river from the steel mills, but near enough. The second interviewer was a rugby fan. And the third was so fascinated by my stories of the mental home, we ran out of time for any more questions.

There was only the final hurdle. The five-minute lecture, on your own chosen subject, which was where Barclay's CD literature came into its own. I was also lucky to be drawn first. I had asked for a blackboard and chalk, which was novel for a start. On it I drew two large circles and began:

"Gentlemen. These diagrams could be rather dull gun emplace-ments, or with only minor additions appear rather more interesting." I stopped and added another very small circle to the centre of each and waited for the laughter to die.

"Nor should you fall into that trap, gentlemen, for as my old anatomy professor used to say, 'The female breast is a snare and delusion, for it is only a conglomeration of fat, tissue and the milk ducts necessary to its function as a mammary gland.' " More laughter, during which I added a straight stroke on either side of the circles.

"Now gentlemen, what you see on the blackboard is a bird's eye view of two Mexicans, riding bicycles."

The old joke with a new twist went down a bomb. I then rather daringly rapped the blackboard, and reflex made them sit up.

"This demonstration has already taught you in 30 seconds two lessons you will never forget about the subject of my lecture. First, command the immediate attention of your audience. Second, use humour as a tool, not a comedy act." I then wrote the subject of my lecture in bold underlined letters on the blackboard: HOW TO GIVE A LECTURE.

"Now gentlemen, I will proceed to teach the rest of you how to pass this lecture test." Which I did, with the aid of Barclay's booklet which was, as you've now guessed, full of instructions on how they should pass on their knowledge when they went back to their CD units, including, of course, the use of the blackboard, humour and all.

It was cheeky, but not overly so. And it showed the initiative those service chappies like. A master stroke, in fact, which I still have the feeling was the clincher that took me to the Mons Officer Cadet Training Unit (OCTU) in Aldershot. I was at the OCTU, accent and all, with the white lapel facings to prove it.

I need only tell you that it was the time when Regimental Sergeant Major Ronald Brittain of the Coldstream Guards put officer cadets through their paces for you to know it was basic training all over again with more of the same and more intense.

With the loudest voice in Britain and bawling in a high-pitched staccato from a barrel chest, Regimental Sergeant Major Ronald Brittain laid down the rules with his opening remark – well, yell – across the Aldershot parade ground.

"You lot iss now offisah cadets an' gennlemen. As you iss offisah cadets, I will call each and every one of you 'Sir'. Each an' every one of you offisah cadets will call me 'Sir'. You will mean it."

I was surprised when this declaration of war excluded the usual seasoning of "bluidy". But it was RB's proud boast that he read his Bible every night and never used an oath in his life. I never heard him swear. I have no reason to doubt him about the Bible. His was the Old Testament faith. Idleness was the worst sin in it. He had discovered a hundred-and-one ways an officer cadet could be deemed idle:

- "Idle on parade" for any offence from a dull button to a thumb 1/16th of an inch off the plumb of the seam.
- "Idle tongue" for failure to respond quickly enough to a question.
- "Idle on a bicycle" for not riding to attention when passing an officer you hadn't seen.
- "Idle in civilian clothes" for leaving a casual hand in your pocket which the RSM thought no gentleman should ever do.
- "Idle on your bed" for being found sitting on it exhausted after a cross-country run.

It was even claimed that he had once come across a young gentleman innocently kissing his girlfriend goodbye outside the station and had put him on a fizzer for being "Idle in the act", not for the kiss, but for not removing his gentleman's trilby before doing so. Out of uniform, every cadet had to wear a trilby in order that he might, even off duty, learn to raise it not only as a courtesy but as a salute to any superior he might meet or as an acknowledgement of the guard's salute at the gate when returning from a night out in town.

Nor was the RSM's own interpretation of Queen's Regulations an idle threat. For such a charge meant you were put on "CO's Orders" which meant lining up outside the Commanding Officer's office next morning, where the RSM would bark out "Idle on a bike, sir" with brief details, and you would take your menial punishment like a man, as you had to. For it was all done under the catch-all Section 40 of Queens Regulations which made an offence of any "conduct prejudicial to good order and military discipline", into which came all the RSM's categories of idleness.

I survived. I even enjoyed the etiquette and other lessons in better living to give us at least the gloss of gentlemen. Manners may not maketh the man. I lean to Rabbie Burns' philosophy that "The rank is but the guinea's stamp. The gowd's the man for a' that." But a little polish on the old Hairy Breeks in me would do me no harm, either. It wasn't changing Bill Anderson. Just disguising him.

I did have a smile when the tailors came down from Hawkes of London to measure us for our No 1 dress uniforms, white Mess monkey jackets, epaulettes, cummerbunds and what have you. First, that attractive uniform allowance did not fully cover it. This led me to my first experience of the credit-worthiness of a gentleman. "Certainly, sir," said the tailor when I whispered my predicament. "It will be quite all right to settle the bill when your allowance is paid. Yes, we do understand you are only paid monthly." The other smile was when the tailor's assistant was measuring us. "Now, sir, have we dealt with you before? If so, you'll be on our books and we won't have to bother with measurements." He must have wondered why I was laughing. All those years of Co-operative suits, blazers and trousers and those awful, sensible yellow cotton vests and underpants – the very thought of my measurements being on the books of some exclusive Savile Row establishment would have made Steel Town keel over with laughter to a long-johned, camisoled, scratchy-vested man, woman and child.

After my final fitting, I tried them all on. The tailored everyday battledress was in a lighter-weight khaki than that of the other ranks. (Once they had been my Naafi oppos [friends], now they were "other ranks". Mons had done its work well. I was even thinking like an officer.) My other new clothes consisted of a smart tweed suit and trilby for leisure; the No 2 dress uniform, worn with shoes rather than boots for Guard Parades and other less dressier occasions, or as an alternative to a dinner jacket when dining in the Mess; the No 1 dress uniform, the one you see the officers wearing at the Changing of the Guard and other formal parades; and the monkey jacket (white tropical and black non-tropical) to be worn with a cummerbund and No 1 trousers for formal Mess dinners. Thinking back, £120 went a long way! In due course, when bits of old uniforms were all the rage, my middle son wore the No 1 jacket to discos and thought himself a real rave in it. To me, they were the passport to yet another new role. I quite liked the thought of being a gentleman.

Two days later, I became an officer, marching up the steps behind the Adjutant on his horse. It was another week or two before I was officially gazetted with the publication of my name in *The London Gazette*. I was no longer 22881263 Gunner Anderson, W. Now I was 432418 Second Lieutenant William Anderson, RA (Royal Artillery).

I now had two even prouder letters after my name. I had rank, too. But best of all I held the Queen's Commission. I hold it to this day, for once you have it as a regular officer, it can only be taken from you by a similar Royal Decree.

The Queen's Commission is an impressive document. A scroll with the Monarch's seal and signed personally by her. No stamps or other fakes. In red ink, in her own hand. I'm sure you won't mind if I give you a taste of it:

> *Elizabeth the Second, To Our Trusty and Well-Beloved William Anderson, Greetings.*
> *We, reposing especial Trust and Confidence in your Loyalty, Courage and good Conduct, do by these Presents Constitute and Appoint you to be an Officer in Our Land Forces from the Nineteenth day of December, 1953.*
> *Given at Our Court at Saint James, the Ninth day of February, 1954 in the Third Year of Our Reign. Elizabeth R.*

That commission and command from the monarch rings down

the ages of history – Drake, Frobisher, Wellington, Admiral Beatty, Jellicoe, Alanbrooke, Montgomery, and your humble Scottish servant, Bill Anderson, ma'am.

I still have my Queen's Commission, rolled up in a cardboard keeper with my Baptismal Certificate, Scottish Leaving Certificate and the Diploma of the Institute of Advanced Motorists.

When I look at it now, the scroll writing and those incongruous capital letters remind me of my mother's letters. I took it home to show her on my first leave as an officer. "Here, Mum, does this help?" I said.

She unrolled it, but it wanted to spring back so I took it from her again and spread it out on the table. I had to bend slightly to do so. She came over and read it, resting her hand on my shoulder, so our heads were close together. (If you'd only been able to show your affection when we were young, Mum. A touch, a look, a hug, a kiss, it might have been so different.) She had finished. She was smiling through the tears, but she didn't say much. "Oh, Bill. And it's signed by the Queen herself. Take it through and read it to your Dad. He'll be so proud of you." It was her way of telling me she was proud of me, too. It was the nearest we ever came to understanding each other. That she could not do it for me. That whatever I chose to do, I had to do it myself. That if I succeeded for myself, I succeeded for my mother and father, too.

I took it through to Dad. He was in bed in the corner room which had been mine. I could see his artificial leg propped up at the end of the bed. The twists of life had made him the child and me the man. I read him the Queen's Commission. He looked at me hard and long. This man who was the father who had been kept from me first by my mother, then by his accident and, in the end, by my obstinacy in leaving home. This man of steel reduced to walking on it. He said nothing. He held out his hand for me to shake. We shook hands and this time it was me who could feel the tears. His hand was offering me recognition and respect.

"Your mother must be pleased," was all he said.

So I had redeemed myself and made my peace with my parents. But there was still one act required of me.

Mum used my Sunday name. "We'll go to church tomorrow, William," she said. She paused and looked at me. "Will you wear your dress uniform? Please?"

My first instinct was to refuse. It was not my way. It was only showing off. Nor was it my need. It was for me to judge myself, not the town. To parade myself was only to admit they were my judges. It was the old *id* (ego) again. But I had learned something from my mistakes. It wouldn't be for me. It would be for my mother. And my father. "Yes, Mum, if that's what you want." It pleased her almost as much as the Commission itself.

"I'm going, too," said Dad next morning. There was no arguing with him. We went in the bus, the kirk bus, that had taken us so often when I was a child. My mother and my father in their Sunday best. Their tall, handsome son, so strong, so proud and erect in his splendid new No 1 dress uniform, with the officer's smart dress cap – just like you see on the Queen's birthday – and one bright pip, shining on each epaulette, sewn on by his mother.

If you are going to do it, do it properly, I told myself. I gave the elders at the door of Dalziel High Church a courtesy salute, slowing it down from the snap of a military salute to that more in keeping with respect for their position in the kirk. I removed my cap and tucked it under my left arm. Then I offered my mother my right arm. She hesitated, then took it firmly and I swear there was almost a twinkle in her eye.

Then I escorted her down the right hand aisle to the pew fourth from the front, the family pew, my father stumping proudly on the other side of my mother, but a pace behind. Every eye turned on us, for it had been a long time since any show of Andersons had been in the High Kirk. My mother smiled to those she knew, like a bride and even saying a word to one or two. I helped her into the pew, then made to let Dad go into the pew before me, as I had been trained. He shook his head. His was the outside seat. So I sat between them, as I had when a child. The last hymn was my mother's favourite.

By cool Siloam's shady rill
How fair the lily grows!
How sweet the breath, beneath the hill,
Of Sharon's dewy rose.

If three of the raised voices were a little trembled, it was of no concern to the rest of the congregation. Their congratulations and questions were to come in the news session that always followed the church service outside in Merry Street.

Lo! such the child whose early feet
The paths of peace have trod,
Whose secret heart, with influence sweet,
Is upward drawn to God.

It was too much. Reconciliation and redemption. A requiescat for past fears and a renewal of future hopes. Not one of the three of us could sing the last verse. My mother took my hand and held it tightly. My father gripped the pew in front of him, letting his walking stick fall against the seat.

Dependent on Thy bounteous breath,
We seek Thy grace alone,
In childhood, manhood, age, and death
To keep us still Thine own.

I was to sing it again at my mother's funeral and did not get beyond the first line before I choked on my tears. By then, I had come to a better understanding of my mother and father. They wanted so much for their family. They offered so much. They gave so much. I asked nothing, but gave too little and too late. But, as we walked from the church that day, I knew that with my Queen's Commission I had given my father back his pride and my mother the final seal of the respectability she sought. It had never been doubted in my brothers and sister.

I had let them down until I could shake hands with my father and my mother could glance round the crowd of well-wishers, smiling but with that Bessie look, the challenge to those who dared whisper. Look at my son. This is the one you said is a university failure who ran away from home. Can you doubt him now or the unquestionable respectability of the mother of a son who holds the Queen's Commission?

Yet, for all any of her family did or did not do, I have never met anyone who did not respect my mother. It was the one word that everyone used about her, even those who had known her as a girl. If she had but known it, she had already achieved for herself what she thought she needed, long before she had the family she thought could achieve it for her. She may rest in peace.

Eight weeks later I was in Hong Kong. But first I went to the Royal Arsenal in Woolwich for a fortnight's final polish as an officer in the Royal Artillery: the mystique of "dining in" and the proper way, the only way, to pass the port; sitting in on court martials; how to conduct a pay parade; man management and morale; the right side to wear a Sam Browne and a sword.

I had not scaled the final heights at Mons OCTU. I did not win the Sword of Honour, nor become the Senior Under Officer nor one of the two Junior Under Officers. My final report was glowing but had a sting in the tail. "He tends to talk too much." So my tongue kept me out of the trio who went off to what was regarded as the glory posting – the Royal Horse Artillery, that stronghold of tradition, right of the line, that fires all the Royal salutes in Hyde Park and dashes about with such verve in the Royal Tournament; and the next two for parachute training and the heroics of the Parachute Brigade. Secretly, I was glad because I did not see myself either trotting along on or behind a smelly horse or falling out of aeroplanes.

But I had been next on the list and that put me top of the next pile of postings – the few that were overseas. The Empire was still shrinking rapidly, so most had to go off and fight boredom in Woolwich, London, Aldershot, Barnard Castle, Otterburn, Salisbury Plains, Oswestry and other such outposts of the Commonwealth.

Many others went to Germany, where most of our Army played cold war. But there were three plums: Singapore, Hong Kong and Korea.

Korea was still being fought over as the protracted peace talks of Panmunjom dragged into their second year. Every officer could put down three preferences. I wrote down Korea, Hong Kong, Singapore in that order. If Bill Speakman of the King's Own Scottish Borderers could win the Victoria Cross with the help of a handful of empty Guinness bottles, what glory called Bill Anderson of the Royal Artillery? I had visions of me sending off the five envelopes. Four with the white feathers for those who had most maligned me in my youth and one inviting Mum and Dad to the investiture at Buckingham Palace. It was not to be. I missed my first war because I was not yet of the age at which the War Office considered officers might be allowed to die. Other ranks could spill their blood on Hill 27 from the age of 18. But officers had to be 21. There was sense in it. An inexperienced, still somewhat immature leader of men, straight from passing the port at Woolwich, might only have spilled more 18-year-old blood. But it denied me the role of Second Lieutenant Beau Geste. That would have been one up on Hairy Breeks.

So I had to settle for Hong Kong. Settle! It was as far as it could be from Gilmorehill, Oban, Hartwood and Hillhead Crescent. And the very name made me tingle with excitement. I collected my tropical kit at the Garrison; all those starched green khaki drill. When new, they made me look like Eric Morecambe in the sketch with Percy Edwards where the creases of his khaki drill rise above his knees every time Percy whistles. Kitted out, I reported to the Land Forces Transport Office in London for my first command.

I was told I was Officer-in-Charge of the troop train from Waterloo to Southampton to embark on the troopship *Uganda*. Be it ever so junior, I was the only regular officer among the batch of National Service officers and men. I was handed a list of men, told not to lose any on the way to Hong Kong, and saluted out. I hadn't a clue what to do. So I stood at the end of the platform, cracking my new leather swagger stick against my leg, and barking in my best Ronald Brittain voice, "Come along there. All troops aboard for

Southampton. Move along, chaps. You're in the Army now." The sight and sound of this young imbecile masquerading as General Haig provoked several reactions.

First, the orderly lines of troops, held by their NCOs awaiting proper commands to embark in soldierly fashion broke loose and made a mass dash for the best seats. The officer had said so. This reduced Waterloo station to a shambles.

Second, said NCOs homed in on me to a man, when the most senior of them, bearing more medals ribbon than Audie Murphy, saluted smartly and said "For goodness' sake stay out of the way and leave it to me, SIR!" thus teaching me the immortal first rule for young officers. Return the salute and say "Carry on, Sergeant."

Third, a small, officious British Railways martinet approached me, moustache bristling. Another veteran. "So you're in charge. I've been looking for you. Why didn't you do as you were told and report to the Stationmaster's Office?", where he led me to sign forms in duplicate, triplicate and quadruplicate to agree I took full responsibility for Steam Locomotive No 145YZ, or whatever, the rolling guardsman thereto, plus 373 passengers in the shape of 361 other ranks and 12 officers, guaranteeing that Her Majesty was to reimburse all parties of the first, second and third incurring any loss of limb, death or any other damage pertaining to, or caused by, said transport and contents.

I got rid of the personnel by conning a signature out of the Transport Officer at Southampton. But no-one ever relieved me of the locomotive. For all I know it is even yet gallivanting through some ghostly graveyard of steam trains doing all manners of damage for which I have yet to get the bill. There is St Peter at the Pearly Gates, in his new British Rail uniform. "So you're the chap who was in charge of that train. I've been looking for you."

I did as everyone else does on any ship, whether troop or luxury cruise, that ever steamed five slow weeks to the Far East. I was sick in the Bay of Biscay. When I recovered I fell in love by moonlight in the Mediterranean, with a Lieutenant Q of the Queen Alexandra Royal Army Nursing Corps who spoke of passion but resisted all further advances on her top bunk. I won a bottle of sherry for third best guess in the draw for the ship's daily run in nautical miles. I got badly sunburned on the 102° beaches of Colombo (thereby earning three extra guard duties for "self-inflicted injury" or as RSM Brittain might have put it "idle sunbathing"). I was fascinated by the goolie-goolie man at Port Said who produced chickens from every part of his reeking anatomy and was conned by the bumboats who sold me an authentic Arab dhow table lamp and a leather wallet, "Souvenir of the Pyramids", which fell apart on first exposure to the tropical sun. I even paid £2 to see "The Only Captive Mermaid in The World" which turned out to be a desiccated dolphin.

I also visited E-Deck several times, as Night Orderly Officer, to make sure no men had escaped. I wouldn't have blamed them. Men are packed in troopships from the top, by rank, and when that runs out, by regimental precedent, down, deck by deck, to the death traps of E-Deck, in the bowels, where the Pay Corps, Army Catering Corps or Pioneer Corps are packed like sardines. It seemed foolish to me to make sardines of the very chaps who paid us, fed us and dug our latrines. Think of what dire revenge they might wreak.

At night, E-Deck had an odour all its own. Diesel oil, smelly socks, sweat and overwhelmed latrines. Add rough weather and heaving stomachs and you have – the night-shift at Hartwood. It speaks volumes for our soldiers that they take it so well, even cheerily, making the best of the worst – be it Balaclava, Tobruk or Belfast, or wherever too much is asked of them.

On the saloon deck, the privileged ate, swam, slept, drank, sun-bathed and made love between the training and lecture sessions for all, including "How to Take Prophylactic Action After Exposure to Venereal Disease".

I lectured in two classes: English – for troops who could scarcely read and write (me – teaching English!); and French Cookery – for the wives. The latter by popular demand after I had modestly admitted to my culinary accomplishments. That was a hoot! I had also polished up my accent enough to be understood even by the exclusively English ear of the most blimpish colonel from service in deepest Poonah "in Indiar, old chap". Or "Africar". Or the other strange lands of his native tongue. So much so, that when my money-making abilities at rubber bridge, played with the junior officers, became the talk of tiffins, I was invited to make up a four with a rear-admiral, a brigadier and the ship's captain, who liked winning money as much as the next man. While E-Deck played "Housey, Housey", I sat back in deep leather in the saloon after dinner, sipping port and puffing cigars, carrying my gouty, grunting partner to another grand slam to the acclaim of "Gad, sir, young Anderson, that was the finesse of a master. Superb tactics, my boy. Have another cigar," as though I had just stormed the heights of Quebec. If my mother could have seen me then!

Then slipping off to the laundry room for another secret and unrequited assignation with my comely Lieutenant Q of the Royal Army Nursing Corps. Ending the evening with a stroll along the boat deck to commune with the deepest blue and starry night sky of the Indian Ocean. Life as a young officer was sweet, especially when he was at peace with the world, and so was his Army. Indeed, I was now a whole man of the world away from Draffen Street and the bare-bottomed toddler in a Co-op vest being scrubbed in the kitchen sink.

I had embarked on the *Uganda* as a raw boy. I left it a man of the world. That Colville blood was starting to tell. I might be an archbishop yet.

I only glimpsed Hong Kong Island as I was whisked by jeep on a Star Ferry to Kowloon, on mainland China, and then deep into the New Territories, to land on that 99-year-lease from Red China, as I was ever after to give it its military designation.

My new home, 14th Field Regiment, Royal Artillery, recently shipped from Korea for regrouping, remanning and recuperation, was in its "forward positions" on the border. I was stood outside the camouflaged Command Post from which emerged my new commander, the grey-haired grizzled, grumpy Col C DSO and Bar, a man of few words, almost shy, but a legend, who promptly scratched his crutch vigorously as he always did when confronted with a new problem, looked me up and down and said, "Anderson, eh. Too young. Go back to camp and grow a moustache."

So I was returned to base, and the Nissen hut which served as officers' quarters where, for the rest of the 14 days in a base camp empty of all but a few maintenance personnel, I grew my moustache which, with the aid of not a little black Cherry Blossom™ boot polish, I was able to present to the colonel when he led the Regiment back from the field.

He was looking at my Army file as the Adjutant let me in. I could not resist it. I came to attention and threw up a smart salute, "432418 Second Lieutenant Bill Anderson, Royal Artillery, reporting for duty with moustache as ordered, sir." Then, remembering just in time, added "Colonel, sir," for all COs are called "Colonel" and not "sir". He was gruff, but he had a sense of humour. "Yes, it does say here you talk too much. Bill, eh. Just Bill, eh?"

"Yes, Colonel. No middle name or titles."

His eyes bore into me from below the hedgerows he called eyebrows. "Either shave it off or use more Cherry Blossom™ until it's fit to be seen," he said. "Now shove off." I saluted, turned and left, to hear him add, "You're a cheeky blighter, Anderson. But I think we can make something of you."

Outside the Adjutant gave me my duty. I was assigned to the Nominal Roll of 13 (Martinique 1809) Battery, Royal Artillery (one of the 14th Field Regiment's batteries in Hong Kong). "You should get on with the Battery Commander," said Jimmy MacLean. "He's a Scot like yourself." As was Jimmy!

Thus began my soldiering in Hong Kong.

CHAPTER ELEVEN

The Worst Cook In The World

14th Field Regiment was a 25-pounder regiment. This meant its 24 guns fired shells that weighed 25 pounds (or roughly 11 kilos). The 25-pounder was the major British field gun during the Second World War. It was a mobile, versatile gun that could take on tanks at close quarters with armour-piercing ammo or spray strong points up to ten miles away with high explosive. For control and command the guns were divided into three batteries and each battery into two troops of four guns each who might be miles apart. As Command Post Officer (CPO), at Battery HQ, I linked and directed the two troops so they could fire singly, in pairs, as troops or a full battery as need be, and still hit the same target at the same time. I loved every minute of it and worked out several technical and gun drill short cuts that made my battery, simply, the best – that is the fastest and most accurate. But only because of the teamwork of a great bunch, some of them seasoned in Korea, who knew they were good; from the signaller who operated the radio links to the gun layer who slapped his bottom when ready to open fire. No other battery in the three regiments present in Hong Kong at this time could touch us in terms of the time between the Forward Observation Officer (FOO) giving us target co-ordinates and my reporting "Echo Ready" to signify the right-hand gun of E-Troop was ready to fire the first aiming shot. Stirring stuff.

But even CPOs like me, and I was now a gazetted two-pipper, a full glorious Lieutenant with nothing second rate about him, had to take their share of the drudge jobs. Periodically, we moved from base camp to take our turn in the forward position. Our guns went into standby in camouflaged pits dug into the backs of low hills near the Chinese border. Every full lieutenant had to do a stint as the FOO.

The name speaks for itself. On the highest point of the front line, the FOO had to observe the enemy and call down gunfire as need be. My turn came around again and I led off my party of eight – myself, a bombardier to share the watch, two signallers to man the different command radios, and four gunmen for guard and general duties.

It was a killing climb, those six miles through the foothills and the long haul up the steep, winding track to the top of the hill, packed like camels, in the humid pre-monsoon heat that even made your bare knees bead with sweat. I can give you an idea of that climb by telling you all our heavier supplies, to the last drop of water in Jerry cans, had to be carted up by a Gurkha troop and their mules and the toughest fighting men and hardiest pack animals in the world both needed three breathers at the rest points hacked out of the hill.

Then we burrowed into the tunnels cut in from just below, and behind, the crest of the hill to take over from the incumbents. First priority was to spend half an hour with the previous FOO, sitting in the camouflaged observation slit cut into the front of the hill below which the meandering ribbon of the pre-monsoon border river cut us off from the spread of paddy-field villages that stretched to the horizon as China.

Just to the right, below, lay Lo Wu station and the pontoon type railway bridge across the river with the rail track that ran straight as a die for countless miles on its way to Shanghai and the heart of mysterious Mao-land, as we called it. It was a scene familiar to many because it had featured on so many TV newsreels of historic exchanges between the West and Red China – the release of Korean prisoners, for example, or refugees streaming out every time there was a purge. My first "fixed" target was to blow up that bridge.

It sounds dramatic. It was the opposite. Boring, humdrum and futile. For a start our Observation Point was the first "fixed" target of the Chinese, so if there had been an invasion, we would have been the first dead, and we knew it. There was no more chance of holding Hong Kong against the Chinese than there was of holding

Hong Kong or Singapore against the Japanese – short of nuclear war, that is.

For 14 days, we would sit there noting their troop vehicle movements and any changes in garrison regiments, vehicles or weapons. There never were any – by day or by night. Every dull daily "same-as-before" was sent through the various intelligence units all the way back to HQ (Far East Land Forces in Singapore). Many's the "Sit Rep Low Wo FOO to GII Farelf" I sent to report that the situation was so normal that we had noted the same old bugler had a new trumpet to blow the Chinese reveille as they raised the Red Flag.

There was one Chinese soldier who shared our jaundiced view of world power. Every morning he stumbled sleepily from his billet down to the edge of the river and looked up to make sure we were awake from the flash of our periscopic binoculars turning onto him as he made the first enemy movement of the day. He would wave cheerily as he pee'd into the river, then give us a very comradely salute with two fingers before returning to less reversionary Western behaviour. I liked him.

One day, I was sitting on the edge of my dugout at the back of the hill. Stewart, the cheery Geordie who was my field batman as well as a driver and signaller, was brewing cha (tea) on the petrol stove (whose black smoke betrayed our position all the way to Peking). I was an officer and gentleman, of course, who needed a butler even in the face of the enemy. But Stewart and I were great mates, of which a wee tale later, and he even voluntarily helped the Chinese servant who looked after my every need back at base. "Would you look at that, sir," he said. "I better lay the tablecloth. It's a visitor." Geordies have a rare sense of humour.

Our "visitor" was still only a small black speck on the yellowed track of the red blaze foothills. I focussed my binoculars on the spot. From a blur, he came into sharp relief as a Chinaman straight from *Chu Chin Chow*. Conical wicker hat, black pyjamas, trousers rolled up from the black sandals on his bare feet, and a bamboo pole slung across one shoulder in such a way the wooden buckets at each end were perfectly balanced. He jogged up and down in counterpoise to the pendulous century of poverty and oppression in each bucket that bowed his shoulders to the weight. A set of Chinese scales, weighing man's woe.

He grew larger and larger, and his buckets heavier and heavier as he struggled on, ever upward, not even stopping at the rest points in case he couldn't start again. A visitor indeed. Though not permitted, I did not wave him away. Not after that climb. If he was a spy, he was a very brave or foolish one and would learn nothing the Chinese did not know already. He stopped at the trench entrance to my dugout. He was middle-aged, but looked older in the way only worn-out workers can. "Me cook," he said, pointing at the pots and other utensils of his trade in the buckets. "Me work for you." So that was it. The Army did employ casual cooks all over the colony. If there were troops, there was the chance of a job, even if it meant climbing Mount Everest. I pointed to Stewart. "Sorry, me got cook. Better you go home." "Me good cook," he insisted, which said nothing for what he could see of the Geordie's kitchen. "He very good cook," I retorted. "Me very very very good cook," he replied, the sharp "r" in each giving lie to the common myth that the Chinese can only make an "l" of it.

This time he did not wait for my reply. He dug into a pyjama pocket. "Me have reference. Very, very good reference" and he produced a page from an Army Message pad which had been unfolded and folded so often the tears at the folds bore testament to the number of times it had been presented for jobs.

It was only as an expression of sympathy that I took it before I sent him on his way back down the hill. I unfolded the page carefully for fear it would fall apart. It was grimy, but still readable. Short, but to the point.

THIS IS THE WORST F…ING COOK IN THE WORLD.

Here was this poor Chinaman humping his tools all over the colony looking for jobs and proudly producing his "very very good" reference from an English officer and gentleman.

He was as baffled by the joke as he had obviously been every time before and started laughing, too, in the way the Chinese do to cover embarrassment. I balled up his reference and threw it on the stove. "Not good," I said. "Me give you no job. But give you much, very much better reference." So saying, I took a GII Intelligence form and wrote "This is the best cook in the colony". He went off quite happy.

For the most part my life in Hong Kong was quite dull. I reverted to playing bridge all weekend with those known as the "Colonel's Cronies". Or my number came up in the latest escort raffle. You lost if you won and had to squire some boring air commodore's daughter to the Queen's Birthday Ball. Until the Colonel went home and he was followed by Major D, my fatherly Scots Battery Commander. It was a sad night for me when another Scot, Captain James MacLean was also "dined out". He, more than any, had smoothed my path, rubbed off my rough edges, toughened me and took me to task until I was not only a bit of a devil, but a damned good gunnery officer whose chaps held him in respect and cheered when he knocked out the Battery bully in the Regimental Boxing Championship. Albeit, in turn, I was flattened in the next round by a Lance Corporal in the Army Catering Corps only half my height, but who knew how to box a Draffen Street brawler.

Though cigarettes at 1s 3d for a vacuum-sealed tin of 50 were already taking their toll not to mention gin and tonic for a few HK cents, I even made the Royal Artillery rugby team in which I scored seven tries – yes, seven – against the Navy. This so angered a gorilla of a Petty Officer, he rammed his bullet head into my navel base, so winding me that I only just had the strength to throw the ungentlemanly punch that landed me in trouble with the Brigadier. I was playing for the Army next time it took on the Navy. The PO was still in their scrum. I dodged him all match until the last ten minutes when he could wait no longer. Though the ball was on the other side of the field, and I was standing still, the fact my back was to him was too much of a temptation. He put in a full-blooded knee tackle that would have made Andy Irvine proud.

I was carried off to spend ten weeks in bed with one ankle in plaster and the other Elastoplasted from toes to knee. It so damaged the Achilles tendon of the broken ankle I was never to play top competitive rugby again. This displeased me no end since a young second lieutenant called Kelly had just become so impressed by my swerve he had written to his father of the young hopeful. As his father was a Scottish selector, Kelly was quite convinced by his reply that it meant a trial for the Dark Blues when I got back to the UK. Thus did an unthinking tar end my international career and every Scots boy's dream of scoring the winning try against England in the Calcutta Cup at Murrayfield (or the winning goal against England at Hampden). I did manage to win the long jump at Regimental Sports Day. Thereby proving not only my jumping ability, but the amazing recuperative powers of youth. Yes, come to think of it, I have had quite a life.

Anyway back to James MacLean's dining-out. James was loved because he'd been a war-time roughneck promoted to fighting Colonel in peace, who'd accepted demotion to Lieutenant to stay in the regular Army. He was a man's man and a fair, honest one at that.

Dinner taken and speeches made, we retired to the new "ante-room" – a long, oblong lounge built against the existing Mess, with the three new walls of a low brick foundation then metal-framed picture windows to the roof. At a "dining-out" the ante-room was the scene of the farewell frolics, usually an innocent game of touch-rugby-without-touching-the-floor or squash played on the billiard table, ten aside, with bare hands and billiard balls. These two Mess games always led to at least one black eye, much broken furniture and many broken windows and fingers. But they were an inalienable tradition going back to Agincourt.

That night we invented a new tradition. James was a great devotee of swimming and water polo. In his honour, we piled all the furniture on the billiard table which became an island as we closed all doors and sealed all leaks while we flooded the new ante-room with the fire hoses to the depth of the brickwork. Then we played a combination of water-cum-polo-polo, mounted on one another's backs – I'd call it "cuddy back". Using billiard cues as sticks and a cushion for a ball, our new Colonel, who was a horsey man, could be heard crying "Tally Ho" as he whipped an unfortunate subaltern round and round the island in pursuit of the winning cushion of the last chukka.

Behaviour that would have resulted in an official punishment for Other Ranks was regarded as typical drunken high jinks in the Officers' Mess, the damage for which was discreetly shared amongst all the officers and gentlemen involved, appearing on our Mess Bills as "Mess Night Extras – 149 Hong Kong dollars". I have a picture of me outside the Mess that night, admiring my gun, fully bulled, to be used as James's carriage to pull him home to his wife. I am finishing the last of a bowl of trifle with my fingers, not a shred of my white Mess jacket or shirt left from the polo, except the torn collar round my neck. An officer perhaps, but a gentleman?

The following day, I was strolling down Nathan Road in Kowloon when I saw myself walking towards me, or all my best civvies, anyway, from my lightweight beige linen suit to my barber's pole striped sharkskin shirt, regimental tie and best shoes. Even my prize rose red silk handkerchief was there, showing its four military peaks from the top pocket. Inside me was my batman, Stewart. I was about to consign him to the death-of-a-hundred-cookhouse-duties when I recalled the previous night. He must have left me too drunk to think I would ever rise again or notice the gaps in my wardrobe. Stewart, ever quick of thought, said "Sorry, sir. Didn't think you'd mind. Besides, I couldn't look like a better man, sir." The appeal to my better nature and vanity cooled my wrath. "OK, Stewart. But they'd better be back in my wardrobe tonight – and not a mark on them." I watched him walk off, strutting like a peacock. He looked like a gentleman. And, let's face it, every bit as much a gentleman as myself or any of the other water-polo players.

I did have one problem in Honkers – my troop sergeant, a beer-swizzling Korean veteran, as tough as the K-rations of the Second World War, and a true professional soldier. He had not taken kindly to the snot-nosed kid from Mons, who thought there was a bit more to officering than saying "Carry on, Sergeant" and nipping off to get more G and T time at the Mess. Especially one with white knees, a Cherry Blossom™ moustache and the long hair I affected at the time. I wanted to make my own mistakes. Sergeant P wanted to make sure I didn't make any mistakes. It was a clash of the new broom and the old besom which showed in a hundred little verbal snipings. "Are you quite sure this is the way you want it done, SIR?" with an emphasis on the "sir" that bordered on the insolent. "If it's not asking too much of a 22-year-old man, can a short officer be consulted before you order the men about, SERGEANT," with just enough emphasis on the "sergeant" to underline that I carried my brass on my shoulders.

It went on thus, neither yielding, until a morning parade on which I could smell more beer on his breath than he could smell gin on mine. "Heavy night, last night, Sergeant?" I asked as we walked out to inspect the Troop, hoping it would give me the edge in the day's manoeuvres. He said nothing, but breathed the other way. I couldn't help pressing home my advantage as he rammed to a halt in front of me to report the Troop ready for inspection. "Thank you, Sergeant. Stand the men at ease." Then, as he turned, I said it, softly enough that it might not seem so, but loud enough that it might just be heard and passed on by the nearest man: "Is that hair or is your neck dirty, Sergeant?" It was sweet revenge for the training sergeant of Oswestry, but a dirty thing to do to my own troop sergeant. Still, this was war. He pretended he hadn't heard. It was all he could do. His hair, unlike mine, was always a short crew cut. So it couldn't be hair and for a long-haired lout like me to suggest his neck was dirty …

Next morning, he was waiting for me on parade in front of the men. He drew the Troop to attention, marched three paces forward and saluted, "Battery Troop ready for inspection, sir." Then, before I could acknowledge it, "Permission to speak, sir?" I could only nod. "Troop Sergeant's neck also ready for inspection, sir." At that, he turned smartly about, to face the Troop and removed his beret to show a shining neck to me and to show the Troop that his shining neck went right up over his skull. He had gone to the regimental barber and had every hair shaved off his head. It shone there in the morning, that golden orb which did not show a hair nor could it hide a speck of dirt. It was open war. "Thank you, Sergeant. That's satisfactory now. Carry on," I stuttered and slunk off like the other lay officers to let the soldier get on with it. But I smarted in defeated silence and long thought until we were once again in forward positions. As darkness fell one night I took Sergeant P and a bottle of whisky behind the Command Post. It was a warm balmy evening, so neither of us was wearing the khaki-drill tops which carried our badges of rank. "Take off your brassard, Sergeant," I said, pointing to the leather wrist band with three brass stripes which was now his only mark of rank.

He needed no other invitation. As I knew I would, I lost the brief and bloody-nosed battle. But I won the war, as I knew I would, with the bottle of whisky, for he was a beer-only man and I was an Anderson. I carried the empty bottle and Sergeant P back to his billet. It was pure John Wayne, but it worked. Thereafter we showed each other the mutual respect of men who have set all differences aside and he became not only the best troop sergeant I ever had, but a friend.

His account of it did no harm to my standing with the soldiery either. Suddenly, I found myself in demand as a "Soldier's Friend". In other words, every rogue in the regiment began to ask for me, as was his right, as Defending Officer at his Court Martial.

It was a task I took more seriously than any other in the Army. I felt a kinship with the less-educated working-class lads who hadn't had my chance to get away from the Draffen Streets and far worse of Scotland. They joined the Army to get away from trouble and only landed in more. I had a technique for them. Plead guilty because they were, and even if they might not be, chances are the Army would say they were anyway, so it saved them hearing weary hours of evidence when their minds were already made up. Thus they had sympathy for the accused's contrition and I could then launch into the Plea in Mitigation allowed in such circumstances, which I had spent many hours researching and two-fingered typing so that, after delivery, it could be submitted for the court records, otherwise it was lost. Not only did my tactics have a high success rate in, at least, reducing sentences, but it was a new role for Bill Anderson, as the Perry Mason of the Far East Land Forces, and my fame soon spread – especially after "The Strange Case of Gunner O".

He was one of those homeless drifters, always in trouble, who somehow end up in the Army. He was a Kiwi, whose parents had separated when he was seven and run off, leaving their four children in an institution, the Anglican Boys Home in Wellington. He ran away, was caught, sent to an aunt who could make nothing of him and returned to another institution which held his two brothers and his sister. Shortly after, his younger brother died and his sister was sent to a different home. He ran away again and was sent to a boys training centre from which, at 15, he was ejected. He held a succession of menial jobs until he was 19 and joined the Merchant Navy which brought him to the UK where he jumped ship, couldn't find a job and landed in trouble. It was the police who arranged for him to join the Army. After training, he was sent to Korea where he earned his Korean Medal with 61st Light Regiment, Royal Artillery, before joining the 14th Field Regiment and ending up in Hong Kong. An institutionalised itinerant, with no family or friends, it's no wonder he was a moody youth who resented authority. And the Army is all authority. So he was in constant, petty trouble until he was unloaded on me as a driver. I got him to behave himself for three months, wangled a stripe for him on the theory that the poacher makes the best gamekeeper. He was never smarter or more efficient than during those three months until he got drunk one night, broke a window in the Naafi and lost his stripe. My noble experiment had failed and Gunner O became a thorn in my flesh as he had with everybody else. But my feeling was for the underdog and I really did believe his Court Martial was a railroad job.

He had married more for company than love and for somewhere to call home. That hadn't worked out for him either. He had pawned his wife's engagement ring to pay off some debts. She was in hospital for a minor op and had threatened to leave him if it wasn't back on her hand when she came out in two days. A Chinese heavy was pressing him for a 700-dollar debt (a loan he'd taken out to set up home). He just couldn't cope.

On pay day, his money wouldn't scratch the surface. So he set off on a binge. I have the list yet – drinking anything and everything in the Nine Dragons Club in Kowloon; the Sun Sun Cafe in Shatin; the Betta Ole in Fanling; the Naafi in Quarry Camp; Wonder Wong's in Kantin; the oddly-named Watson's Cafe back in Fanling; another Naafi at Sek Kong camp; then back to Watson's. It was a pub crawl to end all pub crawls, especially on Tiger beer and every kind of spirit they could offer. And all driving my jeep!

In Watson's, an argument brought the Military Police. Failing to find any other offence, the MPs arrested four of his drinking mates for being "improperly dressed", leaving Gunner O to drink on, while they returned the offenders to the guard room at Quarry Camp. A little later he arrived there, demanding to see them, bawling the injustice of it all. Only to see the Guard Commander officially placing one of his cronies under close arrest. The Guard Commander was wearing neither cap nor belt, in breach of Standing Orders that "He will be properly dressed at all times during his tour of duty". Oliver loudly queried the justice of this when his mates were being celled for "improper dress". He was ordered from the Guard Room, refused, and was himself placed under close arrest at which stage he lost his rag and demanded to see the Regimental Orderly Officer (ROO) who was sent for. Now it may have been coincidence that the lieutenant who happened to be ROO that night, for various reasons, thought Gunner O a thornier pest in his flesh than anyone else's.

He first allowed Gunner O out of his cell, which he shouldn't have done. Then he charged him with refusing to obey a superior officer when he wouldn't return. He also allowed the Guard Commander to get involved in the scuffle to force him back, which should never have happened and when Gunner O was in the cell, ordered the Guard back and went into the cell alone, in breach of Standing Orders, and finally, in breach of Queen's Regulations, he virtually invited Gunner O to have a go at him, too, which he did. When the ROO, not known for his evenness of temper, plus Guard and Guard Commander piled in on Gunner Oliver, the only one to emerge with any real injury was Gunner O. But now they had him. Drunk. Disobeying an order. Resisting arrest. Refusing to obey a superior officer. Striking a superior officer. They had plucked the thorn and so serious was the offence it was a full-blown General Court Martial at Brigade HQ.

My defence was, as always, guilty as charged. My Plea in Mitigation was obvious. Gunner O was a victim of his background, worried, drunk and smarting from injustice while the officer, known to dislike him, made "an error of judgement", if not a clear breach of Queen's Regs, with the inevitable, almost engineered, result.

I had to submit my defence to the Adjutant. Jimmy MacLean wondered if it was wise to make so much of the officer's part in it. It would make me distinctly unpopular in the Mess. I wondered if the charges against Gunner O might be reduced to lesser offences if I glossed over the officer's part. I think it's called plea bargaining. But there was no bargain. I think Jimmy could see the light of injustice in my eye. It was not my popularity at stake, but Gunner O.

I made my plea. Gunner O, with his previous record, expected eighteen months in the Glasshouse. He got a reduced sentence that restored him to my jeep in a couple of months, a much subdued man.

The officer got a quiet rocket from the Colonel. I can give personal testament to his temper. When I went to his hut some months later to pick another bone with him about his high-handed ways, he listened in the doorway, then, looking round to make sure there were no witnesses, gave me a straight left to the mouth. Obviously, I was now in the same category as Gunner O – a thorn in his flesh. I kept quiet about it apart from a visit to the Medical Officer (MO) for my mouth.

The 14th Regiment was coming to the end of its tour when a letter arrived from my brother Ian who had gone to Australia, then New Zealand. He was taking a Kiwi girl home to Scotland, where they would marry. Could I make it back to be his best man?

The timing was awry. It was still six weeks before the Regiment packed up, handed over and embarked for another slow boat home to the UK. Too late.

I talked it over with the Colonel. No, it wasn't a compassionate reason for flying home. But if I could wangle a flight with the Air Traffic Transport Officer (ATTO), he would let me leave before the Regiment. I did it simply by looking sad and saying I had to get home for my wedding. Well, it is the best man's wedding, too. He got me onto a bumpy Dakota to Singapore, where I showed my CO's orders for five weeks of accumulated leave to the ATTO there and, when he started muttering about it being irregular, I gave him the same line, "But it's for my wedding." I was booked on a BOAC Comet carrying officers and NCOs' wives and children home after Christmas and New Year visits. A concession allowed because the war was still being fought from there against the Malay terrorists. Four days to wait.

I spent Hogmanay 1956 in the marble-floored, wood-panelled baronial hall of the Garrison Mess, deserted as the usual inmates joined the festivities at friends' homes. Myself at one end, two toffee-nosed Hussar officers at the other end, on duty next day. At five minutes to midnight, they both yawned and went to bed, leaving me, a Scot, to welcome the New Year with only myself and a glass of whisky for company. That was certainly my most unforgettable Ne'erday until the one after my accident.

So I came home to my brother's wedding, my mum and dad, Barnard Castle and Meg.

CHAPTER TWELVE

Marriages Are Made On The Backs Of Motor Bikes

Marriages are not made in heaven. They are made in dance halls. The sedate St Bernard's of the Palais de Danse may have become the groovy Funky Chicken of Rippers All-Night Rave disco; the diluted orange squash may have been transmuted to a Harvey Wallbanger; the formal to the informal. But the principle remains the same.

Crowd near equal numbers of the opposing sexes together in any suitable hot and sound-proof container in as close a proximity as current conventions allow, add the music of the time and, by the laws of nature, sooner or later, two of them will stick together. They then stick together as often as possible: in backs of cars; on motorbikes if they are Hell's Angels; in draughty closes; behind or in garden huts; on uncomfortable couches; on floors of communal flats; and especially in cemeteries after all-night discos and too many Harvey Wallbangers. Since any of this too closely resembles the behaviour of the naked ape, and our own animal ancestry, civilisation then demands the union be matrimony so that they can stick together as they please.

My own marriage was made by my sister at a Masonic dance and on the back of a BSA 500 motorbike.

I had come from Hong Kong to the boredom of UK soldiering at Barford Camp, Barnard Castle, Co. Durham, of which there is no greater armpit of humanity. Have you ever tried to whoop it up without a local overseas allowance on a wet Saturday night in Darlington? Or find a decent meal on a Sunday drive to Sunderland? The nearest sinful city was Newcastle. After the magnificent borscht, a meal in itself, of Tschechenkov's Russian restaurant off Nathan Road in Kowloon, the soggy chicken curry of the Golden Bamboo seemed not only pedestrian but downright unappetising; the local girls of the Roxy dance hall, with fat legs quick-stepping beneath their dirndl skirts were about as attractive as a wet dishcloth after the flashing thighs of the Golden World. You haven't lived until a Geordie girl says "Wait" and spits out her chewing gum before she kisses you; when she smells of Woolworths and tastes of cod and chips.

Good hearted girls, down-to-earth, with a great sense of humour (and don't they need it), but as romantic as the Tyne Bridge. "If you've finished pawing me, I'll give you a medal for effort." Dampening, especially with the rain dripping down your neck from the broken gutter above her back door.

The only alternative for a young officer of the 14th Field was a hunt ball, dressed up like a dog's dinner, making advances to a toothy debutante in the conservatory, to be told "If you're finished pawing me, I'll give you a medal for effort." Honestly, only the accents were different. And the fat legs were hidden by ball gowns.

Colonel H encouraged us to go to hunt balls, for he had come into his own with the home posting. He was a frustrated country squire. He bought a nearby country mansion from which he could hunt, shoot and fish. He insisted on all his young officers learning to blast pigeons with 12-bores at dusk from the edge of his "copse", recently acquired, which looked like a tired half dozen or so overgrown Christmas trees to me.

He insisted that as "The 14th" was right of the line – the most senior field regiment after The Royal Horse Artillery – we should behave more as such. So stringent new rules of dress were introduced which included wearing "stable belts" to hold up our uniform trousers when we were on maintenance parade with our horse-powered vehicles. He wanted us all to buy more expensive Mess kits with fancy trimmings for Regimental dinners and hunt balls. But the final blow was when he actually stabled four horses next to the gun-towing vehicles shed and announced all officers would learn to ride.

The only horses with which I had ever been acquainted were the Clydesdales that pulled the Co-operative milk. For two reasons. First, on school holidays, if you got up early enough to meet the cart at the stables at 6 am, the milkman would let you ride on the cart and drive the horse, shouting "Giddyup" and "Whoa" just like Roy Rogers, and doing no harm to the horse which knew the route better than the milkman. He might change rounds, but the horse didn't. Second, when any horse passed the house, I was despatched with a shovel to fetch that which it might leave behind for the benefit of my dad's vegetable patch. You had to be careful not to cross the invisible boundaries that marked the divisions between keen gardeners. It was only "yours" if it dropped on "your bit" of the street.

So I refused to enrol in the Colonel's schooling sessions on the lawn outside the Mess, which was now to be referred to as the "paddock". Especially when I learned it would mean a contribution to the upkeep of the hunters on my Mess bill. I was damned if I was going to pay for the Colonel's pretensions. This placed me low on the invitation list to local Colonel-approved social functions, which did not displease me as much as I let him think it did!

But the combination of Geordie girls, toothy debs, home Army bumph and boredom and the Colonel's Hussars did drive me home rather more often than you might have expected from my past relationships there. It was only 200-odd miles away.

So I met Meg. Or rather my sister Betty arranged for me to meet Meg. Betty and Bobby were building a business in Hamilton, on the posh country side of the Clyde from the steel mills of Motherwell. It was a blind date.

"She's a nice girl," said Betty. "Her father has a good business. Her mother's a friend. She's good looking. But she needs a partner to go to the Masonic Ball with them." Her steady boyfriend was engaged elsewhere. Escort duty again! Never mind – as long as she didn't chew gum or have buckteeth, I could stand being a stand-in. She might just be in the acceptable category. Besides which, her breeding and background met with my mother's approval rather more than some of the old flames I had been looking up.

I did, however, partake of a mite too much Dutch courage to face the frolics of the night and arrived late at the ball with a companion of my brother-in-law's, which met with no-one's approval, not least Meg's parents who thereafter never saw me in quite the same light as my sister's glowing testimonial. But Meg tells me that she liked what she saw. And my sister had done her justice. There is a rather curious custom at Masonic balls where all the couples get up to dance, the brothers wearing their aprons and the women all the paraphernalia of the sister crafts. I come from a long line of Masons and my brothers followed my father which I did not. The rebel in me again. So when all the lights went out and the Grand Master called out in the darkness "Brothers, do your duty," I hadn't a clue what secret handshakes, breast baring, Lodge salute or other rite might be required.

"I think you're supposed to kiss me," Meg whispered. So I did. I suspect to this day she invented a new Masonic rite on the spot. But she was no fool, for it launched another branch of the Anderson family. That was 25 years ago. "No, it was twenty-four, dear," she says, hovering over my shoulder again, knowing I am putting our marriage down on paper for all to see – and why should she change her habit of contradicting me in public?

I courted her from the back of Gunner G's motorbike, giving him 48-hour and 24-hour passes to visit his home on the Royal Estate of Balmoral while he dropped me off and picked me up at Hamilton en-route. I went through three pairs of Army boots, worn through at the welts from contact with the road between Barnard Castle and Hamilton as Gunner G leaned the bike right over into the corners to compensate for my weight on the back.

When 24 new gun tractors had to be collected from a Paisley Ordnance Depot, I took a detour and parked them there outside Meg's home – all 24 five-ton, sixteen-wheeled, eight-gear monsters of them. The men enjoyed their cafe break. I got half an hour with Meg and the Strathclyde Constabulary eventually sorted out the traffic jam.

In some ways, it was a curious courtship, in two vastly different worlds. One weekend I would be in Hamilton, pursuing the courting rites of the working-class past – necking in the back balcony of the Odeon and Sunday tea with her parents and family, when her dad would signal I'd overstayed my welcome by yawning, taking off his jacket and shirt collar and rolling up his sleeves. Or, when I was taking too long to say goodnight in the alcove of the front door, he would rattle the key noisily and ask "What are you two doing out there? High time he was away home." What did he think we were doing? Playing Scrabble®?

The next weekend, Meg would be in Barnard Castle, for all the social splendour of a Regimental ball; whirling through the night in Hartnell gowns to oysters and pink champagne for breakfast.

At the biggest ball of the season, one of the Battery Commanders, Major P, was on leave with his wife and offered his house in the married quarters as a temporary maidens' dormitory for the eligible girls who came from all over the country to grace the young officers' arms. (Including chorus girls from the high-kicking line of the London Palladium.)

I took advantage of the Major's hospitality for Meg and that evening we fell for each other. I thereafter proposed to her on the top deck of a double-decker bus carrying us through gloomy dirty Glasgow to do our Christmas shopping by saying "Well, we might as well buy the engagement ring, too." From heady passion among the highest in the land to the prosaic proposal of the lowest. I did tell you it was an unusual courtship. But it was a lovely wedding.

I dare say Meg might have been happier in the end marrying the dull, respectable church organist I stood in for at the Masonic Ball. But she was never able to say that life with Bill Anderson was dull.

CHAPTER THIRTEEN

Who The Hell Is The HON Man?

As I walked slowly forward into the cage, the animal trainer retreated behind me until I was alone, facing the Bengal tiger. This was the beast that had mauled a woman's arm when she had strayed too close to the cage a few days before.

The public wanted Simba shot. I was there to prove she wasn't a man-eater. I raised the whip. "Up, Simba, up!" She jumped onto her pedestal. I took another two paces forward. She snarled. I was so close I could smell her breath. Phew! Like a cannibal with halitosis. I knew, for I had been face-to-face with a cannibal, too.

Simba's paw reached out to flick at me. She didn't like the fool-hardy stranger. She rose on her hind legs and roared, both paws flailing the air. I could feel them ripping through my flesh. I'd made my point. Let's get out of here!

As I left the cage, the circus hands and artistes, who had gathered to watch my heroics, burst into spontaneous applause. For the rows of seats were empty. This was a special morning performance. Just me and Simba.

It was only when I left the cage, I realised the enormity of what I'd done. As the trainer, Charlie Kerr, and Billy Smart's ringmaster, Norman Delborg, crowded round to congratulate me, I sank to my knees, shaking like a leaf. I'd maybe saved Simba's life. But I could have lost my own. Never let Prince Philip say I haven't done my bit for World Wildlife. While he was banging away at grouse, I was saving tigers.

Charlie Kerr, though billed with some exotic name, was a small, balding unremarkable Glaswegian. It was only when he came closer I saw his head was covered with crisscross scars. One of the highlights of his act was letting Simba jump from one pedestal to another, while he stood directly under her flight path. "Sometimes she's a little lazy and lets one paw trail," he said, in explanation of the scars. I fainted again. Norman brought me round. Dear Norman, the archetypal ringmaster who had become my friend during the seven years I had done some stunt or other with the annual Christmas circus at Kelvin Hall. I had tried to ride bucking mules, been a clown, and dear knows what. I had all but wet myself as a knife-thrower's target and brought up my breakfast after a spot of "the daring young man on the flying trapeze", suitably wired for safety. Norman arranged it all – a circus man from his top hat to his tails. His own daughter fell from a high wire in Manchester, broke her back and was paralysed. That night Norman had smiled brightly through the performance before dashing to her side. There was no-one who could replace him. The circus must go on.

Those were crazy years, the seven when I was *The Sunday Post* go-anywhere-do-anything journalist. I sought a fresh challenge every week to titillate the readers of my page. I was a pioneer of the have-a-go journalism that would later also make such good television for people like Peter Purves of *Blue Peter* and reach its craziest heights in *Game for a Laugh*. But "The HON Man" was the original.

Many readers thought that byline hid an eccentric young nobleman who did daft things for kicks. Would that it were so. He was a struggling young journalist doing it for next to nothing to keep a roof over the head of his pregnant wife. The title was an abbreviation for "The Holiday-On-Nothing Man", which was the idea from which it sprang.

My short service commission had come to an end at Barnard Castle. I had passed the vital promotion exam which was the first step to field rank. Colonel H tried to bribe me to stay on – I was a good officer, for all my social failings – by offering me an early recommendation for Staff College, which would have accelerated my Army career like a rocket. But I had become disillusioned with peace-time soldiering. And I wanted to write. Even in Hong Kong

I had been freelancing on the side, from humorous short stories to blank verse for the *Hong Kong Standard*.

I was also being pulled back to Scotland and Meg. So as my commission ran out, I started scanning the Sits Vac again. The good old *Glasgow Herald* turned up trumps, just as it had done at a previous crossroads. "Young man of sound education wanted for training as newspaper reporter, Box 127."

It was another of the discreet ads with which DC Thomson have attracted young people from all walks of life to become part of that amazing publishing empire. After interviews, they made me an offer I could easily have refused. A miserly £7 a week to start in the Glasgow office of *The Sunday Post*. Two things persuaded me to accept. First, I would be paid by Her Majesty for eleven weeks accumulated and terminal leave. The combined pays would give me time to find my feet out of the Army. Second, I had read *The Sunday Post* since boyhood. It was *the* paper in Scotland. What a ploy if I could end up as Editor ...

Three things persuaded me to stay with DC Thomson. I was a natural. I got an unprecedented £2 a week increase after six months. And, at the end of my first year, I got another £2 raise and a private letter from the managing director, Brian Thomson, enclosing a cheque for £47 Variable Bonus (VB). VB was the mysterious system by which Thomson's attempted to hold on to its better talents. Some people had laboured hard for 30 years in Glasgow and never got on this gravy train. Some stuck on VB and never reached the exalted rank of Special Variable Bonus (SVB). I had cracked the system in 12 short months. But it was an iniquitous way of paying people. There seemed no sense to the calculation of the sum you received, which made one suspect it was an arbitrary whim, though, knowing the firm, I have no doubt it was calculated to the last penny. It could seem unfair in its selection of the fortunate few. As inflation raged, it ceased to be a bonus but became deferred salary, which led to a trail of the VB brigade going to their bank managers to arrange annual overdrafts to cover the gap between their monthly salary and the alleged annual income only achievable when VB had been paid in a lump sum. There was no way to budget since you never knew what it would be. Only that it had never been known to be less than the previous year and that, in accordance with Thomson's entire philosophy on pay, it would always be a little more than you'd feared but a lot less than you'd hoped or had good reason to expect. It was a system I sought tirelessly to change, with only moderate success. It was too effective as a carrot for the donkey!

On the strength of my first VB, Meg and I wed in December 1957. We honeymooned in Peebles Hydro in "one double room, containing one double bed, with adjoining private bathroom, at a charge of 39/- per person per day and 15/- per day for the private bathroom" as their letter so coyly confirmed my request! It doesn't sound a lot now, but it was really splashing out then.

To hell with expense, give the cat the canary. I still had what was left of my £400 Army gratuity. I had even splashed out on a 1936 Austin 12, with a leaking "sunshine" roof and wire spoke wheels that were subject to sudden puncture.

We used it for the honeymoon, leaving the reception late to drive to Peebles from Hamilton. It conked out in the middle of the desolate moors south of Lanark. We were still there at midnight, with a blizzard blowing. I had found the cause of the engine failure: a congealed kipper tied on the cylinder head, shorting the plugs, and a tattie choking the exhaust. My family have a perverted sense of humour. But no sooner had I got going again, than the offside rear punctured. It was always the most likely. It was then I had to confess to Meg that the spare was still flat from the last puncture.

There we sat on our honeymoon night, in a blizzard in the middle of nowhere. Me, cold, wet and freezing from my battle outside with the elements of engine, tyre and weather. The rear suspension was up on the jack. Meg, her going-away suit buried in all the clothing I could wrap round her, her tiny feet overwhelmed by an old pair of her mother's boots. Only her nose stuck out of the igloo, and it was quivering – I hoped with cold, otherwise it was an ominous sign. I gave her the small umbrella we always carried for her to put up inside, for the melting snow was now dripping in from the sunshine roof. It was too much. She's sobbing, I thought. On our honeymoon. Not her. She was shaking with laughter. The maelstrom of marriage to Bill Anderson had begun as it went on. If she wasn't laughing, she was crying!

Thank God for the friendly inebriated farmer. He was so delighted by a new story about a honeymoon couple, he couldn't do enough. He went to the nearest village, called out a breakdown truck, which came and fixed the puncture on the spare. Then they waved us on our way – two hours late for the arrival of the old banger with a couple of dishevelled travellers at Scotland's snootiest hotel. Peebles Hydro was where the county set fled for Christmas away from Santa Claus, family and friends. The second day of our marriage got off to a cracking start, too. Having slept so late, we missed breakfast and then had to run the gauntlet of knowing leers to take the car to the village to have the puncture fixed on the tyre that was now the spare.

She wouldn't start. By now our arrival had got around. A row of arthritic old countesses, gouty old colonels, retired somethings-in-the-cities and other weak-chinned or saggy-bosomed celebrities lined up at the glass verandah lounge window to watch my bride of 19 hours pushing our car down the sloping, winding drive, with me inside trying to persuade her to start. When she did, I didn't dare stop and left my newlywed wife standing there, stranded halfway down the drive, with her audience giggling and snorting behind politely raised hands.

We got our revenge that night in the ballroom where a specially hired seven-piece orchestra played to an empty floor. They were too old, gouty, and arthritic or inhibited to risk a public display of their afflictions. Meg and I could cut a mean fish tail in the quick-step and our reverse blocked turn in the samba was a work of art. We danced all night – just the two of us – until the last waltz when even the grateful orchestra stood up and applauded.

On the fourth morning, I was up early and down to Reception before anyone else was about. "Just thought I'd check my bill in case I need to arrange further funds," I told the receptionist. She knew, and sympathised with my ashen face when I saw what meals and extras were piling up. We hurried home from our five-day honeymoon next morning – to our two-room and kitchen, three floors up in a teetering tenement at 32 High Patrick Street, Hamilton.

It had cost me £25 in key money, the infamous bribe handed in a plain brown envelope to the factor – a blackmail of homeless couples that, for all I know, continues to this day, illegal though it is supposed to be.

The rent was £2 16s 10d a month, payable on the 15th, with ten bob a year in advance for the stair light. When the kitchenette window fell out and dropped three floors, dead from dry and damp rot, I consulted the small print in the rent book.

"Any risks of the subjects being in verminous or fungal condition are taken by the tenant who is also responsible for the cost of clearing chokage of all sinks, baths and water closets." Charming!

My total assets were £15 4s 2d with the Bank of Scotland and an income of £11 a week plus VB. Meg earned almost about the same as a telephonist. From here on, it could only be up.

I went back to Port Dundas and the wacky world of the HON Man.

It all started in a Dundee tearoom where my predecessor – John Martin to a few, Mr Martin to the typists and JBM to everyone else – was, as usual, fussing over his diet with a lightly poached egg on toast when the conversation turned to holidays which the harassed waitress obviously overheard. For, looking at JBM's tanner tip, she said "You can't have a holiday on nothing, you know." JBM did not increase the tip. He just said "That's a good idea," and the HON Man was born.

As the HON Man, I travelled twice round the world filling nearly 400 pages with thrills and spills.

In search of stories, I was marooned on a remote island; sawn in half; modelled for Madame Tussaud's; marched with Dr Barbara Moore; was "banged up" in every prison in Scotland; sang with Kenneth McKellar; made a pop record with Mecca (which didn't reach the bottom hundred); had a film test for a Petula Clark movie;

boxed Dick McTaggart; played the rear end of a panto horse; busked in Piccadilly; slaved as a night-shift dustbin man; failed selection as a fighter pilot; joined the Scots Guards; burned £1 million; broke my arm as a stuntman; set up a hitchhiking record from Land's End to John O' Groats; got my eye blackened as a Gorbals rent collector; knocker-uppered Oldham; had my portrait painted; auditioned for BBC news reader; hunted TV pirates; jumped into the Libyan Desert with the paratroopers; writhed with pain as a "bed extra" in *Emergency Ward 10*; delivered a lamb in a blizzard; searched for the Loch Ness Monster; had afternoon tea with a condemned killer; and pawned my medals. I had dinner with the Duke of Argyll in Inveraray Castle one night, and next morning, thanks to the BBC make-up and wardrobe department, squatted in dirty disguise as a pavement artist in Exchange Square, Glasgow, with my begging bunnet in front of some hastily scrawled Picassos, the poster colour paint running with the rain.

An admirer of Wilkie Collins, part of my modus operandi was to find the most terribly strange bed I could on any of my adventures. I slept under the statue of Karl Marx in Highgate Cemetery; in a hobo's flea-ridden hostel; in a tent on top of Ben Nevis; in the White House in the four-poster of President Eisenhower's butler; in a cage at the zoo; in the dormitory of an approved school; in a Soho down-and-outs' dosshouse; in barns; under hedges; in a Fifth Avenue penthouse; on a hammock slung between two Malayan rubber trees.

Including the strangest bed of all which came my way on my first trip which took me all the way round the Scottish coast on one of those tiny Lambretta scooters which were all the rage (and which I even succeeded in taking halfway up Ben Nevis). I can identify the village no more than to say it was a typical Highland coastal village, with one small hotel, a few scattered houses and a Post Office-cum-general store, with a lone petrol pump and a summer sideline in bed and breakfasts. If you've seen one, you've seen them all. But this one was wholly owned and run by a family of two sisters and one brother. Another sister was at university and,

I believe, more of them were scattered round the globe, as tends to happen with Highland families.

Anyway, I booked in for bed and breakfast and was promptly invited to a Highland wedding. You haven't lived until you have been to one of those three-day Bacchanalias. If you ever see a mountain of empty half-bottles of whisky outside a Highland village hall, you will know there has been a wedding.

I enjoyed every drunken, hooching, hootenanny moment of it, to return to the B&B with the two sisters, both of whom I shall describe gallantly as mature spinster ladies. I had no sooner fallen into bed when there was a quiet knock on the door and the younger of the two entered in her voluminous nightie. Was this a further gesture of the true nature of Highland hospitality? She took some persuading to return to her own room to go to sleep and leave me to mine. As she left quietly, so as not to arouse the household, I turned over to contemplate the passion that can beat in the most unsuspected breast. It seemed that I had no sooner done so than there was another quiet knock and the elder sister entered in even more billowing negligee and ampler evidence that anything her sister had, she had more of and knew more about its many uses.

I managed to prevail upon her to retreat, and she, in turn, in her brushed nylon tent, departed. I lay there, wondering if every passing male stranger between the age of 16 and 76 enjoyed the offer of such home comforts; or was it only the normal post nuptial rites of a Highland mating. At which there was another quiet knock at the door. Don't tell me – the youngest sister had caught an express train home from university – not tonight, Mhairi, no way. But it was not her, it was the brother! Not the angry knock of a man about to defend his sisters' honour, either. "Are you asleep?" he asked quietly. I started snoring, very loudly. He had to be joking! Just in case, when he'd gone, I jammed the chair under the door handle, slept only fitfully and was up and away before either the nymphomaniacal sisters or curious brother were awake. To think they led the village to church every Sunday in flowery bonnets and bowler hat.

That story did not reach my family readership. But the others did. I tried out the oddest occupations: Onion Johnny; ballet dancer; Sotheby's auctioneer; barrow boy; Indian pedlar selling bootlaces and lucky charms; cinema usher; advance manager for The Beatles; private detective, fishmonger; coalman; chimney sweep; high building bill-poster; maternity ward orderly; flower-seller; commis cook in The Savoy; tattie howker; debt collector; lay preacher; salmon poacher; school truant officer; school meals disher-upper; Savile Row tailor's dummy; and sheep shearer. You name it, I did it.

I travelled the world in every form of transport too. An outboard-rigged canoe took me deep into the hinterland of Thailand to the "Temple of the Storks" at Wat Phai Lom, to see the same storks that emigrate to the roofs of Dutch villages. A thing of beauty on a birth congratulations card, these storks, en masse, were the dirtiest, noisiest, greediest birds in the world. I was more intrigued by the ancient Buddhist monk at the temple who knew every Burns poem by heart and could recite them in an extraordinary oriental English with a Scots burr. Some wandering Scot in the late 19th century had left a "complete works" in gratitude for the monks treating his wounds. The sage had made a life's study of the volume as a "devotion".

I travelled on the first KLM trans-polar passenger flight from Amsterdam to Tokyo (after they had devised a system of navigation for the crazy gyration of compasses flying over the Pole). I was on the first post-war passenger train allowing tourists into Russia – to find myself accompanied all the way from the Hook of Holland to Moscow by a certain Russian Colonel F, who just happened to be on leave from his job as "a military attaché" at the Hague. The first thing he did was steal the list of useful Moscow telephone numbers I had acquired (since there were no telephone directories available to any such as myself who entered the Kremlin's ken). By scooter, motorbike, horse, camel, omnibus, taxi, rickshaw, mule, yak, boat, plane, train, ambulance, Rolls Royce, bicycle or on foot, it was all the same to me as long as I got the story.

I needed so many visas that I ran through passports like weekly season tickets for the train, and soon had to get rabies, yellow fever, cholera, tetanus or whatever injections in my backside because my arms would take no more. It is easier to tell you that, wherever you put your finger on a globe of the world, chances are I've been there. The only large countries that haven't known my size nines are Australia and New Zealand and that's only because I couldn't fit them in. I once went through all the rigmarole of emigrating to Australia (without revealing my real reason) to see what it was like but had to get off the ship at Naples to fly back to file for my deadline. Next day I was on an American nuclear submarine in the Holy Loch.

I stood in the cemetery on the edge of the Burmese jungle where row after row of white crosses marked the graves of those who died on the infamous Death Railway from Thailand to Burma.

I shared a meal of sparrow breast and rice with Japanese coal miners, on the Tokaido Express taking them to Tokyo where, in those unmistakable yellow helmets and sloganed sleeveless waistcoats, they would hold their annual demonstration.

I haggled with the thief of Baghdad in his Aladdin's cave of silver in the souk. I drank bathtub gin in an Aramco (then, the Arabian-American Oil Company) oil village in Saudi Arabia where it was a race between the American and Arab fire brigades when an illegal still blew up. If the Americans didn't win, someone had to take a flogging.

Really, there was no end to it. It made me the most famous unknown man in the world. Poor Meg. For seven years she never knew whether I was coming or going. Every departure a heartbreak. Every return another honeymoon.

Ewan Colvin was born between me being a knife-thrower's target in the circus and setting up my stall as a flower-seller outside the gates of the Southern General Hospital where every bunch bought another story of suffering or courage.

We moved to a bigger three rooms and kitchen, still in High Patrick Street, between me taking the Road to the Isles for a four-week hiking series and going to London to have my features cast in wax so I might hide behind a curtain and overhear what visitors might say of the HON Man standing in the Royal tableaux.

Graeme Alexander squeezed in between a nine-week epic on Russia and a quick dash to the 1960 Olympics.

I was working so hard for all our futures. It was no picnic. On a three-week trip to New York, I lost over a stone in weight, rushing to cram in a packed schedule of assignments from lift operator in the Empire State Building to exclusive interviews with Jack Dempsey, Helena Rubenstein and Perry Como – all on hamburgers, coffee and three hours sleep a night (to help me cope with the time difference).

It seemed to be worth it. I now had an equally ancient, but lovable 1939 Lea Francis shooting brake. Between my emigrating to Naples and playing against the Harlem Globe Trotters and just before a fortnight's monster vigil in a tent on the shores of Loch Ness, we moved to 19 Melville Gardens, Bishopbriggs.

This was it. The middle class at last! A detached Wimpey villa on an exclusive corner site, with garage, in a typical exclusive estate in a typical commuter suburb. And, when I was home, we entertained with wine on the table or dressed up to go to dinner dances with our dressed-up neighbours. Yes, we were definitely rising in the world. On a £3000 mortgage! That was in 1961. The house which we left in 1962 sold this year for £30,000. My bank balance showed the truth. After four years hard slog, three homes, two children, two cars and various dinner dances, I had exactly £74 16s 8d in the friendly bank manager's cupboard – not much for risking life and limb. I did have a good life insurance policy, though, thanks to a persistent man from "the Pru".

Alan William burst onto the scene in the upstairs bedroom of 19 Melville Gardens. It was the first home fit for childbirth and Meg insisted. I worried myself sick about it. When the district nurse had been up there for two hours, and not the faintest cry to complete the Hollywood picture of the pacing father halting in mid-stride to hear it, I could contain myself no longer and dashed upstairs to see what was happening. Nothing! The pair of them were sitting having a cup of Aunt Peggy's tea – and a cigarette! Alan's undramatic arrival marked the close of another chapter.

I was summoned to a typically secret meeting with JBM in the neutral, security-screened lounge of the Station Hotel in Perth. He had heard I had been "tapped" by John Junor of *The Sunday Express*, which I had, and also by the Mirror Group for a regrouping of the editorial staff of their *Scottish Sunday Mail*, which he didn't know, but I told him.

How would I like to come to head office, just for a week or two? Yes, there would be more money. Maybe as much as £5 a week more! They'd see if my face fitted. Then the clincher. He was thinking of retiring. If it worked out, I could consider myself as being groomed for the job.

Only seven years, well nearly eight, in the business and I was being offered the most almighty chair at the most almighty desk – "Admiral of the flagship of the fleet" as *The Sunday Times* once called me – in the most almighty publishing house in Scotland, if not the UK.

The dream was within my grasp. The week or so stretched to six months in which I was measured up and found to give due value for money. I was told to cancel my room in a Dundee hotel, from which I had commuted home at weekends, and bring Meg up to choose an appropriate house in Dundee which the firm would buy for me as I could never afford the style of dignified Victorian establishment expected of a future editor of a reputable family newspaper.

I traded in the Lea Francis for the £220 second-hand Commer van we used to cheapen our move. I flitted up and down until the five of us moved into the dignified respectable Victorian edifice known as "Fairvale", 1 Muirfield Street, Dundee, where the overworked van gave up the ghost and stayed rusting in the dignified, respectable side drive until I sold it to an itinerant scrap dealer for a tenner.

But we had arrived. From now on it could only be fame and fortune. Or so we thought. In reality, it was only to make me yet another desk-bound executive with high blood pressure, more credit than income, and my success as ephemeral as the circulation figure for the previous week's *Morning Special*.

CHAPTER FOURTEEN

The Best-Read Newspaper In The World

A favourite story of mine is of the six Fleet Street editors who locked themselves in a room, along with a year's copies of *The Sunday Post*, vowing not to leave it until they had analysed the secrets of its success.

Of its success, there was no doubt. No other newspaper in the world had achieved its unique penetration of its circulation area. More than a million copies were being sold every week in Scotland alone, to be read by 70 per cent of the population over the age of 14. By way of comparison a mass circulation popular Sunday paper was delighted with a penetration of 30 to 35 per cent of its circulation area. That was discounting *The Post*'s growing circulation spreading steadily south, plus an overseas circulation in America and Canada especially, where there was a queue outside Smokey Pete's delicatessen in Toronto every Sunday morning for the air-mailed edition.

Little wonder Fleet Street wanted to know the secrets of its amazing appeal and truly remarkable hold on the minds and hearts of a nation. And I could have told them, but I don't want to spoil my story.

The six read and read, on a diet of coffees and pizzas. A week later they stumbled out, unshaven and red-eyed, and their spokesman made a statement.

"No, we haven't found the secret," he said. "But we have reached unanimous agreement about *The Sunday Post*. It's such a damned good read we're all going off to place a regular order with our newsagents."

This then was the responsibility I shouldered after the 30-year term of my predecessor, John Martin. Officially, I took over when he left in December 1968. Unofficially, I had known for a year that it was to be so. I was supposed to be in "double harness" with JBM until he slowly eased out, leaving me to take the strain when I was ready for it. It didn't work out that way, for JBM was a "street saint and office devil". A smiling, charming, old white-haired Christian gentleman to those outside, an impossible, demanding, ruthless tyrant inside. A bit like myself in fact. So it was a trying year until the old bull realised the young bull did not take kindly to being yoked to him and departed. I had a great respect for him as Editor. He had a truly remarkable feel for what was right for *The Sunday Post* but could never make up his mind until he saw it in front of him. He'd no sooner gone than I realised why. It is not what goes into *The Post* that makes it. Like John, I knew that material as soon as I saw it. No, it is what is left out that's the key. The Editor has to be a man who can say "No" again and again and again. This does not make for understanding or popularity with your staff. It does make sure every line in the paper fits the well-tried formula!

Thomson-Leng, the alliance of two business families in Dundee, had a ragbag of interests, from shipping to printing. David Coupar Thomson, who gives his name to the present company DC Thomson & Co Ltd, set out to save the printing firm when it got into difficulties by improving the popular appeal of its publications, like *The People's Friend* and *The Scots Magazine*. There had been a Saturday Sports paper, part of which exists today as *The Dundee Evening Telegraph and Post*, and from that sprang a curious hybrid called *The Post Sunday Special*, which first saw the light of day on 4th October 1914.

By then the struggling printing firm had become Thomson-Leng Publications Ltd, for DCT, as well as being an impossible autocrat, had an uncanny gift for the kind of journalism which appeals to the sentimental and traditional in every Scot – the kailyard formula which is the backbone of Thomson periodicals to this day. Keep it simple and aimed at subjects close to people's hearts. Keep it Scottish. Keep it sincere. Keep it sympathetic. Keep it surprising.

The formula had already proved successful enough to let Thomson-Leng spread to Glasgow, where a Buchanan Street office opened in 1891, as well as a printing works in West Nile Street. In 1906 the Port Dundas plant was built and, like Topsy, the company just "growed and growed".

The Port Dundas plant carried a major share of the production of *The Post Sunday Special* which, on 19th January, 1919, became *The Sunday Post* – the newspaper which has come to inspire such devotion that some folk have been reading it longer than it has existed. Never a week goes by but there's a letter from some oldster to say, "What a marvellous paper. I'm 87 and I've been reading it since I went to school."

The two World Wars helped to make *The Sunday Post* what it is. For its very Scottishness was a breath of home to men at the Front. Its gossipy stories about folk they all knew were a precious link to what men thought they were fighting for. That and the fact that, despite war, strike and pestilence, the Thomsons have always had a happy knack of being able to acquire the newsprint which is the lifeblood of periodical publishers. There were secret reserves (and interests in paper companies) to ensure that nothing stopped the Thomson presses, even on such high days and holidays as Christmas or New Year. *The Post* came round every week as inevitably and reliably as Sunday itself.

Hand in hand with this emerged the most telling DCT dictum of all: "Never lose a reader and the sale will look after itself." Thus the reliable and readable spread steadily, not by promotional advertising, but by the best ad of all – word of mouth. Better one reader you kept for a lifetime than a hundred readers you lost when the advertising stopped. Until the late 1970s the budget for advertising the best-read paper in the world was less than £1000 a year!

So *The Sunday Post* emerged from the two World Wars with a nucleus of faithful readers. But there the sales stuck, until the whirlwind called William Harold Thomson set to work. He had a zest for life allied to an insatiable curiosity that kept him at his desk in the Meadowside building until he was 90 with a mind as active and creative as ever. His body wore out long before his brain.

He was the inquisitive boy who always wants to know everything and won't be fobbed off until he has an answer. In the same breath WHT could ask "Why do so many men drop dead mowing the lawn?" and "Why do so many children turn up their noses at margarine?" That was the very essence of *Sunday Post* journalism – lateral thinking, as I called it when I was trying to modernise the formula.

He found the perfect adjutant in John Martin, my predecessor, who sat in the Editor's chair for 30 years. JBM had an almost feminine intuition for what women wanted to read. He also had a knack of interpreting what WHT knew he wanted, but couldn't quite express. While WHT flitted like a bee from flower to flower, throwing out ideas to fertilise and pollinate, JBM had the single-minded determination needed to distil those ideas into the purest of honey.

This alliance flourished after the Second World War. Their first step was to assess every line in every page of the paper. JBM had to make each piece of writing pass two WHT tests. The first was "Drama Content". Was there enough drama within the paper's articles to make each page and picture more compulsive reading, and thus make more people compulsive regular readers?

Let's see how this would apply to an article on glue sniffing. Other papers might publish a well-researched authoritative, statistical account of the increase in this social menace by a by-lined expert under a heading such as "SHOCK INCREASE IN INNER CITY GLUE SNIFFING". Not *The Sunday Post*. Lateral thinking would take me to an article under the heading "IF YOU THINK YOUR SON IS SNIFFING GLUE" or perhaps "THE BOY WHO WAS KILLED BY A TATTIE CRISP PACKET". I hope you can see the striking difference. The obvious treatment of the subject is a generality, begging the question "So what, don't we know that already?" And the answer is "Yes, and it could never happen to me." *The Sunday Post* angles strike home. Could my son be sniffing glue? What does the article say I should look for? How can a potato crisp packet kill a boy? Who was the boy? Anybody I know? Maybe a neighbour's son?

Now many newspapers will find a similar angle on occasions. But *The Sunday Post* looks for this kind of "idea", rather than "suggestion" on every occasion. Whatever the subject, look for it in personal experience or in such a way the reader can immediately identify with it. A box of chocolates can have drama content if "The Doc" tells you "IT WASN'T ON THE DEATH CERTIFICATE BUT IT KILLED HER ALL THE SAME" – a spot of lateral thinking on the dangers of being overweight! The other lesson that was learned from this is that most of the headings in the paper became compulsive, too. This was honed to the axiom that if there wasn't a good compulsive heading in an article, it didn't "measure up" for the paper:

"All Because He Bent Down To Tie His Shoelace"
"It Could Only Happen To A Golfer's Wife"
"Shocking Discovery In Dad's Wardrobe"
"Just Ask Mr Anderson What He Thinks Of Muckle Flugga"
"If Only Maisie Could Get To Australia"
"She Worries Whenever Her Son Wears Blue Socks"
"Bill Learned The Secret At A Dance In Oban"
"The Man Who Gave Up The Glitter For The Gold"
"It's Too Late For Mrs McGregor"

You want to read about these people, don't you? The art of creating a heading that makes you want to read the article was a science with *The Sunday Post*.

The second test was what WHT called "IMF" and he invented it long before the International Monetary Fund, for it stands for "Interest Motive Force".

Not only were big issues changed from the conventional type of news or semi-news story to the homely, the personal, the unexpected, the controversial or to snippets of human experience that provoked immediate and personal reaction in the reader, but there was also a realisation that for Mrs McGinty there is as much, if not more, IMF in an article that discusses a better way to peel the potatoes or a quicker way to do the washing as there is in an article on another murder in Glasgow. True, the latter may shock her, but life goes on …

The search for IMF went on in all parts of the paper. It was further reflected in the tight sub-editing that became a hallmark of the paper. For that reason, there wasn't a line that wasn't read by the Editor even to the word balloons in *Oor Wullie*; for it was just as important as the big conference of by-lined experts by which others treated the issues of the day. Each short sentence had to have IMF and carry the reader through each paragraph with enough IMF not to stop reading. No article should last longer than the IMF in it. This led quite spontaneously to another unique style of *The Post*: easy reading even on the heaviest subject. No complicated sentences which might interrupt IMF. No long paragraphs. No duplication. No needless words. And no waffle! It was sneered at by stylists and despaired of by pedants, but it worked and made every corner, every line of *The Post* do what it was supposed to do: bring the readers closer to the paper and keep them there.

Out of it grew the habit, which I carried on, of scoring the paper each week on the basis of reader appeal. Did it measure up to the formula? Every article, feature, picture, cartoon, was rated. Was it 100 per cent? 85 per cent? 55 per cent? The more high-scoring items, the better the paper, until a quick run through it, with the eye of experience, could give it an overall score. The worst I ever marked myself was 65 per cent. The best – and it was a cracker – 95 per cent. But it forced the Editor to quickly drop anything lowering the average and so keep up the consistency of the mix. That in itself was another secret of the success of *The Post*. Every week, it was above average for DC and IMF.

It also meant that as features were tried and tested they grew to become regulars, such as "The Doc Replies", "The Queries Man", "Customers' Complaints", "The Honest Truth", and "Can I Help?".

Every Monday morning there were queues at doctors' surgeries all over the country – queues which made doctors shake their heads in despair as they prepared for another onslaught of "Monday Maladies". For whatever the age, sex or infirmity of this mass of suffering humanity, they all had strikingly similar symptoms, could describe them without hesitation, tell the doctor what was wrong with them and demand the cure, which they already knew.

If you asked their GPs what was the cause of this onslaught, they would swear, stamp their feet, tear up a few prescription pads and tell you – *The Sunday Post* – or to be more exact, "The Doc".

The Doc had two places in *The Post*. One was a short article in the centre page which concentrated on a subject of general interest to anyone concerned about their health (which is everybody). This article always carried a heading specially worded to arouse the hypochondriac in all of us. I know, for as Editor, it was a heading I would trust to no-one but myself. I knew the awesome pulling power of the Doc. His every word would be read, consumed, digested and utterly believed so those who trotted off to their own doctor with Monday Malady would be greeted with the impatient question "Look, who do you believe, me or *The Sunday Post*?" A foolish question, for the Doc's word was law wherever the paper was read.

There was another page in which the Doc pioneered the newspaper fashion of diagnosis-by-post, and honed it to a fine art, answering a dozen or so of the more interesting readers' medical queries, with a brief, blunt but friendly style associated with Dr Cameron from *Dr Finlay's Casebook* – a style which the Radio Doctor picked up to become a wartime friend of the family. The implicit faith in the Doc worried me at times. Cancer sufferers, for example, will seek hope from any source even when it is hopeless. There was also a commercial concern for me. For whatever the Doc recommended, from an indigestion tablet to a kaolin poultice, would cause a rush on such products at the chemists on Monday mornings. I had to put a ban on wholesalers ringing up to find out what the Doc was going to recommend the next Sunday so they could stock their retailer's shelves in advance. I wish I exaggerated, but I do not. If he said bananas were good for you, Fyffe's shares went up. When I banned further mention of a rather old-fashioned proprietary cough syrup-cum-tonic, it was discovered old ladies were so addicted they had withdrawal symptoms when they stopped taking it. Another firm whose product he mentioned wrote to say they were grateful beyond measure; before the Doc's seal of approval, they had been on the verge of liquidation.

Medical columns have become common in most of the media. Whatever their form, they all rely on the fact that we are all, by nature, raging hypochondriacs. I am no exception. Only this week, I have had a spasm of hiatus hernia, two coronaries, suspected cancer of the bowel and a small stroke. True, the hiatus hernia was a touch too much Taylor's port at the Lord Advocate's Dinner; the two coronaries were, respectively, arm strain from digging out winter leeks, and a knot of wind from a night of mouth-breathing; the cancer was a diarrhoea bug that was doing the rounds and the stroke was only the dizzy result of rising too quickly from a chair when the Epilogue came on. But the symptoms were real. My fear did the rest. We all fear the worst, don't we? A touch of blood at the toilet and we look out the insurance policies while we rewrite our wills.

Now that men also have a midlife crisis they are allowed to worry about their health and do. But worrying about one's health is the number one obsession in every adult over the age of 16, when it starts with pimples. As a topic of conversation it is second only to the weather. "Good morning. It's a fine day. How are you?" In foreign travel, it is second only to the more urgent calls of nature. Consider that first handy translation in any phrase book. "Excuse me. Can you tell me the way to the toilet/doctor/chemist/station/hotel?" Those are the priorities in life!

Knowing that, you can take my word for it that those letters on "The Doc Replies" page were not made up, as some alleged. There was no need. Our readers could dream up far better symptoms than any sub-editor. They were shortened for brevity and polished for grammar. Otherwise each letter was the product of a very real fear.

They were also answered, despite what some alleged, by a real doctor from a real practice. It was a hereditary asset of the practice concerned. It never ceased to amaze me that the Doc, in thirty words or less could spot obscure ailments which had baffled the combined talents of our National Health Service. Ironically it was that selfsame NHS which was making such a fine job of turning us into more knowledgeable hypochondriacs, with even more obscure symptoms. Why cure a heavy cold with aspirin and two days in bed, which is what the Doc would advise, when it could be tracheatic broncho-pneumonia for which you could demand an expensive course of antibiotics and a week off work?

In this, I have to say the Doc did serve an honest and praise-worthy purpose. He reassured people, particularly the old or sick, that more often than not their worst fears were unfounded. Readers also wrote who were too shy or afraid to seek help from their own doctor (which accounted for many odd epistles from spinsters), or when they didn't think he could help or didn't understand what they'd been told. It's amazing how often a patient is confused by or mistaken about a diagnosis and advice from the medical profession.

So the letters poured in from the naive ("I'm always picking my nose. How do you stop a bad habit?") to the secret tragedies of those whose only source of help was a faceless stranger ("I let my uncle do something I shouldn't. I think I'm going to have a baby. I'm only 15. If I ask my doctor for something to get rid of it, would he have to tell the police?"). I hasten to add I chose not to publish the latter but had some private advice sent to the girl, for I had a personal rule that the paper did not breach a confidence that could land the writer in trouble. But "The Doc Replies" page also provided many funny moments, mostly from the letters that, for one reason or another, could not be published, and authentic every one:

- Should people taking iron tablets have an electric blanket on their bed? Mrs D.
- Could you please explain why I did not bleed when I first had intercourse? I was led to believe all virgins did. Is there some-thing wrong with me? Mrs M.

- Sir, you are a gentleman and a scholar. After your piece about piles, I already feel a different person. May you live long and die a good colour. Mr F.
- I saw my doctor during an attack of asthma. He told me of a new treatment involving pushing something up my passage. He did not explain why or what it would accomplish. Miss R.
- I am hoping you could help me with a problem through your paper. I suffer from primitive ejaculation for which I have seven children. Now I am separated and awaiting divorce, I have had this complaint since I was 16 (I am now 35) and hoping you can help me. Mr T
- If I put "the pill" in my female cat's food, would it stop kittens?" Miss C.
- Every so often my heart goes racing away. It usually comes back after two or three days. "Worried".
- My wife's doctor stopped her pill because of phlebitis in the leg. We've tried the sheath and other things instead, but we don't like any of them, so I have been taking the pill instead of her, one month's supply already, so I would like to know if it is safe to carry on. JW.
- I talk like a girl. Can you get an operation or other treatment to get a stronger voice, for nothing on the NHS? Mr McC.
- Just around Christmas, my mother had a bad bout of influences. DT.
- I am at present male 57 years and have been for the last two years. K.
- Please let me know about a Hyena's Hernia as I have something stuck in my throat and the tablets have done no good. Mr L.
- My doctor told me I have Complications. What is this? Is it safe to take a brandy before I go to bed? Mrs J.
- As a contract fitter moving round the country, I get pains in the kidneys. Is it the change of water or should I switch from beer to gin and tonic? Mr F.
- I have now received my first enema. I thank you very much for looking into it for me. Mr M.

- My wife passes urine 5 or 6 times a night after a prolapse in the Samaritan Hospital. Thanking you sincerely for advice. PS should I just take a sleeping pill? Mr M.
- I went to an ear specialist and he asked about my bowels. What's the connection? Miss W.
- Can a girl lose her virginity without knowing how she lost it? Or is it only her maiden head that goes? Jean and Betty.
- Every time me and my wife have intercourse, she sneezes. Mr G.
- I am 17, male, scholar, studying for Highers in April. I enclose a rough drawing showing how big my testicles are to my penis. I hope this is nothing serious as I must pass my exams. Teen.
- I would like to know whether it is possible to have cosmetic surgery from the NHS to rectify my shortage of organ which is a constant source of embarrassment in sexual relations. Mr S.
- Can an enlarged testicle be caused by a tight cord in the pyjamas? Mr V.
- Dear sir or madam. I have been informed by my doctor I may be prostrate. I thought this was an old man's disease and I am worried because I have just lost my husband. Mrs G.
- Before I met my boyfriend he was bitten by an Alsatian and the doctor told him he couldn't produce. Does this mean that he can't do things into me or only that we won't make children. Miss S.

Funny? Perhaps. But real fears for all that and have you noticed something about the letters? There's a myth that it's women, especially those going through the change of life, who worry unnecessarily about their health. But just as many men let their imaginations run riot. The difficulty for them is they can't swap operations at the coffee morning or confess the most intimate secrets over the garden fence (or unload them on the proliferation of problem pages in women's glossy magazines). Maybe that's why so many men write to the Doc. Perhaps I would have eased more smoothly through my own midlife crisis if I'd been able to share it with a sympathetic ear or eye.

To my certain knowledge, no-one ever wrote to the Doc to say "I am male, 42. I am a paranoid schizophrenic with necrophilic tendencies and a morbid urge to slash loose women's throats." He may have phoned *The Sun* to claim he did it, even if he didn't. But no-one admits to being mad as lightly as they would to having melanoma or Crohn's disease or impotence or bleeding piles, even to an anonymous doctor in a newspaper. Being mentally ill is a taboo, despite the advances in knowledge and the acceptance of recent years. It remains the leprosy of modern society. A nervous breakdown may just be tolerated in one's family. But insanity, now that is a skeleton to be locked firmly away in a cupboard. Or in a mental hospital.

Onto those weekly features were welded series where *The Post* could not only fulfil the wider, ever-changing needs of the formula, but also experiment with ideas that could become the standing features of tomorrow. "Seven Days Hard", for example, added to give a new dimension of hope, everyday philosophy and humour, matured and evolved into one of the best holding features of the paper. "Political Round-Up" condensed yet illuminated politics for Mrs McGinty and I can assure you there were few politicians who didn't read it.

Thus, brick by brick, *The Sunday Post* evolved, deliberately kept to the lowest number of pages possible, so it never outstripped available DC or IMF. Paging was only increased when there was irrefutable evidence they fitted the latest demands of the formula.

I think I can modestly claim to have developed its width of subjects and depth of readership within the formula. Certainly *The Post* withstood far better than most the ravages of a dropping circulation from the early 1960s on, though the competition for dwindling Sunday readership is now fiercer than ever.

The paper's popularity still lies in its extraordinary appeal to the ordinary people whose lives it reflects in a unique way. It is all about people: what has happened, can, might or will happen to them; happened when they hoped it wouldn't or didn't when they hoped it would; the extraordinary that happens to the ordinary. It is about the things we all talk about and hopefully tells us something we didn't know to make us talk about it all the more.

The Sunday Post explored this seam for every new vein of gold, particularly through "invites" – teasing invitations to readers to write on a subject known to be on target:

"The Phone Call That Changed My Life"
"That Knock On The Door At Midnight"
"Why I'll Never Forget My First Holiday Abroad"
"The One Person In All the World I'd Like To Meet Again"
"The Daftest Present My Husband Ever Gave Me"
"Why This Will Be A Very Special Christmas For Me"
"The Operation That Made Me A New Woman"
"A Souvenir I'll Always Treasure"
"The Family Photograph That Tells A Remarkable Story"

The "invites" were legion, and a constant source of unmined human stories. There was no other way to bring these tales to the surface, except, perhaps, by that chance remark our young story-getters were carefully trained to listen for, or to seek out when calling on or phoning their "contacts" in everyday life, from ministers to insurance men.

The "invites" also helped strengthen our rapport with our readers for, in time, much of the content of the paper was actually provided by readers or written from material provided by them. About the people, for the people, by the people!

There were two further vital ingredients in the recipe. Ideas and staff. Ideas were and are the bloodstream of *The Sunday Post*, pumped into the veins that carry the flow from branch offices, contacts, readers, staff, anyone anywhere, to the heart of the Editor's desk, where enriched and revitalised they flow into the arteries of the paper. A Monday morning conversation about the weather between two typists in the office lift could become "Why Does It Always Rain On Sundays?" A snippet overheard at the Women's Guild was a "double" for the centre page, "How Mrs Mathers Makes The Finest Scones In Auchtermuchty". An angry mother in a bike shop could be "Danger Of The Killer Bikes". Or the same mum in a toy shop could be "The Doll With Deadly Eyes". The minister's sermon might give "The Heartbreak That Only A Mother Can Know".

I think you get the idea. Every Tuesday, ideas started flooding onto my desk as a matter of weekly routine – from our main offices in Glasgow, London, Edinburgh, Inverness, Aberdeen and branch offices in between. From the hundreds sifted and selected, I'd maybe only send a dozen back down the teleprinters for investigation.

Putting *The Sunday Post* together was a bit like painting by numbers. Each week we'd start with the 36 or 40 blank pages, not as blank as they looked, for they would be mentally code-numbered for the colours needed to produce the final picture in accordance with the the formula. As an idea came to fruition, another colour would be painted in over its number. Until, on Saturday, sport and news were wrapped round another masterpiece.

An idea was only chosen if it was the right shade. This meant training staff to our way of thinking in order for them to produce the right ideas. As a first salutary lesson, I would often give a new youngster a list of headings with an abrupt instruction to find a story to fit.

Such a list might be:

1. The Woman Who Wanted To Fly Round The World Backwards
2. She Pawned Her Wedding Ring To Pay The Rent
3. He Nailed His Thumb To The Kitchen Shelf
4. A Funny Thing Happened To Tom At The Bus Stop

When the trainee looked blank, he or she would be handed a new, blank, indexed "contact" book (for all the names, phone numbers, addresses that would eventually fill it on every subject and every occupation under the sun). They would then be pointed in the direction of the telephone boxes that filled an end of every main office of *The Sunday Post* and told to phone:

1.   Travel agents and airport airline desks
2.   Pawnbrokers and rent collectors
3.   Hospital casualty departments and do-it-yourself shops
4.   Bus depots and traffic wardens

If you match the second list with the first, you will see how, right from the start, trainees had to plunge into the deep end of the contact system, quickly learning not only to recognise a *Sunday Post* story, but how to get it. It was not unusual for a good trainee to emerge from that first session not with the stories suggested, but with four ideas transmuted into:

1.   If You Ever Lose Your Luggage At The Airport
2.   She Pawned His Best Suit To Pay The Gas Bill
3.   Everybody Wondered About The Minister's Black Eye
4.   So He Sang The 23rd Psalm On The Last Bus To Easterhouse

Again, thoughtful comparison will reveal the merits and immediate rewards of the training system. It was the reason why DC Thomson preferred to take trainees off the street, with no preconceived ideas. It was also an underlying reason for their stand against trade unions, who would have been against this kind of recruiting. DCT also set their face against the sausage-factory products of The National Council for Training of Journalists, who may well have known shorthand, typed with all ten fingers at 60 wpm and been well up in the Town House rules for court reporting, newspaper law and interviewing the Prime Minister, but who were so stereotyped as reporters, they couldn't recognise a *Sunday Post* story in a conversation between two typists in the office lift. You can hand a trainee the tools of the trade, but it's no use if he wants to build St Paul's Cathedral when you want a set of kitchen shelves!

The proof of this pudding is that Thomson training was recognised as the best in the newspaper industry, that same industry whose unions wanted to stop it! An ex-DCT journalist was a valuable asset with an open sesame to any branch of the media.

I can best illustrate this by listing the former occupations of the trainees I took on personally to form a newer, younger team after I sat in the Editor's chair. They were to make their names with *The Sunday Post* or go on to become award-winning and otherwise respected journalists elsewhere: school teacher, carpet factory production controller, tax clerk, office supplies salesman, MA in sociology, Electricity Board clerk, library assistant, art student, insurance secretary, clerk at a college of education and technician with a tarmacadam firm.

I found one of the best of these trainees in a kilt as the "front-of-house" manager for the Pitlochry Festival Theatre.

All were turned, not into reporters, but *Sunday Post* men or women capable of doing any task the paper demanded, from Tuesday ideas to stone-subbing a Saturday news page – in short, they were all-round journalists.

That DC Thomson only paid them as trainees when they were helping to fill the paper from their first day was the price they had to pay for their apprenticeship and the market value it placed on them when they departed. These *Sunday Post* men or women were more specially and uniquely trained than even they realised themselves.

The Sunday Post was different because, from the first day they walked through the door, its staff were trained to think differently! I can recall three illustrations from my own days in Glasgow.

The first was when one of my contacts, a debt collector as it happened, mentioned that there was a rash of illegal money-lending in the Gorbals. That wasn't new. It needed some lateral thinking to personalise it. So I sniffed around and found out that one woman was involved in the ring of money-lenders and she did have a new twist. A mother herself, she knew the value of the family allowance books then issued to mothers to draw the weekly state cash allowance at Post Offices. She held the books as security for her "pay day" loans. She would meet the women who had these loans at the Post Office on the day their allowance was due and only handed back their books just long enough for them to get their money before taking them back along with the allowance (as instalments of the loan repayment). I couldn't name her for legal reasons. But I had a stroke of melodramatic genius and christened her "Mrs Shylock". The story appeared under the heading "Ma Shylock is the Scourge of Gorbals Mothers", which led to police inquiries that put her out of business.

However, there was a heart-stopping sequel. On the Monday morning, the features editor looked across from his internal phone, face ashen. "There's a woman at the counter for you, Bill. She wants to see the reporter who wrote the money-lending story. Her name is Shylock." Honestly!

However, this Mrs Shylock was a perfectly respectable married woman who lived in the Gorbals but she had nothing to do with money-lending. A libel suit – in person! The story had caused her no end of embarrassment. A liberal dollop of *Sunday Post* oil had to be splashed on those troubled waters. It taught me the virtue of lateral thinking but the vice of using names in vain!

On another occasion, I was the down-table junior sub on the Saturday news desk. A five-line brief came to me from a Coatbridge correspondent about a local lad who had died from "natural causes" on a ship at sea. It was the first week of the year and news was quiet. Some lateral thinking inspired me to dare to say to the News Editor "I think there's more to this than is in the brief. It must have happened a day or two ago. It sounds like a page lead to me. Maybe "Hogmanay Heartbreak for a Coatbridge Mother".

"If you think so, do a bit of phoning," said Arthur. I did, then I went out to Coatbridge, spoke to a police contact, went to the mother's home and came back with the front page lead. She had twin sons of 18. She was mourning the death of one twin after a Hogmanay party when the cable came telling her of the death of the other twin on his ship, at sea, 12,000 miles away on the other side of the world.

It is one of the most hated but unavoidable jobs a journalist has to do – intruding into private grief. But *The Sunday Post* was trusted and respected, which made it a lot easier.

As I probed gently, the most astonishing fact emerged – it was exactly a year since she'd lost another son, an engineering apprentice who had been nearly 18 at the time. The only link was alcohol. Each had been indulging in his first Hogmanay as an adult away from the restrictions of home. Some unsuspected allergy had put all three into a fatal coma.

Teenage drinking was just emerging as a problem. It was justifiably a matter of public interest. The mother didn't mind the story being published if it was handled sensitively, for the boys had not been wild or drunks, just working lads with a fatal weakness.

So the five-line brief became the front page lead. Tragedy is never far from any family. It was also my first lesson in newspaper ethics. I felt proud of my scoop but, haunted by the face of that grieving Coatbridge mother, I still felt rather guilty.

My third example of lateral thinking was also a lesson in tactics. In my third year at *The Sunday Post*, I was dispatched to Jedburgh with a photographer, in the thrifty and ancient office Morris Minor, to report on a nasty murder at a dance in the local Town Hall. A local boy had been stabbed to death in the doorway of the hall. The twist to just another fatal brawl was that the police had locked the Town Hall doors and were in the process of interviewing every dancer.

When we arrived, the photographer, Jimmy Hendry, took the "scene-of-the-crime" pictures and left with the car to rush them back to Glasgow. So there I was, on my own, having to compete on a major crime story with gangs of reporters and photographers from every other Sunday paper, who were already rushing around in a fleet of hired cars, scooping up and signing up family, friends and "My All Night Ordeal" dancers.

Even as I got the bones of the story from the police "incident" report, I was thinking that wherever I went, I'd be at least five interviews behind. My best bet was a doorman or someone like that who could fill in some flesh. It wouldn't be a full file, but it would serve the first edition, which went to the Borders, including Jedburgh. So I went to the pub nearest to the Town Hall, where it was all the talk. I chose my moment. "Is there a doorman or somebody I could talk to?" Everybody wanted to help. There were several, all scattered to their homes. "Hey! What about the caretaker? He lives behind the hall" someone suggested. I was out the door even as I shouted my thanks.

I poked around the warren of buildings behind the hall until I found a flight of unlit stone stairs to a door tucked into some brick structure added on to the building. It opened onto the caretaker's cosy flat, his home for donkey's years. Not a soul had been near him. He was bursting to tell it all. He had been there all night and drunk in every detail. He knew every youngster there by their Christian names, who they were, what they did and not a few of their addresses. He knew the name, rank and personal habits of every policeman. He knew the deceased and all his family. He even knew the name and address of the killer, which the police had not yet released.

In half an hour with him, I had it all. Plus a lead on some names and addresses the others didn't have. Three quick calls by taxi and I filed the fullest, most detailed and graphic story then allowed by law. Our Borders edition, front page, which I proudly read in the hotel where I had stayed the night to update it, had all the others whacked hollow. This taught me lateral thinking also needs a little bit of luck!

As I had learned my lessons, I passed them on to my team as I built them up. The misfits from other occupations fitted the needs of *The Sunday Post* perfectly. For they were chosen to be different. From the abrasively ambitious to the abjectly apologetic, they were first of all people before they were journalists. In this way, each could provide at least one colour or satisfy one of the paper's needs, sometimes without realising it. The girl who was a compulsive liar – she couldn't spell butter but was one of the best centre page story-getters ever. The man with the butterfly mind and suicidal wife – he wrote his notes up and down like a Chinaman, in the white margins of his morning paper. I once saw him toying with his cigarettes to come up with the idea "Does The Queen Approve Of Smoking" from the Royal Appointment crest on the packet. That's lateral thinking! There was the boy who wrote articles with imagination and perception beyond his years until we discovered most of it came from reefers smoked in the office loo. There was a touch of eccentricity in all of them, that individual quality of mind that made them journalists in spite of themselves.

Sometimes, when the moon was high, it was like handling a mixed circus troupe of neurotic clowns, pampered poodles, chattering chimps and tigers with toothache, while the somersaulting high fliers soared overhead to the hissing treachery of the snakes in the sawdust and in the centre of the ring I cracked my whip and learned the art of oddball juggling – adding any animal thrown at me to the dozen I already had up in the air.

But I was an animal myself. When the paper was going well, I contented myself by playing the part of the caged Russian bear, cuddly from a distance, but dangerous if you wandered too close, pacing round the room, back and forth aimlessly, until it became a favourite characteristic of young reporters doing their Editor imitation at parties. But when the paper ran into a rut, I became as silent and still as a boa constrictor, withdrawing into my own coils until I had decided where and when to strike. That tight-lipped smile I'd inherited from Bessie was a known warning signal someone or something was about to be crushed until I'd squeezed out the answer I wanted.

I have often been asked what it's like to be the Editor of a national weekly newspaper. I can tell you that it is a hell only another editor can know. You are only as good as last week's issue, so you live a lifetime every seven days, from conception to birth, one day of life and immediate death for there is nothing as dead as yesterday's news, until you are spinning through life at the same speed as the presses and want to shout "Stop Press, I want to get off." I suspect it takes two years off your allotted span for every year in almost any other trade. In what other occupation, the very next day after the product of your heart, mind and soul leaves you, will it be handed back to you wrapped round a fish supper?

I always tried to look six months ahead in planning the paper, the better to avoid being pushed into any passing fad or fancy and to see what long term trends offered a fresh angle to the formula.

It was also why I bristled at those who called *The Sunday Post* the pap of the people, a soft-centred chocolate dummy teat. To counter this, I always pointed to some of the campaigns the paper had fought (not by shrieking to the four winds but quietly, with conviction).

For many years the paper campaigned against the sale of untreated milk which spread brucellosis. This is a particularly nasty disease that affects cattle and can be transmitted to humans via infected milk. In humans it becomes a kind of chronic flu, coming and going, as it flares up or down. It is the devil to diagnose and virtually incurable if not caught early.

The first result of our "Poisoned Pinta" campaign was predictable. Nobody much listened. However, the Milk Marketing Board (MMB) arrived in their Rolls Royce to kick up a stink and threaten us with everything from libel to lynching by the agricultural community whose livelihoods we were threatening. They also stopped their expensive advertising in all DC Thomson publications for more than a year.

But I stuck to my guns. As far as I was concerned, milk was such a basic food in our diet (advertised by the MMB as the purest liquid nourishment) that one case of brucellosis was one too many. Just as the spread of tuberculosis in humans had been greatly reduced by testing cattle (and slaughtering any found to be carrying the disease) and by pasteurising any milk destined for human consumption, so brucellosis in humans could be controlled using the same methods. At the same time, more evidence was reaching the paper from victims whose lives had been made a misery by the disease, which can be devastating in severe cases.

As the political pressure on me also increased, the evidence grew. It was not, as claimed, a few isolated cases. The disease was a constant, stubborn and widespread problem. The irony is that it was the agricultural community who handled or drank raw milk that was worst affected.

Too often newspaper campaigns are given up when they fail to produce quick results to impress readers. *The Sunday Post* persevered over months and years until people began to listen then take action.

The Government introduced a scheme of testing cattle herds to make them "accredited" (free of brucellosis). It was a voluntary scheme. *The Sunday Post* went back into action when there was evidence accredited herds were being reinfected by cattle bought and sold at markets. The system was made compulsory. It is no coincidence that Scotland, where we fought the campaign most intensively, was the first area to have 90 per cent accredited herds.

Then in October, 1981, the Minister of Agriculture, Peter Walker, announced in the House of Commons that Great Britain was now, for all practical purposes, free from brucellosis.

I went home that night and poured myself a large brandy. I hadn't much to show for my life but I had made milk what the MMB advertising claimed it was!

This campaign put us on the trail of another scandal: National Dried Milk (NDM). It started with a trickle of unconfirmed reports that some district nurses, health visitors and doctors were refusing to recommend this state-subsidised powdered milk for feeding babies. Indeed they were pushing much more expensive proprietary brands. I must confess my first reaction was that this was a "backhander" scandal – sales forces handing out perks for pushing their products. I couldn't believe there could be anything wrong with NDM. It had been the saviour of wartime babies along with welfare orange juice. But the evidence grew until it was almost incontrovertible. The post-war formula for NDM had been changed several times. The last change had enriched it with mineral additives – potassium for one. It was well intentioned, but if the feed was not mixed exactly as instructed it was too rich and could poison the baby. There was no warning about any danger on the tin.

This could happen in two ways: a harassed mother who didn't know any better making up baby's bottle in a hurry and not using the measure supplied; or the best of mothers increasing the amount of NDM in baby's feed in the belief it must do the baby good!

When it seemed clear, though there was no proof, that several babies had died in circumstances that pointed to NDM, I decided we had to publish the circumstantial evidence we had. It would not have stood up in court, but it was one of those many occasions when an Editor has to have the courage of his own convictions. The paper's lawyers repeated the classic advice: "When in doubt, leave it out." The story was published.

The reaction was predictable. *The Sunday Post* was slagged in the House of Commons for alarm-mongering based on rumour and speculation. The first flood of letters condemned me for putting young mothers in a needless state of fear. NDM was safe. This included more than a few from the medical profession.

The next trickle of letters brought more evidence. I put teams of reporters out to follow every lead. Every scrap was filed, confirmed and published. As the evidence grew, *The Sunday Times* took up the campaign. Our weight in the north and their weight in the south persuaded the bureaucrats to think again, especially as sales of NDM were plummeting. Warnings were circulated to clinics etc, along with a publicity campaign to make mothers aware of the danger. It was "safe if used properly" was still the official attitude.

Eventually an NDM was produced that could not be misused. So there are not a few youngsters living today thanks to *The Sunday Post*.

There were many other campaigns, for which I must say we were never given much credit. Probably because we went about it in our quiet *Sunday Post* way, shunning sensationalism to drive our message home. They included the "blue flame" campaign against the siting of highly inflammable whisky bonds in the inner cities, often in highly inflammable and inaccessible buildings close to crowded tenements; the "killers-in-your-home" campaigns against the use of ordinary glass in homes, against polyurethane-filled furniture, and against dangerous fairy lights for Christmas trees.

It was *The Sunday Post* that led and won the campaign for a new Great North Road for Scotland, which culminated when Gordon Campbell became Scottish Secretary and we joined forces to bring it about, me with public pressure and him with political pressure in the Cabinet.

One of the most ironic (and I must confess, rather hypocritical) campaigns was against smoking when *The Sunday Post* used all its guns, including anti-smoking stickers and an invitation to readers to join one of our columnists in a national stop-smoking month. It was so successful it won an Ash Award – an award presented annually by the then Government-sponsored Action Committee for Smoking and Health "for public service in the prevention of smoking".

In all conscience, neither the Editor whose idea it was, nor the columnist who wrote it could go to the presentation and collect the framed scroll. For the simple reason we were two of the heaviest smokers in the newspaper industry. In fact, it was impossible to find a non-smoking executive who could go and take the bows. So the Glasgow Editor went – an occasional pipe puffer or after-dinner cigar man. The framed award on the wall became yellow with the stains of rising smoke!

So there were times when the ethics of being an Editor had to resort to the defence of "Do as I say, not as I do." Ethics are a problem! If one village constable goes to help the constable in the next village break up a fight between some farm labourers at the harvest hop can you really permit your splash sub to use the headline "Riot at Harvest Festival. Police Force Doubled"?

If I sound cynical, it is an occupational hazard because an Editor's desk is the repository of all that's worst in human nature. He is assailed daily with disaster, death, tragedy, greed, selfishness and every other deadly sin known to man.

But that was one other reason I believed in *The Sunday Post*. For deep down it believes, as I believe, in the essential goodness of people and the old-fashioned virtues which have stood Scotland in such good stead. I tried to show all was not war, murder, rape, robbing, vandalism, mugging, drugs, drink and despair. *The Sunday Post* went in search of hope and human kindness, and found it often in the most unlikely places.

Take, for example, the letter on the following page from a Fraserburgh couple who had read our story of an elderly Glasgow widow, now a prisoner in her own home from the wounds and fear of twice being attacked and robbed in broad daylight in the street outside her house.

"We own our own cottage in half an acre of countryside, five miles from town. As we have no family, we have ample room. If the lady concerned wishes, we can arrange for her to have a holiday with us and, if she likes us, she can make her home with us."

So wrote Mr and Mrs M, restoring a world-weary Editor's faith in human nature.

"Seven Days Hard" was a column with the specific task of searching for a silver lining. Consider the four mysterious parcels that were delivered one day: one parcel contained a wedding dress; the second a veil; the third a head-dress; and the fourth a pair of white bridal shoes. None of these items had ever been worn. With them was a letter from a Fife widow whose daughter had fought a courageous battle against cancer, only to die before her dream of a white wedding could be fulfilled. Her wedding finery had lain in a cupboard for a year before her heartbroken mother could bear to look at it. She sent it to *The Sunday Post* to pass on to some other bride-to-be, in the hope it would bring her the happiness denied her daughter.

Who says there isn't a destiny that shapes our ends? Almost in the same mail, there was a letter from a Johnstone mother with a husband on the dole, a disabled son and an electricity bill for £193 she couldn't pay. Until her daughter, Jacqueline, gave her the £150 she'd saved up for her wedding.

So one mother's heartbreak and her daughter's sacrifice rewarded another daughter's sacrifice and mended another mother's broken heart. Those were the days it was more than worthwhile to be the Editor of *The Sunday Post*. Those were the stories that restored sanity to the madness of the world. So did our readers come to love and trust their *Sunday Post* and its Editor to have renewed faith in the future.

This closeness with the reader was crystallised for me, in a way

233

I can't fully explain, by the poem entitled "Look Closer" (although it has appeared elsewhere with different titles). It was written by Phyllis McCormack in 1966 when she was working as a nurse in a psychiatric hospital in Montrose. The poem is written in the voice of an old woman in a nursing home who is thinking about her life. It appeared in *The Sunday Post* in 1973 and in other magazines and newspapers all over the world. It says all there is to say about everyone's need for tolerance and understanding, whoever or whatever we may be in the world of today:

LOOK CLOSER

What do you see, nurse, what do you see?
What are you thinking when you look at me,
A crabbit old woman, not very wise,
Uncertain of habit, with faraway eyes,
Who dribbles her food, and makes no reply,
When you say in a loud voice, "I do wish you'd try",
Who seems not to notice the things that you do,
And forever is losing a stocking or shoe,
Who, quite unresisting, lets you do as you will,
With bathing and feeding, the long day to fill?
Is that what you're thinking, is that what you see?
Then open your eyes, you're not looking at me.
I'll tell you who I am, as I sit here so still,
As I move at your bidding, as I eat at your will,
I'm a small child of ten with a father and mother,
And brothers and sisters, who love one another,
A girl of sixteen, with wings on her feet,
Dreaming that soon a lover she'll meet;
A bride now at twenty – my heart gives a leap,
Remembering the vows that I promised to keep;
At twenty-five now I have young of my own,
Who need me to build a secure, happy home;
A woman of thirty, my young now grow fast,

Bound together with ties that should last;
At forty, my young sons have grown up and gone,
But my man stays beside me to see I don't mourn;
At fifty once more babies play round my knee;
Again we know children, my loved one and me.
Dark days are upon me, my husband is dead,
I look at the future, I shudder with dread,
For my young are all busy with young of their own,
And I think of the years and the love I have known.
I'm an old woman now and nature is cruel,
'Tis her jest to make old age look like a fool.
The body it crumbles, grace and vigour depart,
There now is a stone where I once had a heart.
But inside this old carcass, a young girl still dwells,
And now and again my battered heart swells.
I remember the joys, I remember the pain,
And I'm loving and living life over again.
I think of the years, all too few and gone too fast,
And accept the stark fact that nothing can last.
So open your eyes, nurse, open and see,
Not a crabbit old woman, look closer – see me.

See me! Isn't that the cry of us all? And isn't that the key to the success of *The Sunday Post*? That it always tried to do just that.

Postscript

Bill never added to the manuscript after 1982. He retired in 2003.

The many obituaries written about Bill, when news of his death was announced, remain tucked in the back of the photograph album which records much of his life. Many of them used the same photograph. His smile defies the fading newsprint still.

As his staff would tell you, Bill became known as "Flash". Some say it was his fast rise in the DC Thomson firm, such was his journalistic instinct and writing energy and determination, that, at the age of 34, he was appointed Editor.

The truth probably was that Bill bore an uncanny resemblance to the English actor George Cole, OBE (1925–2015) best known for playing Arthur Daley in the long-running ITV comedy-drama show *Minder* and Flash Harry in the early *St Trinian's* films. The resemblance is especially apparent in some of the photographs of Bill's "HON Man" exploits, many of which could have become future *St Trinian's* scripts.

As we now know about Bill's life before *The Sunday Post,* clearly his broad experience from his working-class roots, through childhood, the MV *Marilyn Abbott,* Glasgow University, Hartwood Hospital and his Army days, together with the adventures that only an HON Man could encounter, gave him a unique insight and perspective. He did make a precocious rise to the Editor's chair of *The Sunday Post,* and during his 22 years in charge, it was indeed the biggest-selling newspaper in Scotland. At one point sales reached almost 1.5 million copies which, in a country of five million people, meant that it had the highest per capita circulation in the world. It is still a favourite family newspaper, albeit with more modest readership numbers.

As Editor, he was passionate, tenacious and demanding. Full of ideas, he was particularly proud of two campaigns.

One forced local councils to take the fight to giant hogweed, an invasive plant so noxious that it can cause blindness.

The other, in the early 1980s, was a persistent battle to outlaw unpasteurised (or "dirty") milk, after it was blamed for a health crisis and 12 deaths. In 1983 raw milk was banned, and Scotland was later the first country in Europe to be declared free of the related disease, brucellosis.

Such campaigns demanded unstinting effort, and Bill's work rate was fuelled by a ferocious diet of cigars, of which he would consume six packs each day. Cleaners were regularly obliged to vacuum the ash from his computer keyboard.

Always keen to encourage new talent, in 1989 Bill set up the formal editorial training scheme at DC Thomson, parent of *The Sunday Post*. Many young recruits were in awe of him.

In 1990 Bill left the Editor's chair to become Managing Editor, and the following year he won a Scottish Press Award for his lifetime's work.

Though a traditional newspaperman, he was immediately aware of the impact that the internet would have on journalism, and in the early 1990s he set up Scotland Online, a joint venture between DC Thomson and Scottish Telecom.

In 1991 he became the first Scottish member of the Press Complaints Commission. He was appointed CBE in the same year.

Bill's first wife Meg McLelland, died in 1993.

Away from the newsroom he enjoyed sailing, fishing and dominoes, the latter giving insight to his status as Commander of the Most Excellent Order of the British Empire: CBE (understood by many of Bill's colleagues to stand for "chapping both ends").

Bill and Maggie married in 1999 and had 13 happy years together.

Bill passed away in his sleep, on February 2, 2012, surrounded by family.

His funeral took place in Dundee on February 10 – the day he would have celebrated his 78th birthday. He is survived, missed and remembered by Maggie, his three sons and eight grandchildren, and the very many people he helped and encouraged in his lifetime.

Bill Anderson, born February 10, 1934, died February 2, 2012

Every year DC Thomson presents the Bill Anderson Award for Outstanding Achievement. On it is engraved Bill's favourite exhortation to his trainees: "Use your eyes and ears".